The Politics and Strategy of the Second World War

A series edited by
Noble Frankland and Christopher Dowling

SINGAPORE
1941–1942

LOUIS ALLEN

SINGAPORE
1941-1942

DAVIS-POYNTER
LONDON

First published in 1977 by
Davis-Poynter Limited
20 Garrick Street London WC2E 9BJ

Copyright © 1977 by Louis Allen

Introduction Copyright © 1977 by
Noble Frankland and Christopher Dowling

ISBN 0 7067 0181 X

Printed in Great Britain by
Bristol Typesetting Co. Ltd
Barton Manor, St Philips, Bristol

To Tim, Louise and Felix

CONTENTS

EDITORS' INTRODUCTION   *page* 11

INTRODUCTION: Victory and Defeat   13

    I   Why Singapore?   37

    II   Japan's Course for War   56

    III   The Role of Economic Sanctions   61

    IV   The Role of Thailand   74

    V   Operation Matador   92

    VI   The Approach to Malaya: To Matador or not to Matador?   101

    VII   The Japanese Landings   116

    VIII   The Campaign   121

         i   The defence of Northern Malaya – Jitra, Gurun, Kampar   121

         ii   The sinking of Force Z   135

         iii   The defence of Central Malaya – the Slim River battle   146

         iv   The defence of Southern Malaya – the battle for Johore   151

         v   The battle for the Island   160

         vi   Surrender   175

    IX   What Went Wrong?   185

         i   Yamashita   186

         ii   Percival   188

         iii   Gordon Bennett   191

         iv   Brooke-Popham   193

         v   Playfair   198

         vi   Wavell   199

CONTENTS

X   Who Was to Blame?   202

   i   The Simson case   202

   ii The case for the civilians – Sir Miles
      Shenton Thomas – C. A. Vlieland   212

XI The Factor of Race   247

XII Afterthoughts   264

APPENDICES

I   Casualties   270

II   Percival's 1937 paper   272

III Vlieland's 1940 Appreciation   288

IV   The 'Scorched Earth' Policy   294

REFERENCES   301

BIBLIOGRAPHY   319

INDEX   329

MAPS

	page
Malaya 1941	102
The Japanese invasion	111
The Japanese advance, 8-28 December 1941	125
The sinking of Force Z	140
The Japanese advance, 29 December 1941–31 January 1942	148
The attack on Singapore	153
The fall of Singapore	173

A*

ACKNOWLEDGEMENTS

I am deeply indebted to the publishers and copyright holders of books on which I have drawn, and which are listed in the Bibliography. I owe much to three archivists, each of whom has been more than helpful in finding source material: Mr Fuwa Hiroshi of the War History Room at the SDF Headquarters in Tokyo; Miss Julia Sheppard of the Liddell Hart Centre for Military Archives at King's College, University of London; and Dr Roderick Suddaby of the Imperial War Museum. I am also grateful to Major J. M. Percival for permission to make full use of his father's papers and to Lady Brooke-Popham for permission to use those of Sir Robert Brooke-Popham. I thank Lieutenant-General Fujiwara Iwaiichi for fruitful discussions on *F Kikan* and the Indian National Army. I thank Mr R. Mason Nelson for the loan of his father's work on Changi and a number of other books; Mme Y. R. Medeville for permission to use the memoirs of Amiral Jean Decoux; and Mr C. E. Escritt and Mr Richard Storry for discussion of particular points. I also owe Richard Storry a great debt for allowing me to try out some of my ideas on Malaya at his Far Eastern Seminar at St Anthony's, Oxford. To Dr Noble Frankland and Dr Christopher Dowling of the Imperial War Museum, and Mr Toby Buchan of Davis-Poynter, I am indebted for the scrupulous care with which they have vetted my account. They are not, needless to say, responsible for any errors which may remain, nor for the views expressed in this book, which are my own.

Author's Note: Japanese names in the text are given in the Japanese order, ie surname first.

EDITORS' INTRODUCTION

Numerous books and articles have been written about the weapons, battles and campaigns of the Second World War, and the problems of command, supply and intelligence have been extensively surveyed. Yet, though the fighting has been so fully described from these and other points of view, the reasons why the various military operations took place have attracted less study and remain comparatively obscure. It is to fill this gap in the understanding of the Second World War that this series has been conceived.

The perceptive have always understood the extent to which war is a continuation of policy by other means, and the clash of armies or fleets has, in intention, seldom been haphazard. Battles and campaigns often contain the keys to the understanding of the grand strategies of supreme commands and the political aims and purpose of nations and alliances.

In each of the volumes in this series an important battle or campaign is assessed from the point of view of discovering its relationship to the war as a whole, for in asking the questions Why was this battle fought? and What effect did it produce? one is raising the issue of the real meaning and character of the war.

As the series progresses, its readers, advancing case by case, will be able to make general judgements about the central character of the Second World War. Some will find this worthwhile in its own right; others will see it as a means of increasing their grasp of the contemporary scene. Thirty years have now passed since the death of Hitler and the capitulation of Japan. These momentous events were the culmination of a war which transformed the political and social, the economic and technological and, indeed, the general conditions of society and politics in virtually every corner of the world.

NOBLE FRANKLAND: CHRISTOPHER DOWLING

INTRODUCTION

Victory and Defeat

I

At nine o'clock in the evening of 15 February, 1942, the telephone rang in the house of the Marquis Kido, the Japanese Emperor's closest adviser. It was the Prime Minister, Lieutenant-General Tōjō, with a message for His Imperial Majesty. A telegram had just been received from Malaya. Singapore had fallen. At 19.50 hours on that day, the Japanese Army in Malaya had received the unconditional surrender of the British defenders. An hour later, General Sugiyama, the Chief of Staff, called on the Emperor in person. He was bubbling over with enthusiasm at the speed and courage of the Japanese Army, which had taken the city in such a short time. Kido had an interview with the Emperor the following morning from 10.50 to 11 am, and although they were concerned with routine diplomatic business – the correct form of dress for a proposed envoy to the Vatican – Kido could see how deeply moved the Emperor still was by the news from Malaya.[1]

The Emperor had been bitterly sceptical at first about Japan's preparedness for a southward advance and had upbraided Sugiyama for over-confidence, and for making promises about a speedy ending to the war in China which he had not achieved; but the promises about Malaya had been more than fulfilled, and the Emperor composed a Rescript to his troops:

> Our army and navy [he wrote] working in close co-operation in Malaya, have resolutely carried out difficult maritime escort tasks, transport duties and landing operations, and in the teeth of tropical diseases, and enduring intense heat, they have harried and hunted a strong enemy and broken through his defences at every point, capturing Singapore with the speed of the gods, and destroying Great Britain's base in East Asia.
>
> We express our profound esteem for these deeds.[2]

The Emperor took his white horse to the bridge over the moat from the Imperial Palace, and went out into the winter sunshine. For an hour he sat there, on horseback, the focus of the triumphant gaze of a victorious people.[3] Back in the Palace, he made a decree about the captured city. Henceforth, he declared, it would no longer be called Singapore. It would become 'Shōnan', 'the radiant South'.[4]

One of Japan's best-known novelists, Shiga Naoya, expressed perfectly the kind of satisfaction many ordinary Japanese must have felt when the news came through. He wrote in an essay entitled 'The Fall of Singapore':

> Just recently I read the story of how the US President – during the Japanese-American talks – left for the country to go and eat turkey, without waiting for the arrival of the Japanese envoy Kurusu, who had travelled many thousands of miles, by plane and railway, to meet him. We have seen not only that discourtesy, but also the sight of Churchill losing his temper and making threatening proclamations that he would declare war within the hour if hostilities broke out between America and Japan. In a very short time, that is exactly how things stand today. Has there ever before been such a rapid fulfilment of a prediction? This sudden turn of events seems unparalleled in history.
>
> They are saying in America that they were defeated because they underestimated Japan's capability. But what does the American view of Japan's capability mean? America has made a demonstration to the whole world of her gigantic war budget, her reliance on her own economic power. But the fact that no one has raised the issue of how poor a country can be in *spiritual* power – this the Japanese feel to be very odd.
>
> We Japanese ourselves have been astounded at the spiritual and technical achievements of our armed forces, from the very start of hostilities. When we realize how much of our victory has depended on heaven, we need humility, and every day brings fresh instances of this. The confidence that heaven is with us makes us all the more humble.
>
> Without our expecting it, the unanimity of the entire nation has been achieved. Pro-British or pro-American views are no longer possible in Japan. Among ourselves, we keep a modest frame of mind, we preserve harmony in the

country, and not a single blemish will stain our brilliant victories. It has been a useful lesson for the God-forsaken arrogance of Britain and America. There is cause for rejoicing that hope is born among our young people.

Our spirit bright, clear and calm, we bow with reverence before the spirits of our heroic dead.[5]

II

The day after the Emperor of Japan re-named Singapore Shōnan, the British Prime Minister, Winston Churchill, faced an angry and disturbed House of Commons. Surprisingly enough, their anger and his concern were not for Singapore – at least not at first. His statement to the House dealt with the successful escape of the German battleships *Scharnhorst* and *Gneisenau* from Brest up the English Channel, in spite of British attempts to sink them. *Hansard*[6] devotes three columns to this event, and only one to Singapore, which was the second item in Churchill's speech. He made a plea for no recriminations to be made and did not think a debate would be appropriate.

Both Mr Pethick Lawrence and Earl Winterton, in reply, deplored the impression he gave that to raise queries was disloyal. While the Deputy Prime Minister, the Labour leader Clement Attlee, carefully and industriously drew an intricate pattern of doodles on the paper in front of him, and Churchill pawed the ground angrily with his left foot,[7] 'We are not satisfied' affirmed Winterton, 'with this attitude in the press that you must not ever question the actions of the Government and that all this is inevitable.'[8] He called for 'a Grand Inquest of the Nation on all that has gone on and is going on, for the country is profoundly concerned.'[9] The Labour MP, Mr Bellenger, who had a reputation as the soldiers' MP, re-affirmed the deep disquiet and refused to be put down. 'I go so far as to suggest to the Prime Minister,' he said, 'that there is in the country and indeed in this House at the present moment, a feeling that we have not got the right kind of persons to direct this war to a satisfactory conclusion . . . we have not got the right kind of government.'[10] The House cheered him to the echo.

Churchill's blank refusal of a debate – he had sensed he could not prolong it – gave way to a promise that one would be held, but it would be wrong to debate in the present moment of 'panic and anger'.[11] The phrase was unfortunate, the House thought its courage and wisdom were being disparaged, and protested vehemently. Oddly enough, the concession he made at the end of his speech, 'to tell the House about the Inquiry',[12] did not refer to Singapore but to the German ships. The attack was taken up by the solitary Communist member, for Fife, Willie Gallacher, at which, with a cold humourless smile on his lips, Churchill stalked out of the Chamber, followed by many members. 'I see that other honourable Members are going now,' said Gallacher, not to be outfaced, 'The Führer goes, the yesmen follow. Is it any wonder that we are losing the war; is it any wonder that the Empire is lost, when we have such types as that? They are simply crawlers.'[13] On that occasion, much as the House resented it, Churchill had his way.

But, of course, his own attitude must have been ambiguous. Grievous as the loss of what he considered the 'fortress' Singapore must have been, particularly since it was defended by tens of thousands of troops; and although he had received the news of the loss of the *Prince of Wales* and the *Repulse* as the blackest news of the whole war; yet the main redeeming feature of Japan's entry into the war was never lost on him. Japan's attack had brought America into the war. From that moment, Britain was saved. Whatever happened, victory would come. His inner confidence in this was so profound that it coloured everything else.

His formula for dealing with disaster was a traditional parliamentary one. The days demanded blood sacrifice, and one was made: there was a Cabinet re-shuffle. Captain Margesson left the War Office and was succeeded by his Permanent Under-Secretary, Sir James Grigg, a substitution of a civil servant for a politician which was hardly justifiable. Beaverbrook left the Cabinet, and Sir Stafford Cripps joined it to become Leader of the House of Commons, a chore Churchill found too time-consuming, as he told the House when it gathered again on 24 February to hear his report on the war situation. For two days the British Parliament expressed itself on the recent reverses, but since no particular subject was singled out, the debate ranged first round administrative detail, from Churchill's own nostalgic evocation of the small War Cabinet days of Lloyd George in 1916, to the machinery of the Pacific War Council and Imperial Defence. It was a smoke-screen. There were more urgent matters than committee procedure and he knew it. When he finally came to the business of Malaya, he stalled and proved inept.

The defenceless state of Penang was recalled, in inexcusable terms:

> I saw that some gentlemen who escaped from Penang announced to the world with much indignation that there was not a single anti-aircraft gun in the place. Where should we have been, I should like to know, if we had spread our limited anti-aircraft guns throughout the immense, innumerable regions and vulnerable points of the Far East instead of using them to preserve the vital life of our ports and factories here and of our fortresses which were under continuous attack and all our operations with the field Armies in the Middle East?[14]

No one picked him up on this question-begging allusion, or asked why the intolerable alternative had arisen in the first place, but there was a gasp of disbelief when, without more ado, he told the House, 'I have no news whatever from Singapore'.[15] The House was, as the Glasgow ILP member, James Maxton, reminded it, expecting 'a post-mortem examination of the Government which has failed'.[16]

Some members hauled the debate back to the Far Eastern issues. Sir Archibald Southby said openly what had been at the back of many members' minds, that a tiny fraction of the aircraft which had been sent to Russia should have been made available in Malaya: 'One month's supply of the aircraft sent to Russia would have saved Malaya'.[17] He went on to hope that Burma would be saved, and that

if Britain had to choose between Burma and the Dutch
East Indies she would choose Burma. Mr J. H. Martin
pressed the issue closer. Pre-war ineptitudes in policy-
making were responsible for the catastrophe in Malaya.
But even given these initial blunders, why was there no
policy for evacuating the tens of thousands of troops in
the Island in case of defeat? Why was no effort made to re-
victual the garrison, if it was true that lack of food and
water forced the surrender? Sir Percy Harris was puzzled
by the fact that 'the native population have been standing
by as idle spectators of what has been happening in the
Colonies' as opposed to the 'magnificent fight for their own
country'[18] which the Filipinos were putting up. Mr A.
Sloan, the member for South Ayrshire, had no doubts
about why the public conscience had been so shocked by
the events in Malaya. His speech, more perhaps than any
other, turned the attention of the House to the economic
role of Malaya and to what, in his view, were the shortcom-
ings of those who fulfilled it. It was a legend that lingered,
and one that did great damage:

> Malaya and Singapore were merely names of far-off places
> in foreign lands. They conveyed little to the average mind.
> The general public do not study Stock Exchange reports.
> They are entirely ignorant that rubber, tin and oil are the
> main attractions there. They are in the main completely
> unconscious that this area is the greatest sink of corruption
> in the whole world. They are unfamiliar with the fact that
> these ornaments of British capitalism have done more to
> degrade Britain in the eyes of the East than any scoundrels
> since our depredations in Africa. These tin, rubber and oil
> companies have exploited the bodies and souls of the natives
> of the Far East. Those natives have lived in poverty and
> misery, and the only crime they have committed is to be
> born in the richest country in the world. Those companies
> have made fabulous fortunes . . .
>
> How is it that the natives of Singapore were so indifferent
> to the fate of that island . . . Is there any cause for wonder?
> Their land was invaded by an Imperialist-minded army, but
> they were already dominated by another of the same type.
> What material difference would it make to the Malayans?

Merely exchanging one set of vultures for another, not the difference perhaps of a bowl of rice.[19]

Mr Sloan quoted the despatch from the *Times* correspondent (Ian Morrison) which declared that both officials and British residents were completely out of touch with the people. British and Asiatics lived their lives apart, Morrison had said. There was never any fusion or cementing of these two groups. British rule and culture and the small British community formed no more than a thin and brittle veneer. 'Surely this is about the most complete and damning indictment of British Imperialism ever written,' he went on, and he accused the British companies in Malaya of being more concerned with loss of assets than with loss of soldiers' lives:

> Whatever may be the opinion of the people in this country with regard to the after-war settlement of Malaya, there is no dubiety in the minds of the swindling gang of sharks there. They are less concerned about the loss of life than about the loss of assets.[20]

Dutch capitalism in Java was as bad. The fault went a long way back. The very week fortification of Singapore was begun, the financiers of the City of London loaned to the Japanese £25,000,000 to build a navy for the purpose of destroying the Singapore base which was costing us £20,000,000 to build.

His forthrightness found little response. But Mr Pethick Lawrence claimed that he and others had been saying for years that the administration of the British Colonies was a scandal. For a century before 1929 there had been no labour legislation and no social services: 'The coloured man was the bottom dog who could be exploited to an almost unlimited extent by his white master.'[21] Britain was losing her Colonies in the war precisely because of 'Blimpery' which had remained blind to these conditions.

Leslie Hore-Belisha gave a more balanced view, in which social criticism was fairly mingled with strategic considerations. Britain had lost an important part of her Colonial Empire, and with it a crucial source of supply. Japan had forced an entry into the Indian Ocean and could interfere with communications to the Middle East, India and Australasia. The Colonial Secretary had admitted the loss of Singapore was inexplicable, and it was not anticipated. An army of considerable dimensions had been lost. The mistakes made were not entirely military. Colonial administration left much to be desired. It had not enlisted the support of local people, it lacked imagination and foresight. But it would be unwise to blame exclusively those on the spot. Possibly Colonial administration had become too centralized, its machinery too cumbrous. Those on the spot had been shorn of initiative, and when the need arose, had been reluctant to rely on their own judgment.[22]

Commander Stephen King-Hall forthrightly called what happened in Singapore 'the greatest surrender in numbers of British troops in the whole history of the British Army.'[23] He contrasted the feeling of February 1942 with the mood after Dunkirk. Then, the Prime Minister was the epitome of the nation. 'We felt very near him and he must have felt very near us.'[24] They had been dangerous times, but great times. The times were dangerous again, but there was no more greatness. There was instead a sense of apathy and frustration in the air, 'a littleness'.[25]

Professor A. V. Hill, who sat for Cambridge University, and voiced the mind of the scientific 'boffins', turned crisply to the Navy and accused it of being disastrously out-ofdate. It had persistently clung to the conception of the large capital ship as the basis of the Fleet. These ships could not protect themselves effectively, alone, against enemy air attack. Those who had expert knowledge and had not been misled by tradition had known this all along. The sinking of the *Prince of Wales* and *Repulse* had made it manifest to all. The decisions about the future of the Navy should therefore be taken out of the hands of the admirals:

> These precious ships, each costing some 30,000 man-years to produce, are the greatest liability. The basis of the fleet of the future will be the aircraft carrier. She need not fight the battleship, she can keep out of range and engage the battleship with bomb and torpedo. If that is so, and I think

it is inevitable in the end, a decision should be taken on the matter not solely by admirals and naval constructors brought up in the old tradition, but largely by a combined operational staff, after close consideration of all the technical and strategical questions involved.[26]

Other members used the occasion to query the policy of concentrating the energies and material of the RAF on bombing Germany. Had the role of supporting the Army not suffered as a result? Professor Hill made the same point in reference to the *Scharnhorst* and *Gneisenau*. They sailed up the Channel at top speed after 4,000 tons of bombs had been dropped on or around them:

> Everyone now knows what those who do arithmetic and have an elementary knowledge of the facts knew long ago, that the idea of bombing a well-defended enemy into submission or seriously affecting his morale, or even of doing substantial damage to him, is an illusion.[27]

The blitz had proved it in Britain. Total air-raid casualties since the war began were two-thirds of the numbers lost at Singapore, and there was no question which loss was the greater military disaster. The loss of industrial production in the worst month of the blitz was about equal to that due to the Easter holidays . . .

Captain Lionel Gammans combined strategic considerations with a defence of the Malayan civilian community which had come in for a verbal beating at the hands of Mr Sloan. Captain Gammans had spent fourteen years in Malaya, and had travelled in Japan, China and Manchuria. He was sure the full impact of the loss of Singapore had not yet sunk in. It was a political as well as a military disaster. We had lost half the world's tin and rubber. The Japanese now had raw materials which would permit them to wage a prolonged war. They need no longer worry about tin, rubber, iron ore, fats or oil, and our strategy had been aimed precisely at depriving them of these things. Five million British subjects had passed under enemy rule. He pooh-poohed the notion that local people had not been encouraged to resist. He himself had commanded a company of Chinese volunteers before the war, and it had always been difficult to fill the ranks. They had no desire or aptitude for military service. But as to the ultimate impact of what had happened he had no illusions:

> Perhaps the greatest tragedy of all was the scene on that Sunday morning when the Union Jack was pulled down on the flagstaff on Fort Canning in the middle of Singapore, and that great city, which Raffles founded and our own kith and kin built up, came for the first time under the Rising Sun. Do not let us underestimate the significance of that event. Our contact with Asia has been a long and on the whole an honourable one, and during all those years the Union Jack has never once been lowered. The story of that scene at Fort Canning will reverberate in the bazaars of India, on the plains of China and in the islands of the South Seas when every one of us has long since been dead and gone.[28]

The House of Lords undertook its own inquisition, but profited from a greater supply of information from the Colonial Secretary, Lord Cranborne, making his maiden speech as Leader of the House, than Mr Churchill had seen fit to supply to the Commons. As he saw it, the troops had orders to hold the place to the last, and did so. This valiant phrasing gave rise to sympathetic cheers, but Lord Wedgwood pronounced a gloomier verdict: 'The surrender of Singapore is the blackest page in our military history for all time.'[29]

To some piaculative eyes, it seemed like divine retribution. Dorothy L. Sayers's radio series on the life of Christ had recently been performed on the BBC, and in it the figure of Christ had been directly portrayed. This blasphemous use of God in a stage performance roused hidden ire. One listener wrote in fury to the BBC that the fall of Singapore was God's punishment on the British nation for such a transgression of moral standards.

III

While the debates and the breast-beating continued in Great Britain, and as hubris began to invade the imaginations of the Japanese Imperial Headquarters, when they surveyed the numerous moves made possible by the fall of Singapore, another actor waited in the wings. That actor was Germany.

The Germans naturally wanted to profit from the Tripartite Pact by applying pressure on Britain in the Far East, through Japan. It was more important, at one time, for Japan to do this on their behalf than for her to intervene against Soviet Russia from Manchuria. Many years later, Lieutenant-General Percival, in his book *The War in Malaya*,[30] proclaimed his conviction that the expedition against Singapore was undertaken at the behest of the Germans. But arrangements between Germany and Japan were never so precise as to bring about complex military operations in common; and Japan naturally considered her own needs and interests first.

Hitler himself had already reached certain firm conclusions about Japan four months before he attacked Russia. If he could bring Japan into the war, he could create a war on two fronts against Great Britain, which would lessen the risk of the projected invasion of Russia in June 1941. At his headquarters, on 5 March 1941, a document (Directive No. 24) was drafted which outlined the co-operation he was prepared to give to the Japanese and what he expected to gain from it. The draft was signed by Keitel, as Chief of the High Command of the Armed Forces, but there is no doubt that the views are Hitler's own. He was prepared to strengthen Japan's fighting power by every possible means, and instructed the commanders-in-chief of the various branches of the German Armed Forces to respond generously to Japanese requests for information about the lessons derived from recent campaigns, and for economic and technical assistance. Co-ordination of operational plans was the task of the Naval High Command.

The purpose of all this was to induce the Japanese to take action in the Far East as soon as possible: 'This will tie down strong British forces and will divert the main effort of the United States of America to the Pacific.'[31]

America was not to be drawn in. Quite the contrary: 'The common aim of strategy must be represented as the swift conquest of England in order to keep America out of the war.'[32]

Germany had no aims in the Far East which need interfere with Japanese intentions. He recommended powerful Japanese forces being used to prosecute the same successful warfare against merchant shipping which Germany had undertaken. Japan must obtain territories which would give her raw materials, 'particularly if the United States is engaged'. Deliveries of rubber were vital for Germany. 'The seizure of Singapore,' he added, 'England's key position in the Far East, would represent a decisive success in the combined strategy of the three powers.' [Germany, Italy and Japan][33]

The actual date for beginning operational discussions was left open and the Military Commissions constituted under the Three Power Pact were to deal only with matters affecting the enemy economy. A final note reminded recipients of the draft (only fourteen copies were distributed) that no mention whatever of the proposed invasion of Russia was to be made to the Japanese.

Germany's interest in Japanese intervention in the Far East, *after* Operation Barbarossa began, naturally altered. Not only was it desirable to face Britain with a war on two fronts, by the taking of Singapore and the threat to India, but an invasion by Japan of Soviet Russia's Maritime Province of Siberia would relieve pressure on Germany's eastern front. Japanese troops had already occupied the Maritime Province once twenty years before, in the international attempt to suppress the Russian Revolution. Either way, Japan would be contributing directly to Germany's victory in Europe. But it was not in Germany's interests to bring the USA into the war. The pressure on Great Britain was in fact aimed at keeping the Americans out. A threat to Malaya and India would, in Germany's view, divert US attention from the Atlantic to the Pacific. A shooting war had already begun in the Atlantic between US destroyers and German submarines.[34]

It was, of course, difficult for Japan to reconcile this urging with the strategic requirements forecast by her own Navy: the need to destroy the US Pacific Fleet and so assure the Pacific flank of the operations in South-East Asia.

On the other hand, Germany did not view with any pleasure the likelihood of an agreement between Japan and the USA. Baron von Weizsaecker of the German Foreign Office submitted a memorandum to his Foreign Minister, Ribbentrop, on 15 May 1941, in which he affirmed that 'any political treaty between Japan and the United States is undesirable at present,'[35] fearing that Japan might be lured away by the US, in such an event, from her two partners in the Tripartite Pact. The interruption of the Hull-Nomura talks, when Japan occupied Southern French Indo-China in July 1941, was more to Germany's liking and her Ambassador in Tokyo, General Eugen Ott, expressed his Government's disquiet when the talks were resumed in August.[36] The Germans failed to realize that the ultimate breakdown of the talks would in the end bring about what they least desired, the entry of America into the war.

On 23 November 1941, Ott informed his government that Japan clearly intended to move south, and wanted to know if she could expect German support. Russian resistance by this time was beginning to stiffen, and the Germans were in no position to offer more than moral backing. And they did not know that Japan intended to attack the US (this was two days before Nagumo's fleet set out from Hitokappu Bay to Pearl Harbour). So in the case of their most important strategic decisions of 1941, both Germany and Japan refused to divulge their plans to each other. Ribbentrop spoke to General Ōshima, the Japanese ambassador, in Berlin on 28 November 1941. After that day's council of war, presided over by Hitler, he said Germany's attitude towards the US was changing. The Reich would

back Japan if she went to war with America. He did not
think the US-Japan negotiations likely to succeed and 'if
Japan reaches a decision to fight Britain and the United
States, I am confident that not only will it be in the interest of Germany and Japan jointly, but would bring about
favourable results for Japan herself.'[37] It was just what
Oshima wanted to hear, but he was nevertheless surprised
and asked for confirmation. 'Is Your Excellency,' he asked
Ribbentrop bluntly, 'indicating that a state of actual war
is to be established between Germany and the United
States?'[38] Then Ribbentrop knew he had said more than he
intended. He turned the question by saying Roosevelt was
a fanatic and capable of anything. But Oshima would not
let go and pressed for a precise answer.

'Should Japan become engaged in a war against the
United States,' was the reply, 'Germany, of course, would
join the war immediately. There is absolutely no possibility of Germany's entering into a separate peace with the
United States under such circumstances. The Führer is
determined on that point.'[39]

The German Army seems to have had a somewhat different impression of Japan's aims and intentions from that
gained by the German Foreign Office. This is rather surprising, since Japan's diplomatic representation in Germany was very heavily weighted on the side of the ideas
of the Japanese Army. The career diplomat and future
Foreign Minister, Tōgō Shigenori, had been Ambassador
to Berlin until superseded by his own military attaché,
Lieutenant-General Ōshima Hiroshi, who had the reputation of being more Nazi than the Nazis themselves.[40] Togo
resented the habit of Japanese military attachés of making
direct contact on matters of high policy with the governments of the countries to which they were accredited. It indicated a clear superseding of the normal diplomatic channels by the military, and in fact in the end Tōgō was transferred to Moscow as a result of his opposition to an alliance
with Germany, and his place taken by Ōshima.[41]

The officer who served under Ōshima as military attaché,
the appropriately named Lieutenant-General Banzai, visi-

ted the German Director of Military Intelligence, Matzky, on 4 August 1941 and referred to the possibility of Japan attacking Russia. A minimum of sixteen Kwantung Army divisions would be used, combined into four armies.[42] General Halder, Chief of the German General Staff, noted in his diary that Banzai indicated September 1941 as the month in which this was supposed to happen, and that Vladivostok was expected to be in Japanese hands by November. This meant that although preparations for taking Singapore had been made by the occupation of French Indo-China, further moves in that direction would be postponed.[43]

A month later, Halder noted that the whole picture had changed. 'Situation uncertain,' he jotted down in his diary. 'The Führer does not want to give the impression that we need the Japanese. The [Japanese] Army has got cold feet and looks like doing nothing until further notice. The [Japanese] Navy wants to go into Thailand, Singapore, Borneo and Manila one after the other and believes that America can do nothing to stop them. There may be a change of government and at all events a waste of time.'[44] Some German officers were not particularly perturbed by Japan's change of intent. Colonel Walter Warlimont, Deputy Chief of Operations in the High Command, thought German confidence in the outcome of the Russian campaign was such that when Japan was thought to have made an offer of assistance it had been rejected. 'We don't need anyone,' one officer remarked, 'just to strip the corpses.'[45]

This makes Germany's final decision even more puzzling. Without any assurance that Japan would intervene against Russia (indeed Tōgō had impressed upon Ōshima that no armed clash with Russia was desirable until strategic circumstances permitted),[46] and in open contradiction to the wish, expressed earlier, not to come into conflict with the USA, Germany declared war on the United States once the news of Pearl Harbour came through, but not immediately. Ribbentrop pointed out to Hitler that the terms of the Tripartite Pact bound Germany to assist Japan only in case of an attack against Japan herself. And Japan was now clearly the aggressor. Oshima asked for a formal dec- laration of war at once. On the other hand, the United States had not, so far, declared war on Germany and Italy. In fact there was a strong current of feeling in Congress that the US Army and Navy ought to concentrate on Japan and not take on the added burden of fighting a simulta- neous war with Germany. The existence of this opinion might have made it difficult for President Roosevelt to dec- lare war on Germany.[47] In the upshot, Hitler took the de- liberations out of American hands. 'If we don't stand on the side of Japan', he told Ribbentrop, 'the Pact is politically dead. But that is not the main reason. The chief reason is that the United States is already shooting against our ships. They have been a forceful factor in this war and through their actions have already created a situation of war.'[48] He waited until he could address the Reichstag on 11 Decem- ber. Shortly afterwards, Ribbentrop handed the official declaration of war to the US *chargé d'affaires* in Berlin. It did not, of course, bring about a common strategy be- tween the Axis powers. It merely ensured that they had ranged against them the three most powerful industrial nations on earth.

IV

The original aims of the Japanese assault on South-East Asia were achieved with the conquest of Java: the assur- ance of a source of supply of oil. The establishment of a de- fence perimeter within which they could exploit their gains was accomplished soon after. But further ambitions began to make themselves felt at once, as soon as the phenomenal rapidity of the British surrender at Singapore sank in. Proposals had been made as early as 6 December 1941 – before the outbreak of hostilities – to occupy Calcutta and Ceylon as a way of ensuring that no counter-attack could be made from India.[49]

On 30 December, to the list of naval bases to be secured (Hong Kong, Manila, Davao, Tarakan, Surabaya, Singa- pore) which had been drawn up before the war, the Chief

of Staff of the Combined Fleet, Vice-Admiral Ugaki,
added two further desirable bases, the Anambas Islands,
north-east of Singapore (he spelt them Anaba Islands but
there is no doubt what he meant), and Ceylon.[50] Ugaki
noted in his diary (27 January 1942) that there were four
aims the Japanese forces in South-East Asia ought to bear
in mind:

  i The destruction of the enemy fleet
 ii The destruction of enemy bases and the securing of Jap-
    anese bases
iii The encouragement of anti-British movements in India
 iv An East-West link-up between the Axis powers.[51]

In Tokyo, there were even vaster dreams of co-operation with the other Axis powers to eliminate Great Britain
from the war and force America to a negotiated peace. Yet
even at the height of victory there were those who felt
that the interests of Japan and those of Germany and Italy
did not coincide On 11 April 1942, a Liaison Conference
was held between the Cabinet and the Supreme Command,
to discuss a proposed proclamation by the Tripartite Pact
powers on the liberation of India and Arabia from British
control. Both India and Arabia were the heirs to great civil-
isations and had been for far too long under the heel of the
British. The Tripartite Pact powers would free them.
There was, of course, no intention of substituting Axis
domination for British: the Arabs must liberate Arabia,
the Indians must liberate India, but it was clearly in the
Axis interest to ensure the role this would play in the destruction of Great Britain. A balance sheet was then drawn
up on the value of such a proclamation. It had disadvantages:

  i As far as India was concerned, neither Germany nor Italy
    could intervene actively in her affairs. The responsibility
    for this would therefore fall entirely on Japan.
 ii Neither Germany nor Italy were popular in Indian eyes,
    and it was to be feared that association with them would
    give rise to anti-Japanese feeling there.

The advantages were:

i A joint declaration of this kind about India would ensure the end of Allied propaganda aimed at showing the
Axis powers were divided by incompatible interests.

ii It would be possible, by assuring the Indians that the
Axis had no intention of occupying India, to bring them
round to the Axis viewpoint.

iii There could be great dividends in encouraging the anti-
British independence movement.[52]

The balance was, by and large, favourable to a speedy issue
of the proclamation, but a later Liaison Conference (6 May
1942) received discouraging news from the Japanese em-
bassies in Berlin and Rome. There had been a discussion
between the Japanese ambassador, Oshima, and Ribbentrop, during which the German fear was expressed that to
carry out propaganda concerning Arabia and the Middle
East, in which German and Italian interests were deeply
involved, would lead to exposure of operational plans for
those areas. Moreover, to issue a proclamation of the kind
envisaged would have a profound effect on Turkey, Syria
and Egypt, and it would be as well to delay a little while
this was considered. It might also be invidious to make
propaganda before Axis forces were active in these areas.
The Japanese Foreign Minister saw the point and told
the Liaison Conference that since the Prime Minister,
Tojo, had already made adequate reference to the liberation
of India after the fall of Singapore, there was no need to
hurry the Axis partners into a common declaration while
there were still complications.[53]

The Japanese did not know this, but the real objection
to a common proclamation about India and Arabia came
from Hitler himself and his memories of the First World
War. The day before Oshima met Ribbentrop, there had
been a lengthy discussion between Hitler and Mussolini
in Berlin. When Ribbentrop reminded the Führer that
they had not yet touched on the proposed declaration,
Hitler answered that his position on the matter derived
from a conviction that in the First World War Germany

might have reached a separate peace with Russia earlier if there had been no declaration about an independent Poland. To make a declaration about India and Arabia would simply add support to Churchill, who could then tell the British people that Germany aimed at destroying the British Empire.

Had not the Japanese, Mussolini asked, already made a proclamation of their own? When Ribbentrop replied in the affirmative, the Duce said that there seemed therefore to be little urgency in the matter and it could be left to rest.

Everything depended on military developments, Hitler added. There was no point in such a proclamation until Axis troops were established south of the Caucasus. In the case of India, a military impact by the Japanese was possible, and the interests of Germany and Italy were purely theoretical. The Duce expressed complete agreement. If Germany and Italy were to make a proclamation about Arabia at that time it would be completely platonic (*absolut platonisch*) and he had little regard for platonic affairs.[54]

V

It was therefore left to the Japanese Navy to make the final profit from the fall of Singapore, and the breach in the Malay Barrier. Five days after the surrender, the Combined Fleet held exercises on future operations in the Indian Ocean. The study group which met after these exercises recommended, among other things, the seizure of Port Darwin and the occupation of the neighbouring area of Australia. Like the plan for the occupation of Hawaii, and the occupation of Ceylon, this one was gradually whittled down to a lightning raid on Port Darwin, since the complications involved in taking on Australians on their own territory far outweighed any strategic advantage gained by a Japanese presence. As for Ceylon, there were takings to be had there.[55]

But first there were the Java landings to guarantee. A

combined British-Dutch-American fleet which attempted to destroy the Japanese convoys was defeated in the Battle of the Java Sea (27 February 1942). Against heavy opposition, the Allied force, commanded by the Dutch Admiral Doorman, had no chance. Doorman lost half his force and went down with his flagship, the *De Ruyter*. The Japanese did not lose a ship, and the way to full occupation of the Indonesian Archipelago was open.

On 23 March, the Japanese occupied the Andaman Islands. These lie about 250 miles south-west of Rangoon and not much more from the western entrance to the Straits of Malacca – in fact in an ideal position from which the British might have mounted a counter-attack against occupied Burma and Malaya. After nipping this possibility in the bud, the Japanese Fleet went on the rampage in the Bay of Bengal. Under Rear-Admiral Kurita, the carrier *Ryujo* with six heavy cruisers and a destroyer screen, constituting an ancillary force to Nagumo's main fleet, set itself to raid shipping. At the same time, Japanese submarines caused havoc off the west coast of India. Between 5 and 9 April they sank well over 100,000 tons of merchant shipping.

Admiral Sir James Somerville assumed command of the British Eastern Fleet at Colombo on 24 March. It was a considerable force: five battleships, three carriers, eight cruisers, fifteen destroyers and five submarines (he had been strengthened by the ships that escaped the slaughter of the Java Sea). Acting on intelligence that after its spectacular destruction of the US Pacific Fleet at Pearl Harbour, the occupation of Rabaul, and the raid on Port Darwin, Admiral Nagumo's force was about to repeat the performance at Ceylon, Somerville decided to seek him out south-west of the island, judging he would mount his attack on the bases of Colombo and Trincomalee from that direction. Nagumo's force consisted of five aircraft carriers, three battleships, two heavy cruisers, one light cruiser and nine destroyers. Somerville looked for them, but broke off the search after three days to make for the Maldive Islands and re-stock fresh water.

That search was just not long enough. On Easter Sunday (5 April 1942), Nagumo's carriers attacked Colombo. Ships had begun to clear the harbour the previous day, but there were still two score merchantmen there, and a motley collection of smaller naval vessels. But Nagumo had learned from his omissions at Pearl Harbour. It was imperative to hinder British repairs, so his seventy aircraft did not do much damage to ships beyond sinking a destroyer and an armed merchant cruiser. Instead, they hit the naval workshops and shore installations hard, and caused great damage. Thirty-two RAF aircraft met the attack, and twenty-four failed to return; on the other hand, they inflicted similar heavy losses on the Japanese, which were to produce a delayed effect much later.

Out at sea, Nagumo's force sank the heavy cruisers *Cornwall* and *Dorsetshire*. In the face of these attacks by a combination of powerful forces, Somerville acted with prudence and withdrew to fight another day. His ships moved out of range during the day and although they attempted to close at night they never made contact with Nagumo, who was preparing to strike at Trincomalee, the base on the east coast of Ceylon. The harbour was cleared on 8 April, when news of the approaching Japanese fleet came through. On the 9th, the Japanese sent in fifty-four bombers and forty fighters from their carriers. One merchant ship was sunk, but, as at Colombo, the aircraft hit the shore installations. Five RAF Blenheims were shot down attacking the carrier *Akagi*, and nine out of eleven Hurricanes were lost as they intercepted the attackers – but, again, twenty-four Japanese planes were claimed. That afternoon the Japanese found and sank the Royal Navy carrier *Hermes*, with all its aircraft aboard.

By this time Nagumo was running short of fuel. He had driven the British Navy from the Bay of Bengal and made them run for cover to bases in East Africa, to the western half of the Indian Ocean. His ships had established their mastery of the seas across a third of the world's circumference, from Hawaii to Ceylon. In strikes against Pearl Harbour, Rabaul, Darwin, Java and Ceylon, he had sunk five enemy battleships, an aircraft carrier, two cruisers and seven destroyers, as well as thousands of tons of merchant shipping. His 'planes had shot down scores of enemy aircraft and had pulverised shore installations. All this, without the loss of a single ship from his striking force. Like Yamashita on land, he had converted the image, held by many high-ranking British officers, of the Japanese forces as sixth-rate soldiers, sailors and airmen, into the equally mythical supermen they were to become in the minds of Allied troops for the next two years: the same myth that compelled General Slim, in Burma, to train his troops by putting in attacks at brigade strength against a front held by a Japanese company to ensure there would be some victories to show.[56] It was a very powerful myth while it lasted.

VI

Nonetheless, after the fall of Singapore, the Japanese did two things which proved, in the long run, contrary to their interests.

The losses sustained by Nagumo's aircraft in the raids on Ceylon meant that only two of the fleet carriers in that raid could take part in the Battle of the Coral Sea a month later. The others had to return to pick up new machines and new pilots. The replacements were said to be inferior to the original pilots of his force. If, therefore, Nagumo had not reached out for Ceylon, or if the RAF had been less successful, the carrier group might not have been short of skilled pilots and might have avoided the reverses which were to come, in the Coral Sea and at Midway.[57]

Secondly, on the political rather than the strategic level, the Japanese Army committed a grave error of judgement after the surrender. Although it is true that General Yamashita did not allow the main body of his troops to enter Singapore City, a punitive expedition under Major-General Kawamura, the commander of 5 Division Infantry Brigade Group, was sent into the city to deal with Chinese residents who were known to be hostile to Japan, to have been connected with fund-raising activities on behalf of Chiang Kai-shek's Nationalist regime in Chungking, or to have been members of the Chinese Volunteer Force.

Kawamura's detachment consisted of Kempei (secret police) supported by two battalions of infantry. Thousands of Chinese were herded into concentration camps and questioned. Those who failed to answer in a satisfactory manner were machine-gunned, bayonetted or otherwise done away with. Massive fines were imposed on the Chinese community as a whole.The killing and the terror were such that they reached the ears of the central authorities in Tokyo. The former head of the Kyoto Kempei, Colonel Ōtani Keijirō, was sent out to investigate. He left Haneda Airport on 26 February and landed at Kallang on 6 March 1942. Ōtani spent a total of eighteen months in Singapore and Malaya, being responsible for the preservation of peace and order in the occupied territories. Even though he was a Kempei, and had experience of repressive police activities in Manchuria, it was not long before he realized how contrary to the permanent interests of Japan were the brutal methods of the first few days of occupation. Whatever the political control of the British had been, economic life was firmly in the hands of the Chinese. If the Japanese were to exploit Malaya and Singapore as sources of supply, co-operation between the Chinese community and Japanese military government was essential. As Ōtani points out, it was only natural that Yamashita should want to secure his base by ensuring that all British stragglers should be brought into POW camps and anti-Japanese elements neutralized. But there were sensible and more effective ways of doing this than those used.

As soon as he set up his office in Kempei headquarters, he received an endless stream of Chinese visitors reporting the disappearance of a father, a brother, a son, and in each case the story was the same. They had been arrested by the Japanese Army and nothing had been heard of them since.

So the rumours which had reached Tokyo were true. Even so, Ōtani recalls that such rumours were somewhat

ambivalently greeted there. Some right-wing Japanese re-
joiced at what had happened, since in their view it showed
that the Japanese Army had gone the right way about destroying the base of Nationalist China's anti-Japanese activities in South-East Asia. Others were critical. What had
begun as a *shukusei* (purge) of Chungking Chinese ended
up by being a *bōgyaku* (atrocity) to be remembered along
with the rape of Nanking as one of the biggest blots on the
reputation of the Japanese Army.[58] It was unfortunate for
the future of military government under the Japanese that
it should have started under a reign of terror, which made
a mockery of Japan's claims to be acting as liberator of
oppressed colonial peoples. What happened in Singapore
in the three days 21, 22 and 23 February ensured that
throughout South-East Asia the economically influential
communities of overseas Chinese became irreconcilably
confirmed in their hostility to Japan's New Order.

VII

In this, as in other matters, the seeds of a future Allied
victory were already germinating in the momentary
triumphs of the Axis powers. 'When I survey and compute
the power of the United States and its vast resources,'
commented Winston Churchill, 'and feel that they are now
in it with us, with the British Commonwealth of Nations
all together, however long it lasts, till death or victory, I
cannot believe that there is any other fact in the whole
world which can compare with that. This is what I have
dreamed of, aimed at, and worked for, and it has come to
pass.'[59]

Grievous as the loss of Malaya and Singapore was to
prove, heartbroken as he was on learning of the fate of
HMS *Prince of Wales* and HMS *Repulse*, and of the
humiliation of the British Navy in an ocean it had commanded for nearly 200 years, Churchill judged rightly
that, from that moment, victory was only a question of
time.

I

Why Singapore?

'You had an Alliance with us on Sunday; you broke it on Monday and started a Base on Tuesday. Surely the inference is obvious that you no longer trust us.'[1] The words were spoken by a Japanese general, known for his pro-British views, to the returning British military attaché to Tokyo in 1922. The termination of the Anglo-Japanese Alliance, carried out by a British Government which felt compelled to choose between the USA and Japan, deeply wounded Japanese susceptibilities.

At a time when Russia was the primary enemy in the Far East, the Alliance made good sense. In fact there had been three such alliances from the end of the nineteenth century onwards, all with the intention of countering Russian aggression. If Russia moved against India from Central Asia, Japan would help Britain against her. If Russia moved against Japanese interests in Manchuria Britain would help Japan.

The change in the balance of power after the First World War altered all that. For a time, after 1917, the Russian threat diminished and the German danger was removed in 1918. Then Japan gradually emerged as a threat to British and US commerce in China: she excluded British capital from railway schemes in China and Manchuria, which was a clear erosion of the so-called 'Open Door' policy. Britain began to look again at the strengthening of her position in the Far East. She looked to Singapore.

Exactly two decades separate the decision to build the Singapore Naval Base and its surrender to the Japanese in 1942. An almost uninhabited island in 1824, when it had been ceded by the Sultan of Johore to Sir Stamford Raffles acting on behalf of the East India Company, Singapore had become a prosperous city and port.* But its only defences were a few guns protecting Keppel Harbour. When Admiral Jellicoe toured the Pacific in 1919 to assess post-war naval requirements, he recommended the construction of a base in Singapore, and he had Japan in mind then, three years before the Alliance came to an end. He envisaged the possibility of Japan being able to concentrate secretly enough shipping to carry a strong army of 100,000 men against Singapore. They could capture the base and paralyse the operations of the British Navy. The Washington Conference (November 1921) agreed to limit the Great Powers' naval armaments on a 5:5:3 basis for the USA, Great Britain and Japan, in that order. The *status quo* in the Pacific, radically altered by the growth of the US and Japanese fleets during World War I, was guaranteed by a Four-Power Treaty – Great Britain, USA, Japan and France – and a Nine-Power Treaty guaranteed the integrity of the Chinese Republic, where US and Japanese interests were already seen to conflict. At the same time, US pressure on Great Britain brought the Anglo-Japanese Alliance to an end.

The powers agreed that no new fortifications or bases should be built in the Pacific by Great Britain east of Hong Kong, by the US west of Hawaii, or by Japan in her Pacific Islands. But since Great Britain's interests in the Far East required a naval presence there, or at least a naval availability, and since it was considered unnecessary and costly to maintain two fleets, one in the Western Hemisphere, one in the Eastern, it was clear that the British Fleet, while remaining in western waters, would need a Far Eastern base from which to act. In view of the limitations of the Washington agreements, and as Hong Kong was known to be impossible to defend

---

* Of his political child, 'Singapore is everything we could desire, it will soon rise into importance . . .' Raffles wrote in 1819, '[it] possesses an excellent harbour and everything that can be desired for a British port. . . . We have commanded an intercourse with all the ships passing through the Straits of Singapore. We are within a week's sail of China, close to Siam, and in the very seat of the Malayan Empire.'[2]

for any length of time, Singapore was the obvious site.

An Imperial Defence Conference was held in London in 1922 to decide whether the base should be on the south or north shore of the Island, and the recommendation that it should be on the Johore Strait was accepted by the Cabinet in 1923. The problem of how to defend it arose at once.

These were the expanding days of the infant RAF and the Air Ministry proposed that torpedo-bombers, and not the old-fashioned naval gun, were the best defence against an enemy fleet. His ships could be attacked well beyond the range of any gun, and the bombers themselves could be stationed elsewhere and brought in for an emergency. The Admiralty countered by saying – with some prescience – that heavy guns *in situ* were a real defence, whereas there was always a risk of aircraft not being available.

The bitter lessons of the Second World War make us take for granted the need for air power, and it may seem surprising that the case for the air defence of Singapore, advocated with great passion by Marshal of the Royal Air Force Lord Trenchard, was not promptly accepted and acted upon.

The case *against* Trenchard was, in fact, a strong one. At the time Trenchard was advocating his bombers, it was by no means certain that they could sink a battleship. The examples he adduced (Mitchell's sinking of the *Ostfriesland* etc) were of stationary vessels, not firing heavy barrages, and not manoeuvring to avoid bombs. Even later, in World War II, Bomber Command did not sink a single enemy capital ship with free-falling bombs.*

---

* Dr Noble Frankland has drawn my attention to the fact that this statement ignores the fate of the *Tirpitz*. This 45,000-ton German ship, one of the most powerful naval vessels in the world, was attacked on 12 November 1944 by thirty-one Lancaster bombers of 617 and 9 Squadrons RAF flying from Lossiemouth in Scotland. The *Tirpitz* was lying in Tromsö Fjord, already damaged by a previous raid carried out by RAF planes operating from a Russian base in September 1944. The RAF aircraft encountered no cloud over their target, no enemy fighters and only inaccurate AA fire.

Beatty put up the defence by naval 15-inch shore-based guns to the Cabinet in March 1924, and would have got his case through without difficulty had Trenchard not stonewalled. It was a fact that the gunners would have to *see* the invasion fleet, since radar was not then available, though star-shell could be used as illumination. Shore-based guns were easier to supply and defend than ship-based ones, and their accuracy was likely to be superior to that of any bomber – then or during World War II. So what appeared later to Trenchard's biographer as a nineteenth-century-minded Beatty making a last-ditch defence of outmoded methods was nothing of the kind.[3]

Nor was there any proof available at that time that the torpedo bomber would be effective against modern battleships possessing air cover of their own. Three 15-inch guns were therefore installed at Singapore in the first instance, in 1926, leaving open the question whether a supplementary bomber defence could be made later.

All this assumed – whether air defence or naval-gun defence was employed – that the approach by an enemy would be a frontal assault by a hostile fleet on Singapore Island. Doubts began to be expressed as to the inevitability of this from a very early stage. General Lord Ismay recalled being set an exercise on the defence of Singapore as a student at Quetta Staff College in 1922. He was told to put himself in the place of the Japanese General Staff. He did so, and devised a scheme for landing a force several divisions strong in the north of Malaya or the south of Siam to

---

They dropped their bombs from heights between 12,000 and 16,000 feet. The ship received a number of direct hits, and turned turtle. 1,000 men of her crew were lost, in contrast to the RAF, whose squadrons suffered no casualties.

Even so, it must be pointed out that the *Tirpitz* was a) already damaged, b) lying at anchor in a fjord, and c) the RAF bombers were equipped with special bombs. It was an exceptional circumstance, at a late stage of the war, and the qualifying conditions hardly indicate that its loss can serve as an argument against Beatty's case in the 1920s. (Cf. Sir Charles Webster and Noble Frankland, *The Strategic Air Offensive Against Germany*, Vol. III, London, HMSO, 1961, pp.191-196.)

attack Singapore from the north, while the island was merely blockaded from the sea. On the other hand, he reckoned that no Japanese fleet could risk being annihilated so far from Japan, if a British fleet were in being and ready to move to Singapore at short notice. He never considered a) that there would be no fleet, or b) that the Japanese might 'acquire' bases considerably closer to Malaya than home harbours in Japan.[4]

Official presuppositions about the British fleet and Japanese bases began to be questioned in the late 'thirties. Japan's invasion of China in 1931 and her refusal to withdraw her forces from Manchuria resulted in the League of Nations condemning her as an aggressor. That was in March, 1933. When Japan walked out of the League, one month later, the British Cabinet revised its 'go-slow' policy on the Singapore base, which a need for Service economy had imposed. In 1935, work was begun on further heavy gun emplacements and new airfields were planned – at Kahang in Johore, Kuantan and Kota Bharu – to cover approaches across the South China Sea. They were, unfortunately, sited without consultation with the Army authorities in Malaya, at the end of very awkward lines of communication, which made their defence and reinforcement by land almost an impossibility. This oversight was to be paid for heavily in 1941.

Ismay's Quetta exercise of 1922 has already been mentioned, but little serious consideration had been given to the defence of Malaya as a whole. Any possible thrust southwards by Japan was seen to be barred by the Philippines, with their US garrison and airfields, and by the rich colony of French Indo-China, garrisoned by French and French-trained native troops. The possibility of a naval assault on the shores of Malaya was thought to be pretty remote. The view was expressed cogently by Winston Churchill, in a Cabinet paper written after the beginning of the Second World War (December 1939):

Singapore is a fortress armed with five 15-inch guns and garrisoned by nearly 20,000 men. It could only be taken after a siege by an enemy of at least 50,000 men . . . As Singapore is as far away from Japan as Southampton is from New York, the operation of moving a Japanese Army with all its troopships and maintaining it during a siege would be forlorn. Moreover such a siege, which should last at least four or five months, would be liable to be interrupted, if at any time Britain chose to send a superior fleet to the scene.[5]

Churchill was, in any case, convinced that Japan was too involved on the continent of Asia to risk a southern adventure, and the official view in some quarters – by no means all – in Malaya was very much the same. Some British circles in Singapore were frankly nostalgic for the good old days of the Anglo-Japanese Alliance. The same military attaché – Major-General Francis Piggott – who had listened to Japanese criticism of the end of the Alliance in 1922, passed through Singapore on his way to Japan in 1936. Two civilians, long resident in Malaya, spoke to him in the Singapore Club. Their views were admittedly minority views and expressed in confidence:

> Of course it is very good for trade and for social and sporting amenities to have so large a garrison here, of all three Services and, of course, the Naval Base gives a sense of security – it is a visible, concrete symbol of our power and, let us hope, a deterrent to war. The fact remains, however, that many of us do not feel so safe now as we did in the [first world] war. Great Britain was very busy then in the Mediterranean, in Europe, in Mesopotamia, and the only nation which could threaten us out here, namely Japan, was our good Ally. Yes, we felt safe then. Do we feel as safe now that Japan is no longer our Ally? We wonder very much.[6]

They were right to wonder. That same year, one of Piggott's opposite numbers in London, Major Arisue – he was later to become the head of Japanese intelligence – returned to Japan and advised the immediate stepping-up of intelligence-gathering activities in Malaya.[7] And British commanders on the spot, who knew that the description of Sin-

gapore as a 'fortress' was absurd, had begun to envisage the
need to hold, not merely the Island, but the whole of the
peninsula.

In relation to this question, the wrangle between air
defence of the Island and defence by shore-based naval
guns was a technical issue. The real strategic problem called
into question the whole basis of the defence: did it, or did
it not, involve the defence of the peninsula? The man who
was later to control that defence, Colonel (later Lieutenant-
General) A. E. Percival, was Chief of Staff to the GOC
Malaya Command, Lieutenant-General (later Sir) William Dobbie, in 1937, and in that year wrote an appreciation – 'The Strategical Problems of Singapore' – which
analysed very shrewdly the changes in the international
military situation since the base had been planned, in
1921.[8] Percival's appreciation starts with the assumption
that even if there were not a *British* base at Singapore,
some country or other would have one. Civilians regarded
the defence installations as a nuisance, but that was because they failed to see that they were, to put things at their
lowest, the pre-emption of a hostile presence at the base.
The security of the Naval Base was the justification for the
presence of forces in Singapore. As the 1923 Imperial Conference proclaimed, with the Dominions and India in
mind, the Base was there 'To provide for the security of
the territories and trade of the Empire in Eastern waters'.
Percival split this into three: British lives and property in
China, trade routes to Australia and New Zealand, and
trade routes to India, Burma and Malaya. British capital
assets in China amounted to £500,000,000, mainly in
Hong Kong, the Yangtze Valley, and Tientsin. Of the three
channels leading East (Timor Sea, Sunda Straits, Malacca
Straits) the latter was the shortest. As Raffles had said:
'You take my word for it. This is by far the most important
station in the East, and, as far as naval superiority and
commercial interests are concerned, of much higher value
than whole continents.' Its superiority over the distant
Port Darwin was obvious. Hong Kong was a serious rival,
but it was within a zone in which the British had agreed

not to develop fixed defences, and too close to Formosa (Taiwan) and the Pescadores.

Singapore's defence, according to Colonel Percival, would have two phases: defence until the arrival of the Main Fleet, and offence after its arrival. The enemy could be presumed to want to deny the use of the base to the Main Fleet, and might land to capture 'the Fortress' or damage naval facilities there, perhaps combined with air attack. The defenders should have enough air and naval forces, especially submarines, to make it too risky for the enemy to have his carriers within range. A sudden *coup de main* attack or an attack based on long-term planning might be made by an enemy, depending on the time and the degree of surprise available. If the planning were long-term, intelligence reaching right into the enemy's country should give warning of preparations; or information should be gleanable during the voyage to the point of assault, since he must pass through narrow channels. Certain contingencies might alter this. If the Philippines became independent of the USA, they might be delivered over to the Japanese, a situation which would permit undetected voyages. Increased aircraft range would favour a defence which could use bases in British North Borneo. An enemy would have to establish air superiority, particularly if he lost this element of surprise. This would have to be done 'with carrier-borne aircraft before they can put their shore-based aircraft ashore, because . . . these latter will have been brought to the theatre of operations crated in ships.' It is evident that Percival's exercise for which the paper was written did not envisage the Japanese seizing air bases on land nearer to Malaya than China or Formosa.

The most critical part of the enemy's operation would, in Percival's opinion, be the final approach from his position of assembly to where he unloaded his troops into boats. The RAF must be responsible for watching this, and attack where opportunity offered. Geography would help here, for there were only three good approaches, all narrow: Singapore Main Strait, Rhio Strait, and Durian Strait. If the enemy succeeded in landing and were not

destroyed by beach defences as was hoped, he would be
dealt with by reserves 'which are held for that purpose'.
Other forms of attack might be used, such as attempts to
reduce the fortress by starvation.

Six months later the Committee of Imperial Defence
recorded an appreciation of the defence of Singapore. Its
assumptions are revealing:

  i Even if the Japanese thought there would be 60-70 days'
    delay in the arrival of the British Fleet, they were not
    likely to employ a major expedition in a deliberate at-
    tack, though the possibility could not be excluded.
 ii A surprise attack to capture the fortress by a *coup de
    main* was possible.

Percival and Dobbie disagreed with this conclusion.
Percival prepared a fresh appreciation based on what he
thought the Japanese General Staff would do, rather as
Ismay had done in Quetta. Attack on Malaya was feasible
and probable:

   i The Japanese might use territory in Southern Siam.
  ii Defence of North Malaya and Johore was increasingly
     important.
 iii The Japanese had new combined operations equipment.
  iv A strong Air Force was needed to prevent carriers carry-
     ing special landing craft closing Malayan shores.
   v Arrival of local naval craft, eg destroyers, should not be
     delayed.[9]

The War Office reacted in January 1938 to these proposals as follows:

  a) The British Main Fleet would sail for Singapore no mat-
     ter what the situation in European waters.
  b) The Japanese were heavily involved in China – this had
     been underestimated.
  c) The Chief of the Imperial General Staff did not consider
     provision of a tank unit justified.
  d) There was little money for rearmament.[10]

In view of the crucial importance of tanks, it is interesting to see that Dobbie first asked for tanks in 1937, and his
successor, General Sir Lionel Bond, repeated the request.
(When Percival took over command he submitted an esti-

mate of requirements. His telegram dated 2 August 1941 asked for two tank regiments, about 100 tanks).

Dobbie's insistence on the possibility of an attack from the north is interesting. He described it in May 1938 as 'the greatest potential danger to the Fortress'.[11] Contrary to what had earlier been supposed, the period of the north-east monsoon would permit such an attack; and the jungle was not, in most places, impassable for infantry.*

This perceptiveness was not confined to the soldiers. C. A. Vlieland, the colonial civil servant and controversial figure who was Secretary for Defence, Malaya, from December 1938 to February 1941, made much the same analysis, though his views on the fashionable exaggeration of the role of Singapore itself were diametrically opposed to Percival's. Vlieland's very radical Appreciation is dated July 1940.[12] Its first claim is its most important: the idea that the defence of Singapore itself is of prime importance should be discarded. Its loss would not be fatal provided the peninsula were held. The real threat from Japan was from the north. He recalled that the GOC in 1925, General Sir Theodore Fraser, had warned that Singapore would never be safe until the British held Lower Thailand. This was not the aggressive ambition it appeared to be. Fraser and Vlieland were sure that Lower Thailand could perfectly well have been *purchased* from the Thais, in all amity, at this time.

---

* 'The views held on the practicability of landing on the East Coast during the N.E. monsoon are really quite simple. In 1936 the general view, supported by the Navy, was that a landing was impracticable. Dobbie and I did not believe it, so we held a T.E.W.T. [tactical exercise without troops] at Mersing as a result of which the conclusion was reached, with which the Navy agreed, that, while landings could take place during the N.E. monsoon, there were periods of two or three days at a time, increasing as the monsoon reached its height, when landings would be difficult. Therefore, as Combined Operations have to be very carefully timed, we concluded that the Japanese would be unlikely to attempt a landing during the height of the monsoon. It appears that the Japanese also came to the same conclusion, because the 8th Dec. was about the latest date on which they were prepared to make the landing.' (Percival, in comments on Sir Shenton Thomas's *Comments,* page 1. Unpublished TS, Percival Papers).

Specifically, Vlieland rated the chances of a direct assault on Singapore as negligible. There were slight chances, no more, of subsidiary landings on the southern section of the east coast (ie south of Kuantan). Invasion in force of the Kelantan coast, on the other hand, he regarded as certain. This would follow the programme he was sure the Japanese had in mind: conquest of Indo-China for rice and as a base; Thailand, for rice; Malaya, for wealth and prestige; the Dutch East Indies to complete their southern empire. Once they landed in Kelantan the Japanese would cross to the west coast and sweep down the western coastal plains. They should be stopped decisively at an early stage, preferably north of Alor Star. If they were not, it would mean the loss of the whole of Malaya, including Singapore. Japanese air-power would be land-based, and decisive.

At a time when almost no one in England saw the risks in this light, Vlieland's prescience is phenomenal.

He had answers, too. Civil life should be disturbed as little as possible. There should be no preliminary havoc. Civilians should not be mobilized. If the volunteers were called up they should be used where their expertise could tell, not simply as soldiers. Alor Star was the key to the whole defence and the main Japanese thrust should be stopped as near to the frontier as possible. The main British effort should be concentrated on the defence of the north-west plains, subsidiary thrusts via Kroh-Baling or Kroh-Grik-Kuala Kangsar also being blocked. A thrust from Kuantan might be made but could easily be blocked. If the Japanese once succeeded in driving the British out of the north-west plains, disaster would follow inevitably. No area south of Kedah, with the exception of Kampar (though that was turnable via the Telok Anson-Bidor road from the coast), offered the same advantages to the defence, which could operate on interior lines in well roaded and highly motorised country.

Vlieland knew there were British plans to move into Thailand. He disapproved, because he knew the Government would never countenance a move until the eleventh hour, which would mean leaving prepared positions for unprepared ones. The open country in Kedah, into which the Japanese would have to debouch from narrow defiles, was perfect for defence, and could be strengthened by satellite airfields and supplementary roads, 'What exactly should be done' he concluded, 'is of course a matter for the Service professionals, but it seems to me, as a civilian who is at least familiar with the terrain, that it would not be difficult to make northern Kedah into a modern equivalent of a "fortress", which Singapore most emphatically is not'.

It emerges quite clearly from these various sources that, although there was some division of opinion about whether Singapore as such should be defended – Percival for, Vlieland against – the possibility that it might be approached overland from the north was envisaged in almost the same way as the invasion actually took place in 1941.

But this realization came into conflict with ideas about Singapore prevalent in London: that it was a 'fortress' and that the Japanese, to reach it, would have to cross hundreds of miles of narrow seas. The likelihood of the beleaguered fortress being relieved was dependent on the arrival of a British fleet, originally within seventy days, extended to ninety days in July 1939, and to 180 days three months later.[13] But this itself was in turn dependent on Great Britain not being at war simultaneously with Germany, Italy and Japan – precisely the situation which occurred. Nor were Japan's footholds on South-East Asia considered, because at the time she did not have them. These half-military, half-diplomatic footholds in French Indo-China and Thailand radically altered the security of the approach routes. In a later memorandum, Vlieland implied that the acquisition of bases in French Indo-China should have been no surprise to the British:

> The collapse of France certainly made things a little easier for the Japanese and a little harder for us, but that was all. The long-standing Japanese plan, as I envisaged it, always involved the use of Indo-China as a springboard and they must have been prepared to put in any necessary military effort to secure it.[14]

This is no doubt true but it may be questioned whether, if France had remained an undefeated military power in Europe, Japan would have risked becoming involved in a campaign to seize those bases. It would have meant lengthening her lines of communication if she did not, but this might have been preferable to a full-scale war with France. As it was, the defeat of France in June 1940 solved the problem. Indo-China was, on its own, in no position to resist Japanese demands, and concessions were granted in the north in 1940 and in the south in 1941.

Even before these Japanese encroachments, Dobbie's successor as GOC Malaya, Lieutenant-General Sir Lionel Bond, submitted a new assessment in 1940 in which he envisaged having to hold the northern frontier for several months, for which he would require four divisions and two tank regiments. These demands might be reduced if the RAF could guarantee the destruction of a Japanese seaborne expedition before it landed, or could at any rate ensure that it could not maintain its base.

Although both the Governor, Sir Miles Shenton Thomas, and the Air Officer Commanding, Far East, Air-Vice-Marshal J. T. Babington, disagreed with Bond on almost everything else, they accepted that only a strong air defence would remove the need for a large standing garrison for Singapore. On the other hand, Babington was a firm believer in the defence of the Peninsula as a whole. So too was Ironside's successor as Chief of the Imperial General Staff, Sir John Dill, who knew Percival well, and thought highly of him. At a crucial moment in British history, August 1940, between the Fall of France and the decision in the Battle of Britain, the Chiefs of Staff issued a fresh appreciation of the situation in the Far East.

They were not sure Japan would risk confrontation with Britain or the USA. If she did, her first move would be into Indo-China or Thailand, to be followed later by an attack on the Netherlands East Indies. This would precede any direct attack on Singapore. In Britain's situation at the time the wisest course was undoubtedly to avoid war with Japan and to make a general settlement with her, including economic concessions. If this proved impossible, Britain should play for time. The Fleet was still the ultimate basis of defence, but it would be an inadequate one until Germany and Italy were defeated. Britain should withdraw her garrisons from north China, and should not reinforce Hong Kong. It would be necessary to defend the whole of Malaya, and in the absence of naval reinforcements this would have to be done by the RAF. The Chiefs of Staff suggested that twenty-two squadrons (336 aircraft) would be needed. The squadrons in Malaya should be modernized and brought up to establishment by the end of 1941.

Much was to happen before then. The air defence of Britain put a strain on aircraft production, and Germany's invasion of Russia in June 1941 diverted to Russia aircraft which could have been sent to Malaya. Between the German invasion and the winter of 1941, it has been estimated that fifty-three British merchantmen sailed for Russia, carrying war equipment which included 200 Hurricanes. The Chiefs of Staff protested to the Defence Committee that 'these aircraft would pay a better dividend if sent to the Far East and to the Middle East and/or Turkey'.[15] Whether much profit would have been gained by letting Turkey have them is highly questionable. But they might have made all the difference in Malaya.

But even before Russia came into the war, the Chiefs of Staff held out little hope for a real reinforcement of the air strength of Malaya. On 10 January 1941 they signalled the Commander-in-Chief, Far East:

> We agree that 582* aircraft is an ideal, but consider 336 should give very fair degree of security, taking into account experience in Middle East . . . Malta and defence of Great Britain. *Japanese should not be over-estimated* [*My italics*]. The target of 336 cannot be increased before end of 1941 and remains subject to general situation and supply of aircraft.

---

* Brooke-Popham testily annotated this figure: 'I am not clear where they got the figure 582 from, the number asked for from Singapore was surely 566.' In fact, the conference of commanders in the Far East, held in October 1940 (before Brooke-Popham's arrival) had named the higher figure. He should, of course, have known.

... Suggested air reconnaissances South China Sea appear too ambitious ...

... Anti-tank artillery not available, but anti-tank mines will be despatched.

Tanks cannot be provided at present.[16]

The Official Historian remarks that the decision limiting British aircraft in the Far East to a hoped-for 336 by the end of 1941 became known to the Japanese.[17] A document recovered from a Japanese aircraft which crashed in China nearly a year later gave this figure as Japan's estimate of Britain's Far Eastern air strength.[18]

The Japanese seem, too, to have been *au fait* with the Chiefs of Staff's appreciation – though whether that of August 1940 or that of 1941 is not clear. Sir Cyril Newall, Chief of the Air Staff, wanted to appraise Brooke-Popham of their decisions and decided to send the full details not by aircraft but by what was deemed a more secure method, by ship. The ship in question was sunk by a German submarine, the captain of which removed the documents before sinking the vessel. One of them was the Chiefs of Staff Appreciation, which was found in Berlin after the war, with a minute to the effect that it was clearly important and should be transmitted to Tokyo. So on Britain's general stance and capabilities in the Far East the Japanese can have had little to learn.[19]

Even the low figure of 336 aircraft then had a setback. Churchill sent the Chiefs of Staff a strong rebuke when they next met on 13 January 1941:

I do not remember to have given my approval to these very large diversions of forces. On the contrary, if my minutes are collected they will be seen to have an opposite tendency. The political situation in the Far East does not seem to require, and the strength of our Air Force by no means warrants, the maintenance of such large forces in the Far East at this time.[20]

So instead of the 582 aircraft asked for in 1940, instead of the scaled-down figure of 336 promised for the end of 1941, the RAF had only 158 planes when war broke out. But even this low figure is deceptive: for the most part they were obsolescent types, slow and unwieldy bombers such as the Swordfish and Wildebeeste, and fighters such as the American Brewster Buffalo which arrived in February 1941 and had a theoretical maximum speed of 295 mph. Only Hurricanes could match the Japanese Zeros, which averaged 325-335 mph at 18,500 feet, and even Hurricanes could not manoeuvre as well as the Zeros below 10,000 feet.

In spite of their obsolete machines, some RAF representatives were incredibly optimistic about their effectiveness, before war broke out. Many years later, Percival wrote to Professor J. R. M. Butler,

Although it was apparent to most of us, including apparently the C-in-C, Far East and the AOC, that our Air Force was too weak to do much damage to a seaborne expedition before it could establish a bridgehead, yet at a Joint Staff Defence Conference held, I think, about August 1941, the view was officially expressed by the C-in-C's Air Representative (Gp. Capt. Darvall) that we could rely on the Air Force destroying, I think, about 70% of the ships of an invading force before it landed. The trouble all along was that most of the Naval and RAF senior officers were *far* too optimistic as to what they would be able to do.
(Percival 'Comments on *Grand Strategy*, Vol. III', 7 January 1962, Percival Papers)

Percival was – to some extent – right to exempt Brooke-Popham from this ill-considered optimism. Some months before Darvall expressed the above views, Brooke-Popham wrote to the Permanent Under-Secretary of State for Air, Sir Arthur Street:

The AOC (Babington) and his Staff have had, and are having, a great deal to do and think about and are doing well. But there is a peculiar undercurrent here which, if it were flowing through any organisation other than the Royal Air Force, one might term inferiority complex . . . one of the big contributory factors is that the RAF are flying aeroplanes of obsolete design and of ancient vintage and there are no reserves to keep them going if war should start. Our Singapore flying boats ought quite definitely to be scrapped

and some of the boats would undoubtedly be condemned as
unfit to fly by a technical board ...

He then added, naturally perhaps, but a little confusingly:

> I want to make it clear that I have not the least anxiety
> with regard to their determination if it came to a scrap, or
> their confidence that in spite of their handicap as regards
> equipment that they are capable of taking on any number
> of Japanese squadrons or Japanese ships.
> (15 January 1941, Brooke-Popham Papers, v/2/3)

On the other hand, in their depreciation of the future
enemy which lay behind this unwarranted optimism, the
army officers Brooke-Popham met were equally remote
from realities. 'I was amused by one battalion commander'
Brooke-Popham wrote to General Ismay, 'who while we
were standing together looking at his men said "Don't you
think they are worthy of some better enemy than the Japanese?" . . . I also got a similar remark from the Colonel
of the Argyll and Sutherland Highlanders yesterday; he
has trained his battalion to a very high pitch for attacking
in the type of country one gets near the coast and said to me
"I do hope, Sir, we are not getting too strong in Malaya,
because if so the Japanese may never attempt a landing." '
(Letter to Major-General Sir H. L. Ismay, 3 February
1941, Brooke-Popham Papers, v/1/5.) Colonel Stewart
need not have worried. When he was promoted to Brigadier, he was to lose nearly his entire brigade at the hands
of a single Japanese tank column – less than a year after he
spoke to Brooke-Popham.

The reinforcements which came were not aircraft but
men. The 8th Australian Division, under Major-General
Gordon Bennett began to arrive in February, and in April
two brigades of 9th Indian Division (Major-General A. E.
Barstow) came from India – without artillery. There were
changes in command, too. Air-Chief-Marshal Sir Robert
Brooke-Popham, with a tiny staff, came out in November
1940 as Commander-in-Chief, Far East to deal with major
questions of military and political strategy. He was sixty-
two, had already retired from the service, and had spent

some time as Governor of Kenya. If the defence were to
rely on air power, his appointment made some sense, and
he made some headway in sorting out the complexities of
military and civil organization in Malaya. Brooke-Popham
was a man of varied experience and considerable shrewd-
ness. He had a very difficult brief. The over-riding priorities of home defence in 1940 compelled him to accept the
limited resources offered (but never completely supplied)
by the Chiefs of Staff. He had to bear in mind London's
policy of doing the utmost not to provoke the Japanese into
offensive action and at the same time make a show of confidence in the inadequate means at his disposal to resist
them, if bluff and diplomacy failed. This gave him a tricky
time when confronted by an inquisitive press, and to some
correspondents he undoubtedly conveyed the impression
of the senior British officer in the traditional role of Colonel Blimp. The American reporter Cecil Brown, of the
Columbia Broadcasting System, who had already tangled
with British military censorship in the Middle East, saw
Brooke-Popham at a number of press conferences and interviewed him privately. 'He had an odd abashed, friendly
manner, and a high, breaking voice,' wrote Brown, who
described him as a giggly, boyish, country squire when
laughing off difficult questions.

Yet Brooke-Popham was no blimp. Physically very
tough, and quick-witted, he was an astute judge of character. He lacked decisiveness at a crucial moment at the
start of hostilities; but more important was the fact he
seemed to share the conviction of several commanders that
the Japanese would not be a dangerous enemy. When he
toured Hong Kong at the end of December 1940 he went
up to the frontier with China, where the Japanese Army
was already in occupation. He looked across at them:

> I had a good close-up, across the barbed wire, of various
> sub-human specimens dressed in dirty grey uniform, which
> I was informed were Japanese soldiers. If these represent
> the average of the Japanese army, the problems of their
> food and accommodation would be simple, but I cannot
> believe they would form an intelligent fighting force.[23]

On the civil side, the Governor was the tip of an umbrella under which came the Colony of the Straits Settlements (Singapore, Malacca, Penang, Province Wellesley), the Federated Malay States (Perak, Selangor, Negri Sembilan, Pahang) and the Unfederated Malay States (Johore, Trengganu, Kelantan, Kedah, Perlis). The Governor was also High Commissioner for the States, which were governed by their own sultans, the Federated Malay States having also a form of federal government at Kuala Lumpur. But the States had to be dealt with separately, not as a single entity, which created problems of consultation. In addition, Brooke-Popham was not the only Commander-in-Chief in Singapore. The Commander-in-Chief, China Station, Vice-Admiral Sir Geoffrey Layton, had moved his headquarters from Hong Kong to the Naval Base at Singapore, and he was responsible, not to Brooke-Popham, but to the Admiralty in London. The various local commanders had been instructed to carry on their usual administrative and financial relations with London – the Air Officer Commanding, Far East, to the Air Ministry, and the Governors of the Straits Settlements, of Hong Kong and Burma (all were within Brooke-Popham's purview) to the Colonial Office.

There were changes in the garrison. Once 9th Indian Division arrived, III Corps Headquarters was formed to be responsible for the defence of Malaya north of Johore and Malacca, using the 9th and 11th Indian Divisions. This was put under the command of the victor of Keren, Lieutenant-General Sir Lewis Heath. In April 1941, Air Vice-Marshal C. W. H. Pulford relieved Babington as AOC Far East and Lieutenant-General A. E. Percival succeeded Bond as GOC Malaya, in May. In August, Churchill despatched the Chancellor of the Duchy of Lancaster, Duff Cooper, to Singapore to act as resident Minister of State and political overlord.

The new brooms had arrived. All began to sweep busily in different directions.

II

Japan's Course for War

Japan's course to war upon Great Britain and the attack upon Malaya were predictable. Once she had embarked upon her policy of carving out an empire for herself, based in part upon her conquests in China which began in real earnest in 1937, and euphemised as 'The China Incident', Japan was bound to come into collision sooner or later with those powers whose economic or emotional ties with China compelled them to oppose her. The collapse of Holland and France in 1940 laid open their eastern dependencies to Japanese aggression, and the British defeat at Dunkirk indicated that Britain herself would hardly be in a position to resist Japanese encroachments. Japan joined the Tripartite Pact on 27 September, 1940, linking her fortunes with those of Germany and Italy, but also ensuring that Japan retained a free hand in dealing with the Dutch East Indies. The discussion at the Imperial Conference of 19 September 1940, showed that the Japanese Government was fully aware of the likelihood that signing the pact would make future agreement on policy with the US extremely difficult. But the Army was pressing to conclude an agreement with a victorious Germany, and, as the Foreign Minister, Matsuoka, pointed out:

> We are a great power with a strong navy in Far Eastern waters. To be sure, the United States may adopt a stern attitude for a while; but I think that she will dispassionately take her interests into consideration and arrive at a reasonable attitude. As to whether she will stiffen her attitude and bring about a critical situation, or will levelheadedly reconsider, I would say that the odds are fifty-fifty.[1]

Those odds altered considerably in the course of the next fifteen months, during which Japan mapped out her course of aggression with greater precision. The decisions were taken in a way that had become customary since 1937. The Supreme Command, consisting of the Chiefs of Staff of the Army and Navy, was responsible for planning and operations. They reported directly to the Emperor, but they and their Vice-Chiefs also met representatives of the Cabinet every few days in what were termed 'Liaison Conferences' (*Renraku Kaigi*). The Cabinet usually fielded the Prime Minister, the Foreign Minister, the War Minister, the Navy Minister, and other ministers of state such as the Finance Minister if required. The secretariat of these conferences consisted of the Cabinet Chief Secretary, the Chief of the War Ministry's Military Affairs Bureau, and the Navy Ministry's Chief of the Naval Affairs Bureau. The purpose was to obtain a common line between Government and the Supreme Command.

When major issues were involved, the debates were repeated in the presence of the Emperor and the President of the Privy Council in what were termed Imperial Conferences. As a rule, the decisions had already been taken, and the Imperial Conferences were basically rubber-stamping ratifications. On occasion though, the Emperor did intervene and asked the occasional embarrassing question, or probed a minister or two; but by and large his role was not to speak, merely to be present.

Throughout 1940 and 1941 the conferences dealt with the problems of Japan's conquests, in particular the solving of the China Incident. The supplies sent to Chiang Kai-shek by Britain and the US were delaying a settlement. They had to be stopped. Of the two routes, the Burma Road, which the British under pressure agreed to close for three months in October 1940, was the less important. Most of the supplies were shipped through the port of Haiphong and along the Yunnan railway. French Indo-China was therefore the target for Japan's policy. Northern Indo-China was 'occupied' in the summer of 1940, when the Governor-General (first General Catroux and later Admiral Decoux) found it impossible to resist Japanese demands. The following year, Southern Indo-China was similarly occupied. At this point, the US Government decided that draconian measures of economic reprisal should be invoked to force Japan to withdraw from Indo-China. Embargoes had been used before: in July, 1940 there was one on aviation fuel, in September on scrap iron, in November on exports of iron and steel to Japan. On 25 July 1941, Japanese assets in the US were frozen. This was not a direct retort to the occupation of southern Indo-China, but a response to the wishes of Chiang Kai-shek. As it happened, the following day Japan made public her intention to occupy strategic areas in southern Indo-China, and on 28 July began off-loading troops in Saigon. The US reacted again. On 1 August 1941, the final step of imposing an oil embargo was taken. The net effect of these measures was that Japanese trade was limited to Manchuria, occupied China, Thailand and Indo-China.

The situation between Japan, the USA, and Great Britain was narrowing towards a conflict. The Japanese Premier, Prince Konoye, had dismissed his war-like Foreign Minister, Matsuoka, in July 1941, and told the US Ambassador, Joseph Grew, on 6 September 1941 that he felt personally responsible for the deterioration in Japanese-US relations, and would like to be personally responsible for improving them. He suggested a direct meeting between himself and Roosevelt, in Honolulu or Alaska, to achieve this, and as a beginning declared that he accepted Secretary of State Cordell Hull's 'Four Principles':

   i respect for the sovereignty and territorial integrity of all nations;
   ii non-interference in other countries' affairs;
   iii equality of commercial opportunity;
   iv non-disturbance of the Pacific *status quo*, other than by peaceful change.[2]

Roosevelt did not consent to the meeting, because he thought exchanges at ambassadorial level had produced no good results, and he did not anticipate any from an encounter between Konoye and himself. He was by no means sure that Konoye could take the rest of Japan with him, particularly his military colleagues, in a policy of concession.

He may well have been right in thinking things had already gone too far. The Japanese service chiefs had already given Konoye to understand that they would not withdraw from China, and America would not lift the oil embargo unless they did. Besides, South-East Asia was now regarded as the next objective.

Konoye met Grew on the evening of the same day (6 September 1941) on which the most fateful of all the Imperial Conferences had met. At that conference the decision was made for Japan to be prepared for war even if this involved the USA. At the same time, all diplomatic means were to be employed to reach an agreement with the USA and Britain, but if negotiations came to nothing, then Japan should determine on war with the USA, Great Britain and the Netherlands. That conference sealed the fate of Malaya and Singapore.

Certain documents presented to it made quite clear that the Japanese Government was fully prepared to take the risk of war with the USA and Great Britain in order to continue its policy of building up a New Order in East Asia: 'The building of the New Order will go on for ever, much as the life of our State does'.[3] If Japan were forced to go on making concessions to the Americans, her Empire would ultimately lie prostrate at the feet of the United States. Such a war would be long, no one knew how it would end, and it would be impossible to expect America to surrender. On the other hand, factors might be produced which would lead American public opinion to desire to end the war, such as Japanese success in operations in South-East Asia or the surrender of Great Britain:

At any rate, we should be able to establish an invincible position: by building up a strategically advantageous position through the occupation of important areas in the South; by creating an economy that will be self-sufficient in the long run through the development of rich resources in the Southern regions, as well as through the use of the economic power of the East Asian continent; and by linking Asia and Europe in destroying the Anglo-American coalition through our co-operation with Germany and Italy. Meanwhile, we may hope that we will be able to influence the trend of affairs and bring the war to an end.[4]

The French collapse gave Japan her opportunity. General Catroux, who had become Governor-General of French Indo-China in August 1939, telegraphed Marshal Pétain on 18 June 1940 that if France were to conclude a separate peace with Germany, it was still necessary to co-operate with the British in the Far East, where both France and Britain were facing the same enemy, Japan. In addition, it was vital that Indo-China should continue to be able to draw minerals from India and supplies from elsewhere in the British possessions in the Far East. In a later telegram to the British government Catroux added that the British decision to go on fighting received his full support; he sent a copy to his own government at Bordeaux to make it clear that, in spite of the Armistice, Indo-China and he himself, as Governor-General, intended to pursue the war against Germany at the side of Great Britain.

The previous day, 19 June 1940, he had received an ultimatum from Tokyo, which gave him a breathing space of only twenty-four hours in which to give in to Japanese demands or be invaded. In the end, whatever his protestations, Catroux was forced to accept the Japanese demands, which kept increasing throughout 1940 and 1941.

The Role of
Economic Sanctions

Two factors affected British economic policy towards the
Far East after the fall of Holland and of France in the
summer of 1940. One was the need to ensure that supplies
from the French and Dutch colonies did not reach Germany. The other was to try and prise Japan away from
her conquests in China. Sometimes these purposes coincided, sometimes they clashed: because a prime condition of achieving the first aim was to ensure that Britain,
while apparently on the verge of defeat in Europe, did not
become involved in hostilities with Japan. This meant being
able merely to irritate the Japanese without going far
enough in inconvenience to produce a cause of war.[1] 1940
saw many rapid changes. In May discussions began for an
Anglo-Japanese trade agreement. Germany's victories in
Europe changed all that. The occupation of Holland and
the fall of France made French Indo-China and the
Netherlands East Indies vulnerable to pressures from Germany and Japan. Before Germany attacked Russia in June
1941, it was still possible for goods to be channelled to
Germany from the Far East via Japan, Vladivostok and
the Trans-Siberian Railway. The situation became acute
after 17 September 1940 when Japan ceased to be an un-
friendly neutral and allied herself with Germany and Italy
in the Tripartite Pact.

For the Americans, the situation was ambiguous. Japan's
conquests since 1931 had given her areas of Manchuria and
North China which ensured that, with her own production,
she could run her war with Chiang Kai-shek largely from
her own resources. Largely, but not totally. She had coking
coal from North China for her steel industry, but she also
needed scrap iron to feed it. Her own iron ore production
was too small. She also needed ferro-alloy ores, and de-

pended on supplies from abroad for these. Nearly a third of her iron and steel scrap came from abroad, mostly from the US. Likewise over 80 per cent of her iron ore. The United States was still, in 1940, Japan's biggest supplier of commodities needed by Japan to continue her war against China.[2] Above all, she had no oil, no rubber. These now lay tantalizingly just beyond her grasp in Malaya, French Indo-China, and the Netherlands East Indies.

In the case of rubber, German needs in 1941 were also considerable. The Germans expected to consume 122,000 tons of rubber that year, and their domestic synthetic production could only provide 62,000 tons. They had stocks of 21,000 tons and expected to be able to import the remaining 40,000 tons: 4,500 from Brazil, 6,000 from Netherlands East Indies and 30,000 from French Indo-China. Given British control of the Indian Ocean, the latter supplies could only come through Japan and Japanese-held territory. The British Ministry of Economic Warfare was therefore concerned to ensure that supplies of rubber to Japan from these sources did not exceed what Japan herself required, so that no surplus could be exported to Germany.

But it was impossible to achieve complete consistency. Japan needed rice, and Britain had the possibility of restricting exports from Burma. On the other hand, Burma depended on her rice exports, and as her European markets had disappeared, she had half a million tons to dispose of. There was no question, then, of cutting off the Burmese nose to spite the British face. Similarly, though the USA had confined the export of aviation fuel to countries in the western hemisphere (31 July 1940), thus depriving Japan of a source of an important strategic material, there were political repercussions. Japan increased the demands she made to Netherlands East Indies. Within the US Government, opinion was divided. The service ministries urged the cessation of all oil supplies to all foreign countries. The State Department successfully resisted this, but could not prevent the export of iron and steel scrap being restricted to countries of the western hemisphere (16 October 1940).

This was not economic warfare. It was a policy of pin-
pricks. It infuriated the Japanese without compelling them
to change their policy. The USA was suspicious, in any
case, that Britain was seeking to involve them in war. Even
on 10 February 1941, when Roosevelt was sure a Japanese
attack upon French Indo-China, Thailand and possibly
Malaya and Singapore was imminent, he told Lord Halifax,
the British Ambassador in Washington, that the US would
declare war if Japan attacked American possessions, but
he was sure the American people would not support such
a declaration if the Japanese restricted their attacks to the
Netherlands East Indies or to the British Empire in the
Far East. The Americans were convinced that Singapore
could not be defended; and war in the Pacific would only
divert materials from the Atlantic, where the war would
be decided.[3]

Until the freezing of Japanese assets in the summer of
1941, the American attitude seems pusillanimous beside
that of the Dutch. Between September 1940 and June
1941, the Netherlands East Indies Government held off
pressures from a succession of Japanese delegations. Yield-
ing a minimum of concessions, they continued to resist the
Japanese will to penetrate economically into the Netherlands East Indies. Japan first asked for oil, to offset the
American cuts. The Netherlands East Indies government
said it could not compel the oil companies to sell, and referred the Japanese to the companies themselves. A delegation was to be sent to Batavia (now Jakarta) on 16 July
1940 headed by General Koiso, later Japanese Prime
Minister. But Koiso had made in public some remarks
construed as offensive by the Dutch, and they refused to
receive him.[4] The Japanese were compelled to replace him
by their Minister of Commerce, Mr Kobayashi. To ensure
the Japanese did not feel entitled to enlarge the negotiations to include political discussion, the Governor-General left the exchanges to Dr van Mook, his Director of
Economic Affairs. The Japanese complained that his
rank was too low for him to carry out discussions with
Kobayashi who was, they pointed out, a cabinet minister.

The Dutch promptly elevated van Mook to the rank of Minister Plenipotentiary, and the talks began.

Estimates of Japan's oil holdings by the Americans and the Allies were that Japan could carry on a war against Britain, the Netherlands East Indies and the US for nine months with the stocks she already had. The obvious deduction from this was that if there was an effective stoppage from all oil-producing areas, Japan would be forced to attack the Netherlands East Indies and take the oil she needed. The Japanese demanded 3,750,000 tons of oil from Royal Dutch Shell and the US company Standard Vacuum (whose participation in the talks was frowned on by the US Government, which, however, imposed no sanctions on the company*). The export rate at the time was 600,000 tons. The companies made a counter-proposal, which the Japanese were forced to accept, of around two million tons. A Japanese request to allow her experts to visit the refineries and production sites was refused.

At the end of October 1940, the Dutch in Java told the Netherlands Government, then in exile in London, that French Indo-China had agreed a set of supplies to Japan for the period November 1940 to January 1941, and suggested that this indicated the need for comprehensive restrictions on exports to Japan, particularly tin and rubber from Malaya and Netherlands East Indies. But neither British nor Americans could countenance action which might lead to open war. They could not offer help to the Netherlands East Indies if the Japanese used military force to back their demands.[5]

At the Imperial Conference held on 19 September 1940 to consider the consequences of Japan's joining the Tripartite pact, Prince Fushimi, the Navy Chief of Staff, pointed out that in spite of the indications of the President of the Planning Board, Hoshino, that Japan might be able to obtain oil from the Soviet Union and also from Germany

---

* The Standard Oil Company had already (before September 1940) tried to sell to the Japanese its holdings in the Netherlands East Indies because it feared losses from war (Ike, *Japan's Decision for War*, p.9).

(who was supplied from the Soviet Union and Rumania and was said to have ample stocks as a result), Japan could not rely on these sources. She could not carry on a war on the basis of her own stockpiles. 'In the end, we will need to get oil from the Netherlands East Indies,' he assured the conference. 'There are two ways of getting it – by peaceful means, and by the use of force. The Navy very much prefers peaceful means.'[6] That this was a hopeless ideal was underlined by Hara Yoshimichi, President of the Privy Council, who made what was to be Japan's case for war as clear-cut as possible:

> You cannot carry on a war without oil. The capital in Netherlands East Indies oil is British and American, and the Dutch Government has fled to England; so I think it will be impossible to obtain oil from the Netherlands East Indies by peaceful means.[7]

Lieutenant-General Tōjō Hideki, then War Minister, expressed the Army view, which was opportunistic:

> As for the Netherlands East Indies, it was decided that we would try to obtain vital materials by diplomatic means, and that we might use force, depending on the circumstances.[8]

The meeting concluded with both Army and Navy welcoming the Tripartite Pact. But Prince Fushimi, on behalf of the Navy, sounded a final caution about taking every possible measure to avoid war with the United States, to avoid friction with third parties in carrying out the 'southward advance' by peaceful means, and to control anti-British and anti-American statements and behaviour.[9]

The negotiators for the Netherlands East Indies were under no illusions about the possibility of preventing Japan from having their oil and keeping the peace at the same time. 'The Indies were probably the main Japanese objective,' wrote van Mook later, 'if they did not want to succumb miserably and disgracefully, they would have to fight anyhow. But for a sudden and complete change of fortunes on the European and African battlefields – which did not occur – the attack would come and come suddenly: since her trade with the world had disappeared, every succeeding month weakened Japan's position by a depletion of vital stocks.'[10]

There were certain practical problems involved in holding the Japanese at arm's length. The Japanese delegation and its numerous staff began to look as if they were permanently installed in Java, and they must have been a source of precious information for the Japanese Army and Navy as the constant staff changes sent messengers back and forth between Batavia and Tokyo, under the shelter of diplomatic immunity. Even though Kobayashi's successor, the experienced diplomat Yoshizawa Kenkichi, a former Foreign Minister, proved more courteous and sophisticated than his browbeating predecessor, the Dutch were more than pleased when he acknowledged defeat, and returned to Japan with very little in the way of concessions to show for months of hard bargaining.[11] Some seven weeks later, on 26 July 1941, a Reuter telegram gave Java the news that the USA had suspended financial and economic intercourse with Japan. The Netherlands East Indies followed suit. As van Mook points out, the American and British embargoes would have been fruitless if the Netherlands East Indies had not joined in.[12] The Japanese protested. But from 28 July 1941 contacts between the Netherlands East Indies and Japan virtually came to an end.

What had produced this American action, so different in spirit and intention from the attitudes of 1940 and early 1941? A new ambassador, Admiral Nomura, arrived in Washington in March. Conversations began with Cordell Hull, the Secretary of State, in which Nomura suggested a termination of the 'China Incident' by a mutual acknowledgement of the independence of Manchuria, but insisted on maintaining some Japanese troops in China. These proposals, presented on 12 May 1941, were to be accompanied by a resumption of normal trade between Japan and the US, particularly in the procurement of certain natural resources: oil, rubber, tin, and nickel.

The British viewed with extreme unease Hull's willingness to exchange views of this kind with Nomura. Eden wired that Matsuoka, the Japanese Foreign Secretary, was clearly intending to withdraw from China but to keep the positions Japan had acquired in Manchuria, Indo-China and Thailand, driving a wedge between Britain and the US in doing so. The terms of the telegram were withdrawn by the British ambassador Halifax when Hull expressed pained resentment that the British should doubt either his good faith, or his sagacity in dealing with the Japanese.[13] Britain's fears were explained by the fact that she felt her efforts to impose economic restrictions on Japan were having some success. In addition, distinctions had carefully been made between strategic materials, on which partial or total embargoes had been placed, and civilian commodities, trade in which was still largely free: raw cotton, the largest single import from the British Empire, was free from restrictions, and foodstuffs were not reduced below normal quantities.

It was Japanese miscalculation over their occupation of the southern half of French Indo-China which brought matters to a head. Both the British and US governments knew that Japan intended to make such a move. Halifax asked Roosevelt on 7 July 1941 to announce that if Japan made a military move into southern French Indo-China then all possible economic pressures would be applied against her. Roosevelt was undecided on the wisdom of an announcement beforehand. He was not sure it would deter the Japanese. It might have the contrary effect of playing into the hands of extremists. He told Halifax to speak to Sumner Welles (Under-Secretary of State acting as Secretary in Hull's temporary absence), who told Halifax he had always advised Roosevelt to apply a complete economic embargo on the Japanese as soon as they committed any overt act of military aggression but that he did not favour announcing such an embargo in advance, for the reasons Roosevelt had given.[14] Both Welles and Roosevelt were wrong. The Japanese were convinced that the Americans would do nothing. American reticence assured them that if they moved into Indo-China's southern airfields there would be no violent reaction in Washington. They were surprised when there *was* such a reaction. It was clear to the British that, although military conversations with the US early in 1941 had left the initiative in Far Eastern matters in American hands, the Americans were not intending – at least the State Department was not – to sever *all* trade connections with Japan. Stanley Hornbeck, Hull's Far Eastern adviser, told a British representative that he thought there might be an embargo on petroleum products, but that United States supplies of silk from Japan were vital and no embargo would be imposed on them.[15] British anxiety was that America might impose an embargo but would not back it by the threat of force. If Japan did not back down, but preferred to use force southward instead, the British and Dutch would be left to resist such aggression on their own, as a result of collaborating with a country which would go only so far in imposing her will. British uncertainty about how lenient or harsh the US Government intended to be continued right up to the final declaration. It was not known at any stage whether the US would support them if the Japanese used armed force to retaliate. Nor did the freezing of assets take place with simultaneous effectiveness in all fields. Throughout August and September, as the measures began to take effect, the State Department realized that what had happened ultimately was a declaration of economic warfare against Japan.[16]

If the Liaison Conferences are anything to go by, Japan's initial reaction, voiced through the new Foreign Minister, Admiral Toyoda Teijirō, was not to take the embargo as a lethal blow at all. Anticipating fairly precisely what would happen, he declared at a Conference on 24 July 1941,

> The occupation of Indochina will exert an influence on the United States; they will adopt a policy of putting an embargo on vital materials, freezing Japanese funds, prohibiting the purchase of gold, detaining Japanese vessels etc.
>
> Among the items included in the embargo on vital materials will be raw cotton, lumber, wheat and petroleum. As for cotton and lumber, we have already taken steps. Since America is sending wheat to China, we can somehow or

other get round the embargo on wheat. [*A clear indication of how trade still flourished between occupied and unoccupied China!*] Although petroleum causes some anxiety, it is unlikely that the United States will impose a complete embargo on it.[17]

Toyoda was more concerned about the freezing of cash and securities. Japan had 550 million dollars' worth tied up in the USA; the US had 300 million dollars' worth in Japan, which left Japan the vulnerable side at a disadvantage of 250 million dollars, when the assets were balanced off. The result would be a shortage of the funds needed to buy petroleum and would cause much hardship. Ōgura, the Finance Minister, had told Toyoda that freezing funds *would* cause hardship, and he proposed to write a letter to the American Secretary of the Treasury, Henry Morgenthau, in a private capacity, to see what could be done to alleviate this.[18] (The letter was, in the event, postponed.)

A later Conference (5 November 1941) took a more serious view. In an overall survey of Japan's economic prospects, the President of the Planning Board, Suzuki Teiichi, reckoned the total oil to be stockpiled by December 1941 at 1.11 million kilolitres, for Army, Navy and civilian consumption. His view was that it would be difficult to carry on a war against the US, Britain, and NEI while still maintaining hostilities against Chiang Kai-shek. But since initial victories were more than probable, he thought the increase in morale resulting from them would turn the Japanese people towards a greater production effort, and at the same time persuade them to reduce their consumption. 'In terms of maintaining and augmenting our national strength, this would be better than just sitting tight and waiting for the enemy to put pressure on us.'[19] If war were avoided, and Japan attempted self-sufficiency, he warned against optimism about synthetic petroleum. After three years the Army and Navy would have difficulty in meeting their needs, and it was 'well-nigh impossible to achieve self-sufficiency in liquid fuels in a short period of time, depending only on synthetic petroleum. It is estimated that even if we take strong measures, at least seven years will be required.'[20]

Kaya, the Finance Minister, expressed his misgivings in a series of rhetorical questions, though he prefaced these by a claim that Japan had been able so far to carry on operations in China smoothly as far as financing the war was concerned. But what if operations were to be extended?

It is clear that when we begin military operations in the South, additional large expenditures of Government funds will be needed to cover them. Can our national economy bear the burden of such large military expenditures? Especially, are they feasible when the probability is high that the war will be protracted? Will there not be unfavourable effects on finance? Isn't there danger of a vicious inflation as a result of these expenditures?[21]

Kaya also hinted at the hard times Japan's military adventure south would bring upon the nations of South-East Asia and the Indies. These countries had imported materials of all kinds in large quantities from Japan. Once the areas were occupied by Japanese forces, he said, their imports would cease:

Accordingly, to make their economies run smoothly, we will have to supply them with materials. However, since our country does not have sufficient surpluses for that purpose, it will not be possible for some time to give much consideration to the living condition of the people in these areas, and for a while we will have to pursue a so-called policy of exploitation. Hence even though we might issue military scrip and other items that have the character of currency in order to obtain materials and labour in these areas, it would be difficult to maintain the value of such currency. Therefore, we must adopt a policy of self-sufficiency in the South, keep the shipment of materials from Japan to that area to the minimum amount necessary to maintain order and to utilize labour forces there, ignore for the time being the decline in the value of currency and the economic dislocations that will ensue from this, and in this way push forward.[22]

'Of course,' he added, and the codicil boded no good for

the millions of people Japan was soon to conquer, 'it is to be recognized that the maintenance of the people's livelihood there is easy compared to the same task in China because the culture of the inhabitants is low, and because the area is rich in natural products.'[23]

So whatever the slowness and uncertainty about the American freezing of Japanese assets, whatever the difficulties felt by the British in ascertaining just what were the details of the policy to which they were committed in a more or less blind fashion, three months of embargo reconciled the Japanese Government to the prospect of war against European possessions in South-East Asia, with a concomitant preventive strike against the Americans. For their part, the Americans thought the British were very cautious in committing themselves and in letting the US know the precise limits of that commitment. In a memorandum dated 21 July 1941, Stanley Hornbeck, the State Department's Far Eastern Advisor, noted that he had asked Noel Hall, British Minister in Washington, to discuss the proposed economic embargo measures with Dean Acheson. Afterwards, he [Hornbeck] had asked Hall what the British proposed to do. They would denounce certain commercial treaties, was the answer. They would 'tighten controls' of exports and imports. But Hall did not know what his Government's intentions about freezing assets were. He added that Japanese trade with the UK was not significant in volume, but that with the Dominions and Colonies it was considerable.

Hornbeck viewed Hall's comments as 'inconclusive and not very comprehensive' and added a final comment:

I am of the impression that the British government has rather vague and rather limited intentions as regards economic pressure against Japan, and that the British Government's chief interests as regards such conversations is to find out what this Government has in contemplation and have itself in position to offer to this Government suggestion or advice.[24]

On the other hand again the British must certainly have

been puzzled had they known how little punitive intention was to be shown by the US Government. State Department correspondence at the time shows that, far from deliberately and publicly relating the freeze to Japan's occupation of bases in southern French Indo-China, a pretence was to be made that they were to retain materials for the USA's own defence, and that no reference to Japan or to China was to be made.[25] Of all the factors involved in setting Japan finally on the road to war, it seems that the freezing orders of July 1941 were the most crucial. Yet the initiator of these orders, the United States Government, seems to have entered upon them without, at first, a full knowledge of their likely impact. And the collaborators, Britain in particular, were committed to a course of action of which they did not know the details until the last minute:

> On 27th September, [writes a British official historian] the [British] embassy, after reporting that Hull was highly gratified with this co-operation [*a standstill on trade between Japan and the British Empire, and a cessation of oil exports to Japan from the Netherlands East Indies*], emphasized the decisive potentialities of the new economic weapon. The United States had discovered *by accident* [my italics] the technique of imposing a total embargo by way of the freezing order without having to take decisions about quotas for particular commodities: it was now in a position, if it wished to do so, to state that the Japanese had imposed the embargo upon themselves by their lack of loyalty to the American freezing regulations. Hull however insisted that the utmost secrecy was necessary; the United States Government would not admit that any connivance with the British Government was taking place.[26]

So from the end of September until the outbreak of war, Japanese trade with the US, Great Britain and the Netherlands East Indies more or less came to a standstill. Even so, there was no agreed plan of action concerted between Britain, the Netherlands East Indies and the US, nor did the American State Department give the British a full prediction of its future programme for Japan.

The British Foreign Office believed it was the American view that the Japanese were bluffing, and the economic embargo was the final card played to call that bluff. Once Japan's stocks were exhausted, she would have to give in to the demands made upon her by Cordell Hull in his conversations with Ambassador Nomura, who was joined by Kurusu Saburō in November as special envoy. The almost total cessation of exports to Japan was bound to bring her face to face with an unpalatable alternative: either she must give up her policy of expansion in Asia which had been the cornerstone of her national development for decades, or resort to war. There had always been ways, hitherto, of disguising the crudity of this alternative. After July 1941, there was none. The policy-makers in the US and Britain must have had rather different views on the duration of the crisis. If oil is taken as the crucial stock, American estimates of Japan's oil reserves were far higher – by a factor of two – than the British estimate. By the end of 1941, the US Government reckoned Japan would hold around ten million tons. The British Ministry of Economic Warfare calculated she would have just over five million tons. The British estimate was much closer to the mark (the US Strategic Bombing Survey later gave the actual figure as 6,690,000 tons for December 1941) and it must therefore have seemed to the British that the pressure on Japan was likely to produce results, one way or another, much more rapidly than the American policy-makers envisaged.

The role of economic embargo in forcing Japan to the position of desperate choice is clearly emphasized by the British official history; which adds that the weapon of maritime blockade was the real weapon which ensured the Allied victory in the war which the economic embargo had precipitated:

> In the end Japan was brought to unconditional surrender without an invasion of her home islands, and after devastating and expensive air attack; there seems every reason to think that the same result could have been achieved more economically by blockade alone.[27]

IV

The Role of Thailand

The role of Thailand in the events in Malaya in 1940-41 has been examined historically from one side or another – Japanese or British. In fact, sympathy must go to the Thais themselves during this period. The only independent country in South-East Asia, Thailand was placed in an intolerable position by the pressures of powerful neighbours.

Thailand was a monarchy, ruled in practice by a military dictator, Pibun Songgram, after the coup d'état of 1932. Power was, however, shared between Pibun and his colleague in the coup, the lawyer Nai Pridi Panomyong, a friend of Britain and the US, as was the Foreign Minister, Nai Direck Jayanama.

Resurgent Thai nationalism was shown by the rejection in 1939 of the old name Siam, used by Europeans and Americans, for the name Thailand ('Freeland'). Britain was unwilling to use it, because it was symbolic of military pro-fascist nationalism on the lines of that which seemed to be taking over Japan. British writings of the time always use the name 'Siam'. And there was irredentism. Like other countries of South-East Asia which had a past of greater glory than their dependent present, Thailand had once ruled a much larger territory. Four provinces of Northern Malaya, Kedah, Perlis, Kelantan, and Trengganu, had once been Thai territory, and were ceded to Malaya in 1909. Parts of the Shan States, Keng Tung and Mong Pan, now under Burmese (ie British) rule, had once belonged to Thailand. So too had an area west of the Mekong which the French had incorporated in 1904 into Laos and Cambodia.

The Japanese were not slow to profit from this irredentism in 1940, when France's weakness made it impossible to defend the frontiers of French Indo-China. War broke out in November 1940 and in spite of frantic efforts by Sir Shenton Thomas, the Governor of the Straits Settlements, and Vice-Admiral Sir Geoffrey Layton, C-in-C, China Station, to act as mediators in the dispute, it was Japan who succeeded in imposing herself in this role upon the warring parties. The mediation unhesitatingly gave Thailand part of Indo-China on the right bank of the Mekong bordering Laos. It also established the Japanese in a position of great influence in Bangkok, where hitherto the major influence had been British. Brooke-Popham wrote ruefully to Ismay, 3 February 1941, that in spite of the efforts he, Shenton Thomas and Layton had made from Singapore to bring about an end to hostilities between the Thais and the French, the Japanese had stolen a march on them and scored a diplomatic victory. The Japanese had 6,000 troops in Tonkin to reinforce their 'mediation', and could send planes and tanks to Bangkok if they chose, as well as an 8-inch cruiser off Saigon, 'whereas we couldn't send a man or a gun'. But he was convinced nobody was to blame for this, and added:

> Another thing that I am quite certain about is this. We played absolutely square and openly both with the Thais and with the French. But the fact that they double-crossed us* merely proves whom we can trust in future or rather whom we can't, but it in no way alters the fact that we must go on playing straight and not try to imitate their duplicity. For one thing Englishmen are naturally very unskilful liars and for another, from my dealings with Iraqis and Egyptians I am quite certain that one confuses a deceiver far more by telling the truth than by trying to imitate him.[1]

The British Minister in Thailand was a principal factor in the maintenance of British prestige there, and an interesting figure in his own right. Sir Josiah Crosby was a man who knew the Thais intimately, spoke their language well, and was desperately anxious not to involve them in international conflict. His eagerness to prevent this, at all costs, without doubt influenced the advice he gave the

---

* The phrase seems strong in this context.

government in London, and the authorities in Singapore. Although Brooke-Popham had only been in his command a few months when he wrote to Ismay, he had already summed up Crosby's attitude to the Thais:

> I feel that Josiah Crosby, our Minister in Bangkok, was, at any rate on this occasion, too much inclined to rely on his former knowledge of the Thais and the former friendship of the Thai Ministers for him. He didn't seem to realise the rapidity with which the situation was changing. One so often finds people who have been a long time in one place and who have a genuine affection for the people, getting into the position of believing 'These people are my friends, they will never deceive me.' I don't in the least wish to suggest that Josiah Crosby should be moved, in fact I think it would be a great mistake to do so at the present time. Further, he has doubtless realised his mistake, but to my mind it emphasises the need for some independent source of information, which is in hand here.[2]

Crosby's pressure played a crucial role in the development, or rather lack of development, of British strategic plans for the Kra Isthmus, where the Japanese were to land in December 1941.

But the situation really goes back to the outbreak of friction between the Thais and the French in Indo-China. The French had other problems in 1940 besides the Japanese. Vietnamese insurgents were in open rebellion in the Langson area, close to the Chinese border, in the autumn, and were repressed with some harshness. The Thais had signed a non-aggression pact with the French on 12 June, but instead of ratifying it they proceeded to reclaim the lost provinces of Cambodia (Battambang, Sisophon, Siemreap) and part of Laos. There was some ethnic justification for Siam's claim on Laos, since the Thais and Laos are akin. But the Khmers of Cambodia are not connected with the Thais, and the case there was not only weak but put with extravagant violence by Pibun, who claimed the entire kingdom of Cambodia as historic Thai territory.

A series of clashes between French and Thai forces

escalated in January 1941. French native troops were half-hearted, and their equipment was poor. They were defeated in Cambodia by the Thai army. In a tit-for-tat action, French naval forces entered the Gulf of Siam on 17 January 1941 and in two hours put paid to the Siamese navy at Koh Chang. 'It was', says Decoux of this not particularly glorious encounter, 'the only pitched battle fought by the French Navy during two world wars.'[3] At this point the Japanese put forward their plan to mediate between the two belligerents. The meetings were held in Tokyo, with the French ambassador to Japan leading the French delegation, and Prince Varnvaidya leading the delegation from Bangkok. The upshot was that neither party was satisfied, but Japan consolidated a position of authority as mediator. Japan took advantage of her newly won prestige to extend her diplomatic representation in Siam. She had had no consular representatives outside Bangkok before. But in 1940-41 she established two consulates, one at Chiengmai in the north, and one at Singora, in the far south, close to Malaya.

There were other repercussions, particularly in Anglo-French relationships. The Governor-General of French Indo-China, Admiral Jean Decoux, was convinced that the French Minister in Bangkok, Lépissier, was thoroughly inept and slavishly subservient to the notions of his British colleague. The situation did not lack a certain piquancy, since the British Minister, in an earlier stage of his career as British consul-general in Batavia, had also carried out the functions of consul-general of the French Republic. In this position he had, in 1925, welcomed to Batavia the young French naval officer who was later to become Governor-General of Indo-China during the Japanese occupation. Decoux remembered Crosby's *entregent* and spirit of intrigue, and described him as a Jew with a lively mind and supple intelligence, who spoke French correctly and was a connoisseur of fine French wines. Unsuspecting Frenchmen therefore took him, Decoux wrote later, as a friend of France, but the reality was slightly more complex. 'I did not for my part suppose for one single instant, from the very day I met him, that he would ever contemplate compromising, in any way whatever, the interests of the British crown, or risk his own personal situation, in order to ensure the safety of French interests. The contrary would have been surprising.'⁴ Crosby's endeavours to have Thailand sign a pact of friendship and non-aggression with Great Britain were the natural outcome of his ambitions, says Decoux. Crosby therefore was, in French eyes, prepared to back Thailand against French interests in Indo-China. 'I would prefer to see the Siamese established on the mountain ranges of Annam than the Japanese army penetrating into Thailand,' he is rumoured to have confided to a colleague, and, through M. Garreau, the French *chargé* in Bangkok, the phrase was not long in reaching Decoux in Indo-China.⁵

Decoux heard other rumours filter through from Bangkok, too. He wired the French ambassador in Washington on 23 November 1940 that Crosby maintained to the Thais that the British government was fully in sympathy with them in demanding territorial restoration at the expense of French Indo-China.⁶ That Decoux's suspicions of Crosby's statements were not unfounded is shown by a conversation which took place in Washington a week before that telegram was sent. The Chief of the Division of Far Eastern Affairs in the State Department, Maxwell Hamilton, was visited on 18 November 1940 by Nevile Butler, the British chargé d'affaires. Butler put the issues which were currently occupying his government's mind in relation to the dispute between Thailand and the French. The British feared most of all that Japan would establish herself in southern French Indo-China and make arrangements with Thailand for use of military bases there which would bring the threat to Singapore much closer. 'Would it be preferable,' Butler wondered,

> for Thailand . . . to take over certain portions of French Indo-China rather than for Thailand to feel estopped from doing so by the attitude of the British and the American Governments? Should Thailand take over Indo-Chinese territory, would not Thailand be disposed to resist Japan

78

and not to agree to give Japan military bases in Thailand?
Should Thailand make no move to take over Indo-Chinese
territory, would not Thailand feel that it had been estopped
from such action by the attitude of the British and American
governments and would not Thailand be more likely to agree
to give Japan military facilities in Thailand?[7]

When he asked Hamilton what the US view would be,
the reply was that use by Thailand of military means to
reclaim territory which now belonged to another country
would serve to stimulate aggression and in the end be
disastrous to Thailand itself.

A different, more balanced version, was given by the
chargé's namesake and cousin, R. A. Butler, then Under-
Secretary for Foreign Affairs, to Johnson, the American
chargé in London, four days later. Crosby was doing his
best in Bangkok, he told Johnson, to discourage Thai attempts to make demands on French Indo-China, because the British wished to encourage French resistance to
Japan. By the same token, they were not encouraging the
de Gaulle movement in Indo-China, though de Gaulle
had sympathizers there. 'To strike the balance between
Thailand ambitions and stiffening of Indo-China resistance was a ticklish job.'[8]

On the other hand, Americans in Bangkok were sure
Crosby was playing a very tricky game. The US Minister
to Thailand, Grant, wrote to the State Department on 26
November 1940 that the *Bangkok Times*, a British-con-
trolled English-language newspaper, had hinted that the
French in Indo-China should accept frontier rectifications
with Thailand. Grant was sure the article had the fullest
approval of the British minister. 'I repeat,' he added, 'that
the British here are apparently ready to make almost any
concessions in the Indo-China affair solely in their own
selfish interests and without regard to us or our Far Eastern right of transit.'[9] Crosby was perhaps less tricky than
Grant believed, for he had expressed himself clearly
enough to Roger Garreau, the French chargé in Bangkok,
in terms which Garreau had promptly reported to the
Quai d'Orsay, who in turn conveyed them to Robert

Murphy, the US *chargé* in France, in pained uncompre-
hension. The British were in no position to restrain the
Thais in their attitude to Indo-China, Crosby had said,
as such an attempt would only throw them more and more
under Japanese influence. Even if he could take such a
step, he would not do so. It was much more to British
interests for the defence of Singapore to see aggressive
Thai troops on the Mekong as a defence against Japanese
forces pushing through Indo-China with the Malay peninsula as their probable ultimate objective. (The terms are
very similar to those reported to Decoux.)[10]

The French were puzzled by Crosby's attitude. They
were not sure whether it really represented the British
Government's view, or whether, as Ostrorog, Acting Head
of the French Foreign Ministry's Far Eastern Division
put it, Crosby was 'another case of too much zeal on the
part of a small Colonial-minded administrator with which
class the French have had so many previous difficulties
even at times when their relations were the closest.'[11]

In spite of R. A. Butler's soft words in London, it seems
likely that Crosby was in fact expressing a governmental
view – and no doubt it coincided with his own, though his
later account of these matters sounds very pro-French.
The proof of this lies in a later conversation held with
Sumner Welles, US Under-Secretary of State, and Nevile
Butler, on 23 December 1940. Butler admitted that
Crosby had favoured the rectification of the Thai/Indo-
China boundary, at the expense of Indo-China, with the
consent of the British Government.[12]

The upshot of this early situation was as follows: Japan
established herself militarily in Northern Indo-China, and
as a power to be reckoned with in the counsels of the Thai
government. French Indo-China had not only looked to
Britain and the US for aid and failed to obtain it. Her
authorities, and the authorities in Vichy, were sure the
British had connived at their humiliation. No doubt Vichy
had been greatly at fault too. France had begged the US
to sell a few aircraft to supply the Indo-China garrison
and the request had been refused. But the refusal was

perfectly justified. The Americans saw no reason to release to France aircraft which they could use themselves, while the French still had at their disposal, in Martinique, 100 modern aircraft which they could have shipped at once to Indo-China. The claim that such a transfer was forbidden by the armistice arrangements with the Germans was not accepted by the Americans. Indeed it is difficult to see the Germans objecting to a transfer aimed merely at safeguarding a French colony. But whatever the reasoning, the upshot was that French Indo-China was, in effect, abandoned to Japan's aggressive designs and Thailand lay open to them.

Not that the Japanese themselves were absolutely sure of Thailand's peaceful collaboration. At a Liaison Conference in Tokyo on 11 June 1941, in reply to a suggestion from the Army Chief of Staff, General Sugiyama, that Japanese troops should move into southern French Indo-China, the Foreign Minister, Matsuoka, said that if Japan did this, it would provoke retaliation by Great Britain and the United States, and British troops would move into Thailand. If French Indo-China were to be invaded – and frankly he preferred to exercise pressure indirectly instead, ie through Germany acting upon Vichy – then the Japanese should go into Thailand at the same time. This would inevitably involve the British. Sugiyama did not think so. A show of Japanese strength would ensure the British did not intervene. With heavy irony, Matsuoka replied, 'From the point of view of diplomacy, I would like to go on a sudden rampage, but I won't because the Supreme Command tells me not to.'[13]

Sugiyama need not have worried. A couple of months after that Conference, the Defence Committee in Great Britain recommended a joint warning to Japan by the United States and Great Britain that if she treated Thailand as she had French Indo-China, it would lead to war. This was moved during the absence of Churchill on the American visit which led to the Atlantic Charter, and the Committee hoped he would obtain Roosevelt's acquiescence in such a course. But the Chiefs of Staff did *not* think action by Great Britain alone was possible, if Japan occupied even the Kra Isthmus, that part of Thailand bordering on Malaya. Without United States support, they felt, Great Britain had not enough men or ships and would have to accept a Japanese *fait accompli*. If not backed by the United States, any warning to Japan would be bluff. The Defence Committee – then chaired by Attlee – nonetheless agreed to move troops to Singora in Thailand, without starting hostilities against Japan, if the latter came into northern Thailand.[14]

The general tenor of Japanese conferences in the summer of 1941 was that it would be appropriate to enter southern French Indo-China, because the United States would not stop such a move, particularly when the issue between Germany and Russia was still undecided, with the advantage to the Germans. It was also felt that pressure against Thailand, with its even more obvious implications for Malaya and Great Britain, should be postponed.

In August the situation developed further. Anthony Eden, the British Foreign Minister, said that a Japanese occupation of Thailand would have 'grave consequences' and he advised the Thais to resist Japanese aggression. Some days later the British Ambassador to Tokyo, Sir Robert Craigie, had a conversation with Matsuoka's successor as Foreign Minister, Admiral Toyoda Teijirō, the details of which are rather surprising in view of the impression the British forces in Malaya were trying at that moment to create in the Japanese mind. The Japanese press had claimed that Eden's speech proved Japan was being encircled by the ABCD powers (America, Britain, China and the Dutch). The British were not, Craigie affirmed, threatening Japan. 'We cannot increase our forces in Singapore and Malaya because we do not have the ships,' he told Toyoda, 'although we are increasing aircraft. Hence we cannot advance into Thailand.'[15]

Craigie declared he was sure Japan's aim was to drive Britain out of Thailand, and he pointed out that Britain would be satisfied as long as she acquired rice, tin and rubber and could be sure these materials were not sent to Germany.[16]

When he presented the report of this conversation with Craigie to the 40th Liaison Conference (14 August 1941), Toyoda used it as evidence that the problem of the freezing of Japanese funds could be settled if the *military* advance south were halted. He assumed the economic advance could go on. It was clear, too, that British troop strength along the Thai border was weak. Tōjō was not interested: the acquisition of Thai bases had already been approved by Imperial Conferences several times and it was too late to change that policy.[17]

The Imperial Conference on 5 November 1941 brought the Thai issue up again. Japan wished to enter into an arrangement for the transit of troops, but was prepared to use force if Thailand refused. Hara, President of the Privy Council, pointed out:

> If we allow time for negotiations, Great Britain will learn about them. In that event, the intentions of the Supreme Command will become known to the enemy . . . If you are going to use coercion, it will be coercion, and not negotiation for a close military relationship. This approach would affect our relations with Thailand in the future.[18]

Tōjō, who had become Prime Minister by this time, answered that the Japanese had been working on the Thai Prime Minister, Pibun Songgram, to win Thailand over to the Japanese side and set up the close military relationship Hara referred to. There were delicate points. Militarily, Japan would have to make landings in Thailand, and it would not do to let this be known too early. In the talks that were proposed, if the Thais did not agree, it would be necessary to act in any case. The documents presented to the conference specified three points to be demanded of the Thais:

1 Transit of Japanese troops and use of facilities.
2 Steps to prevent clashes with Thai troops.
3 A mutual defence pact to be signed if the Thais wished it.

But before negotiating to secure these aims, Japan should not show any particular change in her attitude towards Thailand as great care had to be taken to keep secret the plans to begin the war. There would be promises to respect Thailand's sovereignty and territorial integrity. And there would be perks: 'In order to facilitate our negotiations and depending on Thailand's attitude, she may be secretly told that in the future she might be given a part of Burma, or perhaps Malaya.'[19]

Hara raised the problem of Thailand again in the Imperial Conference which took place immediately before the outbreak of war (1 December 1941). Would Thailand ally herself with Japan or with Great Britain, he wanted to know. What would happen if Thailand opposed Japan? What did Tōjō intend to do?

Tōjō was quite frank. He did not know, even at that late hour, how the Thais would react, or which side they would choose. Thailand herself did not know, she was in a quandary. Peaceful means to ally her with Japan were desirable, but the time factor was vital. Early aggressive action could be damaging, so too could delay. The Japanese intended to broach matters just before war began, and to make the Thais agree to their demands. It was planned to do everything to prevent her from resisting, even though, if the worst came to the worst, force might have to be used.[20] Ike's *Japan's Decision for War*, from which these accounts of the Imperial Conferences are taken, does not contain the translation of the February conference (1941) which dealt with policy towards French Indo-China and Thailand, but a note adds that the document referred to established the objective of a 'close and inseparable military, political and economic union between Japan, Thailand and Indo-China.'[21] In fact, the record of the conference and document in the *Sugiyama Memo* shows that the Emperor put a number of questions to Sugiyama and his naval colleague on the plans for air bases in French Indo-China and Thailand. When the Emperor asked what air bases the army had in mind, Sugiyama answered 'Saigon and Phnom Penh'. These were air bases which must be prepared if future operations were considered. In addition, Tourane and Nha Trang were important for landing operations against Malaya. The Emperor then asked if air bases had been required from Thailand and the Naval Chief of Staff answered that it was as important to have air bases in Southern Thailand as in the Saigon area. Surprisingly, Sugiyama added that Saigon was really vital, but that he had not given too much thought to Southern Thailand. Generally speaking, the plan was to avoid the use of military force and proceed as much as possible by diplomatic means.[22]

In Bangkok itself, the Japanese were as eager to precipitate a violation of Siamese neutrality by the British as the latter were to inveigle the Japanese into preceding *them*. American codebreakers kept their own intelligence services informed of this, but it is not apparent from Brooke-Popham's papers that this intelligence was passed on to him. A message received on 1 December 1941 outlined a Japanese plan 'to entice the British to invade Thailand and thereby permit Japan to enter that country in the role of defender.'[23] This secret information was based on a radio message to Tokyo, dated 29 November 1941, from the Japanese ambassador in Bangkok. Commander A. H. McCollum, the head of the Far Eastern Division of the Office of Naval Intelligence, catalogued a number of espionage activities uncovered from signals intelligence:

(a) The Japanese consulate at Singora was manned by four Army intelligence officers.
(b) A consulate had been established at the northern railhead of Chiengmai.
(c) Army communication personnel and equipment were present at Singora, Bangkok and Chiengmai.
(d) Four Army and Navy officers under assumed names had been sent to the Embassy in Bangkok. The Ambassador had received instructions not to interfere in the work of these men.
(e) A chain of drug stores manned by intelligence agents was in process of establishment.
(f) Japanese Army doctors under assumed names were in the hospital at Bangkok.

(g) At the end of November 60,000 Bahts were sent in gold to the Ambassador at Bangkok with instructions to hold it for emergency intelligence use.

(h) At least two sabotage agents had been sent into Singapore.[24]

And, in this kind of game, it would be surprising if the British were not doing the same kind of thing. Late in November 1941, the Japanese Consul-General in Bangkok, Asada Shunnosuke, returned from Tokyo with new instructions for the approaching emergency. He did not know when war was to be declared, but he knew something was likely to happen pretty soon. During the night of 1 December 1941, he was awakened in his private residence by a messenger. Asada had just returned by military aircraft from Tokyo, not by scheduled services, and he was a little surprised that anyone should know he was back in Bangkok. A package had just been handed in at the Embassy for him, the Messenger said. Asada looked at the address: ASADA ESQR. It struck him as an odd way of addressing him. Bangkok correspondents didn't use 'Esqr' as a rule. Opening it, he read on a half-sheet of ordinary typing paper the phrase: 'THE BRITISH ARMY WILL OCCUPY SOUTHERN THAILAND A WEEK FROM NOW'. It was, of course, unsigned. Agents came in and out of the Embassy with all kinds of information, Asada knew, and it was not his first contact with it. But this kind of precise information was unusual.

He remembered then that he had received an offer of secret intelligence from a source inside the British Legation. About two or three months before, he had been introduced by a clerk at the Embassy to a man who described himself as the archivist at the British Legation. 'I am an Iranian,' this man had told him, 'and I have worked for many years as archivist at the British Legation. But Great Britain is the enemy of my country [*Great Britain had occupied Iran in October 1941*] and I hate her. I have heard rumours that Japan is going to attack Singapore. I pray to God that is true. My job puts me in touch with many secret documents, and I am sure they will be of use to you in your plans for Singapore. I want 1,000,000 yen for the information. You can pay me after the fall of Singapore.'[25]

Asada's caution, when faced by this letter, which he thought might well have been sent by the Iranian archivist, is understandable. It would profit Great Britain not at all, he knew quite well, to infringe Thailand's neutrality first. Surely this *yami jōhō* ('black market intelligence') was intended to precipitate action by Japan, which would provide a pretext for action by the British? In other words, running through Asada's head were exactly the same reactions which operated in Brooke-Popham's case some days later, when he was faced with the information that a Japanese convoy was approaching the shores of Thailand : was it not a foray designed to induce the British to act first?

The state of uncertainty on both sides prevailed until the Japanese moved into Thailand with their armies – in fact shortly after.

British military contacts with the Thais were still very friendly until quite late in 1941. In July, Sir Robert Brooke-Popham met the Thai Colonel Sura Narong, who had a message from his Premier, Pibun Songgram. Pibun wanted Brooke-Popham to know that he was pro-British and anti-Japanese. His son was in England and his other children in America. Was that not proof? But if the Japanese used force against him he could not resist, and so far England had not helped, nor had the US. The C-in-C Far East was asked to realize that this was the explanation of the attitudes Pibun was at times forced to adopt.

Brooke-Popham accepted this, he told the Colonel, but countered by saying that Pibun must recognize *he* had difficulties, too. He could promise Pibun at that time no support from Malaya. Great Britain was fighting in Western Europe and the Middle East and had lost equipment in Greece and elsewhere. Output was increasing but was still below 1941 requirements. Early in 1942 things might improve and he might afford the Thais some help then, if only from the air. The proper course for the Thais to take was to play for time, to avoid concessions as long as possible, and then to give way as little as possible, until Britain could assist. Though even then he could not say whether such help would be direct support or a supply of munitions.

Sura Narong said Thailand needed tanks, anti-tank guns, anti-aircraft guns, and fighter aircraft. Even twenty tanks would be welcome, and the Thais would accept British instructors with them. He was sure Brooke-Popham would welcome that.[26]

Similar hints were being dropped in Singapore by Thai officials. The American journalist Cecil Brown, of the Columbia Broadcasting System, talked to the Thai Consul-General in Singapore, Luang Vudiasora Nettinate, on 5 August 1941. He was pro-British and anti-Japanese, the Consul told Brown. Thailand wanted to maintain her neutrality, but would defend herself. She had 400 aircraft of Japanese and US makes and 300,000 trained men with modern equipment. If Japan invaded Thailand, there was a fifty-fifty chance the Thais would resist. They could hold out for three or four months, unless the Japanese put in a naval attack, in which case he didn't think the Thais would last much longer than twenty-four hours. They only had a small navy and very few shore batteries. Brown hinted that Thailand had already a secret agreement with Japan and Germany, and Nettinate indignantly denied this. He added that the Thais didn't want the Japanese mediation in the war with Indo-China, but couldn't help themselves.[27]

On the evening of the same day, Brown went along to interview Tsurumi Ken, the Japanese Consul-General, whom he described in unflattering terms as a man with the air of a good fellow and the eyes of a cut-throat. Tsurumi was, he was sure, operating an espionage organization in Singapore. Never one for finesse, Brown asked bluntly: 'Are you going into Thailand?' Tsurumi fenced: 'We have economic interests there.' Brown pointed out that one of Japan's aims was to close the Burma Road, and that obviously operating from Thailand would make that much easier. 'Then you have,' he persisted, 'a definite military objective outside of other considerations for invasion of Thailand?' Tsurumi merely laughed, and answered 'Yes'.[28]

A month after these two interviews, Brown saw the Thai Consul again. This time the Consul upped the odds.

'We are swinging away from the Japanese,' he told Brown,
'I can assure you that ninety per cent of the Thais would
fight a Japanese aggression. Why, we would even oppose a
British aggression. We would fight anyone who tries to attack our country.' Brown was not convinced. 'I hope so'
was all he said.[29] But he was interested to notice that
Brooke-Popham gave a similar impression at a press conference a week later (16 September 1941). Relations with
Thailand, Brooke-Popham told the assembled newspaper-
men, had become more friendly. The Thais had begun to
realize the British could help them. They were becoming
more independent-minded, having realized it was uncom-
fortable to be too economically dependent upon Japan.
Brown cut through the cosiness, and asked: 'Sir Robert,
would you be prepared to go to the help of Thailand?'
Brooke-Popham airily waved a hand, and refused to answer a question that implied too many assumptions. Brown
dug in: 'If Thailand were invaded by the Japanese and
they called on you for help, are you prepared to give that
help?' Brooke-Popham fenced, and gave the only honest
answer possible: 'If the order comes from Whitehall, I'll
carry it out.' In that answer lay the doom of Operation
Matador, and of the chance to intercept the Japanese before they got to Malaya.[30]

That Britain alone could not stop the Japanese going
into Thailand was admitted to Cecil Brown by Admiral
Sir Geoffrey Layton on 11 August 1941. 'Even if America
came in,' Layton told him, 'I don't believe Japan would
stop.' He didn't believe, either, that the British could drive
them out, once they were established in Thailand, though
he believed their sea communications could be pulverized
and they would then collapse. He also gave Brown the
line proposed by the Defence Committee in London,
though without saying it was an official line: 'The most
possible action, the most probable that would succeed, is
to dispatch to Singapore some portion of the American
fleet and a public announcement that if the Japanese go
into Thailand it would be a *casus belli*.' If that were stated
definitely, he thought it would make the Japanese refrain

from going into Thailand at all. On the other hand, if the Japanese *did* move, the British would not attempt to stop them, unless they came further south, though he was not precise about what he meant. He then told Brown to cross that statement out.[37] Brooke-Popham gave Brown exactly the same answers, but to Brown's statement, based on what the Thai Consul had told him, 'The Thais say they will fight if they are attacked by the Japanese,' Brooke-Popham countered with 'Yes, if they are not bought out by the Japs'.[32]

Visits of Thai officers to Singapore continued until early December. In a memorandum on the Malayan campaign [*Some Personal Observations of the Malaya Campaign 1940-1942*], Lieutenant-Colonel B. H. Ashmore, who was GSO/II (Operations and Training) at Malaya Command HQ, records that information on Thailand was obviously lacking even up to a few days before the attack. A high-ranking Thai officer visited Ashmore's office in Singapore on 3 December 1941 to discuss the possibility of receiving a 'Christmas hamper' of arms and ammunition from Britain to assist in defence against the Japanese. Ashmore noted indignantly that this request was made five days before Thailand's complete hand-over to Japan, and that the officer must have been aware of events and feeling in his own country. He came as the fully accredited representative of the Thailand Army and Ashmore had been given full authority to discuss weapon matters with him. 'He did not learn a great deal from me' Ashmore wrote later, 'but he was conducted on a tour of the defences of Singapore.'[33] In the event, that officer did not return to Thailand, but was arrested and made a POW. Percival himself was, not unnaturally, suspicious of the colonel's visits – once in July and once in November. Not that he suspected the colonel himself of playing a double game – had he not been trained at the British Staff College? – but he thought it possible he had been sent to throw dust in the eyes of the British. If the Japanese had not been in close touch with certain highly placed Thai officials at the same time the colonel was in Singapore, they would never have been able to make all the secret preparations in south Thailand to anticipate their landings. Nor would the Thais have opposed the British entry into their territory as they did.[34]

And yet, just before war broke out, a young British diplomat on Crosby's staff, Andrew Gilchrist, was quizzed by the Thai Foreign Minister, Nai Direck Jayanama. He asked Gilchrist what aid Thailand could expect from Britain in the event of war, and Gilchrist was forced to give the usual dusty answer. Nai Direck then told him: 'If the Japanese do invade us, I know that Nai Pridi and myself will never accept the situation. You may be sure we will work against them. I want you to understand this, because you are my friend.'[35]

V

Operation Matador

The role of Thailand is important in relation to Malaya for a number of reasons. The Japanese needed to land troops in the Kra Isthmus to capture airfields close to North Malaya and to put their forces within striking distance of the road down the west coast; and they needed transit rights for the invasion of Burma. But the British also had plans for Thailand, and these crystallized into what came to be called Operation Matador. It was never carried out. But it has been the source of as much controversy as many an operation which really took place. Its preparation took up the time and energies of Indian troops who might have been better employed preparing defences. It finally placed a burden of choice on the shoulders of the Commander-in-Chief, Far East, which he seems to have been unwilling to bear. And the delay involved in the final wrangles about whether it should be mounted or not resulted in dismay for the troops involved and a clear advantage to the enemy.

Matador was discussed in London by General Percival before he left to take up his appointment as GOC Malaya (16 May 1941). The problems were not new to him though the scene had changed considerably in the four years since he had served as Chief of Staff Malaya Command in 1937. It was now impossible to send the Fleet to the Far East, the Chiefs of Staff wrote in their appreciation of August 1940. Communications and aerodromes in Thailand had developed, and, with the increased range of aircraft, this constituted a greater threat to Malaya. But even in 1938, General Dobbie had written

> It is an attack from the northward that I regard as the greatest potential danger to the fortress. Such attack could be carried out during the period of the north-east monsoon [ie October to March].[1]

Brooke-Popham told Percival to consider the possibility of moving into Southern Thailand as a preventive measure to seize the ports where the Japanese might land. The matter was discussed at several conferences. But he was told that Matador was not to be put into effect without reference back to London. It was to be done only when it became clear beyond reasonable doubt that the Japanese were approaching the shores of Thailand. As Percival points out in his despatch, by the time permission had been asked for and obtained, the opportunity to act would have been lost.

Militarily, there were great advantages in Matador. The enemy could be caught on his landing beaches and annihilated there; and the additional aerodromes could be used by the RAF and denied to the Japanese. There was a proposal to make Matador more ambitious by moving troops right up to the narrow neck of the Kra Isthmus, but there were no resources for this. Even for Matador the troops could hardly be spared, and the task of preparing it was given to 11 Indian Division, which was to occupy the port of Singora and take the aerodromes at Singora and Patani, on the coast of the Gulf of Siam. There were obvious disadvantages too: opposition from the Thais had to be reckoned with, since they had declared they would resist any aggressor, and the troops would be losing the advantage of fighting from prepared positions.

The decision was ultimately taken to operate Matador during the north-east monsoon (October-March), if there were a favourable opportunity. Singora would be captured by an advance by road and rail, and a defensive position held north of the little junction of Haad'yai. This was not the only road into north Malaya from Thailand, and the Patani-Kroh road had to be considered too. In this case, there was a suitable defensive position thirty-five to forty miles across the border, at a place called 'The Ledge', where the road was cut out of a steep hillside and could easily be blocked by demolitions. It was at all times regarded as essential that twenty-four hours' start ahead of the anticipated time of a Japanese landing must be given to 11 Indian Division. Otherwise, instead of carrying out a

93

denial action, they would be faced with an encounter battle with an enemy who had landed tanks, while they had none.

Plans were worked out, Thai currency put in reserve, and pamphlets written in Thai for the local population. About thirty British officers in plain clothes – some of them very senior indeed – slipped across the border as tourists to reconnoitre the ground. As in most situations of this sort, they met a number of Japanese officers, similarly garbed, and similarly employed. They often stayed in the same rest-houses.[2]

Percival realized that 11 Indian Division was being asked to do more than was reasonable, and on his behalf the C-in-C Far East's Chief-of-Staff, Major-General I.S.O. Playfair, sent a long signal to the War Office on 20 August 1941 saying he thought Matador should be strong and that he accepted Percival's view that it should be operated by a brigade group in addition to 11 Indian Division.[3] Percival was afraid lest the drain on his resources for Matador, once war was declared, would leave him weaker than he wished to be in Johore. There was, too, the internal security problem, which is rarely referred to in this connection, but was a factor in Percival's mind: the brigade at Haad'yai could thereafter not be used for internal security in Perak, Kedah or Penang, and in May there had been some unrest in plantation and mining areas.

The feasibility of Matador did not depend merely on the troops Percival had available. It depended partly on the attitude of the Thais, and, much more, on that of the Americans. In the early planning stages, the likelihood of American support for such an action did not seem great, and without it Britain could be branded as an aggressor and deprived of the help she needed. Late in 1940 the Assistant Naval Attaché in Washington had been shown certain US naval defence plans, in strict confidence, but obviously on the understanding he would transmit them to the British Cabinet. They were held to reflect the views of Admiral Stark, the Chief of Naval Operations. Besides anticipating complete Axis control of the Mediterranean, the plans said that a war between Japan and America would take the whole of American resources, and help to Britain in the Atlantic would be reduced accordingly. A strictly defensive war against Japan was to be waged, if it were forced upon the Americans, and this might mean accepting the loss of the Philippines, Borneo, the Netherlands East Indies and Singapore. This did not move the British Prime Minister as much as it might have done. Almost until the outbreak of war, he was sure the Japanese would not attack Malaya in great strength. If war came, their navy might harass trade, but that was all.[4]

Until almost the last minute no certainty was offered to Brooke-Popham that the US would support Matador. Late in November 1941 he sent a number of telegrams to London asking for his position to be more clearly defined. 'We realize your difficulty,' the Chiefs of Staff wired him back on 25 November,

> but His Majesty's Government cannot be committed in advance to automatic reaction to any particular situation . . . we cannot in advance of the event give you authority to act. You should however as soon as any situation arises which in your opinion is likely to lead to MATADOR make all necessary preparations to enable you to do so. But you should not repeat not order any actual move into THAILAND without specific instructions from His Majesty's Government. We estimate that His Majesty's Government's decision should reach you within 36 hours in receiving a report of any Japanese move.[5]

'Slow', scribbled Brooke-Popham in the margin of the telegram at this point. It was more than slow. It was a guarantee of failure. Any period longer than twenty-four hours would ensure the Japanese had landed and the result would be not a forestalling action, but an encounter battle. Three days later Brooke-Popham sent another 'MOST SECRET' and 'IMMEDIATE' wire asking to be kept informed of the Washington talks between Hull and the Japanese envoys Nomura and Kurusu.

> The Press in the Far East is full of rumours about the KURUSU talks and the fluctuations of opinion are most violent. We ourselves are completely in the dark except for

Press reports. You will realise how important this matter is
to us especially if the breakdown stage is approaching.
Please keep us fully informed.[6]

The British Cabinet decided to sound out the view of
the Dominions. The Australians replied on 30 November
that if Thailand were attacked the British Commonwealth
should intervene, whether the Americans participated or
not. Curtin, the Prime Minister, said that Australian information, at that time, was that no definite understanding on armed support from the Americans could be anticipated. New Zealand's telegram arrived half an hour later
saying a Japanese occupation of Thailand should be fore-
stalled, but added the rider 'if the United States Government are in general agreement and are willing to proffer
such assurances of assistance as the American Constitutional situation will allow.'[7] Smuts cabled from Africa that
weight should be given to the commander on the spot; and
added his conviction that the US would in fact support a
move. The Canadian reply did not come in until the following day, 1 December. It was negative: 'So long as there
is any uncertainty about the degree and immediacy of US
support it would be a terrible mistake to commit any course
of action which might result in a war between Japan and
the British Commonwealth of Nations.'[8]

These replies were considered by the Chiefs of Staff,
who were already of the view that Matador would precipitate war, and should be avoided as long as it was not known
what the Americans would do. Churchill notified the War
Cabinet that the Chiefs of Staff maintained their attitude,
with a qualification: action could be taken to protect Britain's vital interests. But what were they? 'An occupation
by Japan of the Kra Isthmus could only be with the object of attacking Singapore,' said the Chiefs of Staff, but,
they added, incomprehensibly, 'it would not be itself an
attack on our vital interests.'[9] Churchill backed their view.
We ought not to assume, he declared, 'that the outbreak
of war between England and Japan would necessarily precipitate the United States into the war. There was a strong

party in the United States who would work up prejudice against being drawn into Britain's war.'[10] He had already suggested to Roosevelt a joint declaration, secret or public, to Japan, warning her against further aggression. The Thai Prime Minister had done likewise. He would be more ready to resist Japan if he knew such a warning had been made. We should not, therefore, 'resist or attempt to forestall a Japanese attack on the Kra Isthmus unless we had a satisfactory assurance from the United States that they would join us should our attack cause us to become involved in war with Japan.'[11]

Early in the afternoon of 1 December 1941, Roosevelt had a conversation in Washington with the British Ambassador, Lord Halifax. He had been considering some statement on the Japanese moves to reinforce their position in Indo-China, and he wanted the British Government's reaction to certain hypotheses. In the case of a direct attack against the British or the Dutch, 'we should obviously be all together.'[12] But the issue might not be presented so plainly. What would the British Government do if the Japanese reinforcements had not reached Indo-China and they did not give a satisfactory answer to his query about where their reinforcements were going; and if they were going to Indo-China what was their purpose? A second hypothesis would be: if their answer were unsatisfactory and their reinforcements had *not* reached Indo-China. The third was: if the Japanese moved against Thailand without attacking the Kra Isthmus, or merely extracted dangerous concessions from Thailand. Halifax's impression was that Roosevelt seemed prepared to support whatever action Britain took in any of the hypothetical cases.

Halifax was told to pass on to Roosevelt the British Government's impression that a Japanese attack on Thailand was now expected and that it would include a seaborne expedition against the Kra Isthmus. As soon as it was clear that Japanese ships, under escort, were nearing Thailand, the British proposed a descent by sea [*sic*] on the Isthmus to hold a line north of Singora.[13] [No descent by sea is referred to by Percival or Brooke-Popham.] What

D 97

would the Americans think of this plan? The telegram to Halifax resulted from a compromise between differing points of view: that of the Foreign Office and that of the Chiefs of Staff. Always cautious on this issue, the Chiefs of Staff wanted to be certain of American support before they acted. The Foreign Office thought a definite assurance unlikely. If the British waited until they got one, it would be too late to move. They thought the Americans should be told we would act unless the US Government offered a direct dissuasive.[14]

The response from Roosevelt was better than expected. The British could count on American support, even though some days might pass before it was given. The British could promise the Thais that, if they resisted, their future independence would be guaranteed. He was prevented by the US Constitution from making the guarantee himself, but he was sure the Americans would support a British one.[15]

A British answer to Roosevelt's hypotheses was telegraphed on December 3. The first one, based on an assumption the Japanese had not yet reinforced their troops in Indo-China, was already out of date: the British knew such reinforcements had already arrived. It was proposed that the US, British and Dutch should warn Japan, if her answer were unsatisfactory, that she would use Indo-China as a base for future aggression at her peril. If the Kra Isthmus were attacked by the Japanese, the British would advance along the Isthmus to a point north of Singora (though Churchill on 2 December was sure that a Japanese attack on Kra was unlikely for several months). In fact, provided American support were forthcoming, the British would make the advance if the Japanese attacked not merely the Kra Isthmus but anywhere else in Thailand. It would be preferable to enter the Isthmus at Thai invitation, but since British help to resist aggression elsewhere in Thailand could not be promised, the Thais were unlikely to view with enthusiasm the occupation of Singora alone. It was recognized by the British, though, that it was unrealistic to ask the Thais to resist the Japanese on the basis of a British guarantee of future independence.

This would be asking them 'to accept the virtual certainty of partial extinction in order to ensure their ultimate independence.'[16]

No answer had yet been received from the Japanese when, on 3 December, Roosevelt saw Halifax again to discuss the British reply to his questions. The President was a little unsure about the British phrase 'use of Indo-China as a base for further aggression.' Did this mean an *act* of aggression, or building up a base *for* aggression? He accepted the operation into the Kra Isthmus if the Japanese attacked Thailand. American armed support could be counted on: though Roosevelt added that he thought the Japanese would in fact attack the Netherlands East Indies. He agreed that a warning should be given, but thought he should write directly to the Emperor. Halifax countered by suggesting that the letter to the Emperor might constitute the warning. Roosevelt agreed, and said he would decide on 6 December, after receiving the Japanese reply to his enquiry.[17]

At a War Cabinet meeting on 4 December, Halifax's telegrams giving these views from Roosevelt were handed round, to the great satisfaction of all present. Churchill said instructions could now be sent to Brooke-Popham to put Matador into effect if necessary. The telegram was despatched on 5 December.

> H.M. Government has now received an assurance of American armed support in the following contingencies: -
> (a) If we undertake MATADOR either to forestall attempted Japanese landing in the KRA ISTHMUS or as a reply to a Japanese violation of any part of Thailand.
> (b) If the Japanese attack the DUTCH EAST INDIES and we go at once to their support.
> (c) If the Japanese attack us.
> Accordingly you should order MATADOR without reference to home in either of the two following contingencies: -
> (a) You have good information that a Japanese expedition is advancing with the apparent intention of landing on the Kra Isthmus.

(b) The Japanese violate any other part of THAILAND (SIAM).

In the event of a Japanese attack on the NETHERLANDS EAST INDIES you have authority without reference to home immediately to put into operation the plans which you have agreed with them.[18]

As Brooke-Popham scribbled on a note attached to his telegram, this was a big step forward. 'Invasion of Thailand, or *threatened* invasion of KRA, are now both covered by this authority. But the case of an attack on British territory has NOT yet been answered . . .'[19] He sent off a further cable to London to clarify this issue: should he order MATADOR without reference back, if *British* territory were attacked? He received an answer to this on 8 December, by which time it was long past serving any useful purpose.

No doubt, at this stage, Brooke-Popham was playing his hand more cautiously than the situation warranted. But it must be remembered that his main brief when he took up his post as C-in-C Far East was to avoid war with Japan. He had been bluffing for the past twelve months. Acutely aware that the British Empire was already stretched to its utmost, he did not relish the thought that a mistaken judgement of his might plunge that Empire into a war which should never have happened. His mood was echoed by General Playfair, his Chief of Staff, who observed, when the telegram from London arrived. 'They've now made you responsible for declaring war.'[20] Brooke-Popham wanted to operate Matador. But he needed to be cast-iron sure of his grounds for doing so. *How* he acted upon the authority finally given him must be considered now in some detail.

VI

The Approach to Malaya:
To Matador or not to Matador?

The signal for war to begin was flashed from the flagship of the Japanese Combined Fleet at 5.30 pm on 2 December, 1941, the day Admiral Sir Tom Phillips's Eastern Fleet put in to Singapore. 'NIITAKA YAMA NOBORE 1208' was the brief message. 'Climb Mount Niitaka 1208', in other words, hostilities against the USA, Great Britain and the Netherlands begin on 8 December.

The convoy which was to invade Malaya – the Malaya Force – left Samah Harbour on Hainan Island on 4 December, under the command of Vice-Admiral Ozawa, C-in-C, Southern Expeditionary Fleet, in the flagship *Chōkai*. Eighteen transports carried 20,000 men of General Yamashita's 25 Army behind a screen of cruisers and destroyers. The day was fine and the weather calm as they set course for Malaya at sixteen knots.

The spearhead of the invasion was to be 5 Division (Major-General Matsui) which was well trained in landing operations and was to secure Singora and Patani, then push south into Malaya at once. 56 Infantry Regiment of 18 Division (Lieutenant-General Mutaguchi) under the command of Major-General Takumi, and known as Takumi Force, was to land at Kota Bharu. It, too, was seasoned from campaigning in China. Both of these forces had as their primary task the achievement of Japanese air mastery over Malaya. The airfields in Kedah were to be taken by 5 Division as it made for the line of the River Perak. Those in Kelantan were to be taken by Takumi Force. In this way, the British would be unable to strike back at the Japanese from their northernmost airfields. The Japanese also intended to ensure they should not be reinforced by air from India: 143 Infantry Regiment of 55 Division (Uno Force) was to land at a number of points on the Isthmus

Malaya 1941

of Kra and cut across the Peninsula at its narrowest part. Here, at the tip of the tongue of Burmese territory that runs parallel to Thailand, was the airfield at Victoria Point, a vital staging post in the journey from India to Malaya. With Victoria Point taken, aircraft reinforcements to Singapore would have to go by sea.

The only force of 25 Army which was to move by land was the Imperial Guards Division. It was stationed in Cambodia, and was to cross the Thai frontier into Battambang Province, which had been ceded to Thailand under the mediation with French Indo-China earlier in the year. It would then move directly on to Bangkok. The Japanese hoped the threat of this powerful force would persuade the Thais to a peaceful settlement. If this did not work, they would take Bangkok by force anyway. Unlike the other two divisions under 25 Army's command, the Imperial Guards had no battle experience. They were a purely ceremonial force, and although they acquitted themselves well in Malaya, Yamashita never overcame his mistrust of their commander, Lieutenant-General Nishimura, nor his distaste for the attitudes of the Guards. Yamashita, who had only taken over his command a month before, did not trouble to use the fourth division – 56 Division – which had been allotted to him. It was held in reserve for a possible landing at Endau or Mersing, but never used, and was finally sent to Burma.

The fine weather was no blessing at this stage. Secrecy of movement was essential and a visibility of over thirty kilometres was a hazard: if the Malaya Force were discovered, there was a risk that war would break out *before* 8 December, in which case the US Fleet at Hawaii would be on the alert and the chance of a surprise attack on Pearl Harbour would be lost. To deceive neutral shipping or prying aircraft, the fleet was to appear to be sailing south for Saigon, turn west on 5 December, and finally northwest on the 6th into the Gulf of Thailand before the convoys dispersed to the landing beaches. It would appear to have set course for Bangkok after rounding Cape Cambodia. Deception might not work, and more ruthless measures had been envisaged to preserve secrecy. Japanese aircraft would attack and sink any submerged submarine within a radius of five to six kilometres of the convoy. Submarines beyond that limit, or on the surface, would be left alone. Aircraft which tailed the convoy were to be attacked, others merely to be observed.[1]

The first security scare came on 5 December, when the destroyer *Uranami* intercepted a foreign merchant ship ahead of the convoy to starboard. While it was being searched – it was a Norwegian vessel en route from Bangkok to Hong Kong – the main convoy came up and the escort commander, Vice-Admiral Kurita, ordered the ship to make eastwards until the convoy had passed. He signalled the *Uranami* not to release the Norwegian ship without smashing its wireless. The convoy had already been instructed to treat ships flying the flags of Norway, Denmark, Panama and Greece as if they were American or British.[2]

A much greater danger occurred the following day, 6 December, at 1340 hrs, when the convoy was 150 kilometres south-east of Cape Cambodia (Point Camau). Every ship in the convoy spotted an aircraft on the distant horizon. The 'plane kept appearing and disappearing between the clouds and the Japanese could not be sure whether it was hostile or not. They soon knew. It was British. It came up to the convoy, circled, then began to shadow it, keeping at a safe distance, out of range of the anti-aircraft guns.

Ozawa had a hard decision to make. True, Imperial General Headquarters had given permission to shoot down American, British or Dutch planes, if they were reconnoitring operation areas or troop convoys. On the other hand, caution was needed, since rash action might impair the secrecy of the operations timed for the 8th. He had other information, too. A DC3 carrying a staff officer from Imperial General Headquarters had made a forced landing near Canton, and it was not known what had happened to him. He was carrying secret documents giving details of the operations and there was still some doubt whether or not they had fallen into the hands of the Chinese Army. The Japanese had information that the US Army had put its air forces in the Philippines in a state of emergency, which reinforced the doubt. If Ozawa sent aircraft to shoot this British 'plane down, hostilities with Great Britain might break out earlier than planned. Yet he had his convoy to consider. It was to strike Japan's major blow at the British Empire. If the plane continued to observe and report, the Malaya Force might never reach its objective. Ozawa sweated this out for over an hour, then signalled 'Large-type British aircraft in contact. Shoot down.'[3]

It was 1500 hrs, and the whole Japanese fleet – through home waters and right across the Pacific – had been observing wireless silence. There was a moment of great tension in the Combined Fleet and at Imperial General Headquarters when the signal broke the silence. 'It was,' wrote Admiral Ugaki, Chief of Staff of the Combined Fleet in his diary, 'like living through a thousand autumns in one day.' Not that he had any doubts about the ultimate outcome. 'What we are living through is a great drama for the human race,' he continued, 'in which the fate of the nation and countless lives are at stake. But there is no anxiety. What will be, will be. This "will be" is the will of the gods. And the country of the gods moves in accordance with that will. Therein lies our strength.'[4]

But the response to the signal was slow, since the convoy's direct escort had not arrived because of bad weather, and the aircraft disappeared. It was in fact a Hudson from the Australian squadron stationed at Kota Bharu, piloted by Flight-Lieutenant Ramshaw. Kota Bharu reported his sighting at once to Air Headquarters, Far East, and the news was flashed to London. Ramshaw pinpointed the convoy, but he miscounted – he made out twenty-five transports in one convoy and thought he saw a second convoy of ten transports, each with cruiser and destroyer escorts. The count of ships varied with further sightings, but whatever the detailed figures it was clearly a considerable force. It was a remarkable performance by the pilot, who was hampered by broken cloud and flying at the limit of his Hudson's range, 300 miles from the coast of Malaya. The results of this reconnaissance were also reported to Phillips in Manila. He promptly broke off his conference with the American commanders and prepared to return to Singapore, signalling *Repulse*, which had been ordered to Port Darwin, to hurry back. Percival was in Kuala Lumpur that day, conferring with Heath. He received a message shortly before 1500 hours that two Japanese convoys had been sighted, eighty miles ESE of Point Camau, steaming westward. Percival and Heath traced their course on the map and saw that if they kept west they would hit the coast of Thailand near Singora. Heath put 3 Corps in the first state of readiness and instructed Major-General D. M. Murray-Lyon, the GOC 11 Indian Division, to be prepared to operate Matador at short notice. Percival left Kuala Lumpur at half-past four in the afternoon, and was back in his own headquarters by 6.30 pm. Judging from the size of the expedition, he naturally assumed Matador would have been ordered and was surprised it had not been. He then learnt that the sighting signals referred also to a much smaller convoy steaming north-west which had given Brooke-Popham pause.

After consultation with Admiral Layton and Phillips's Chief-of-Staff, Admiral Palliser, Brooke-Popham concluded that the large convoy would probably follow the smaller one round Point Camau on a north-westerly course, possibly making for the anchorage at Koh Rong on the west coast of Indo-China. He did not consider he had enough information to order Matador and requested further sea searches. Pulford, the Air Officer Commanding, Malaya, realized the urgent need to keep the convoys under observation, and a Catalina flying-boat was sent out to make contact during the night. It failed to do so, and a second one was despatched on the morning of 7 December. Meanwhile Admiral Ozawa had acted on the correct assumption that the Hudson had signalled to its base his convoy's approach. If the British Fleet were to come for him, or if a bombing raid were to be mounted, it would be on the morning of the 7th. So he ordered watch to be kept

from 0300 hrs on the 7th, one hundred sea miles off Kota
Bharu. There was heavy rain and zero visibility, and his
eleven observer and six sea reconnaissance aircraft reported
nothing. But on its way back, one of the sea reconnaissance planes, piloted by Reserve Second-Lieutenant
Ōgata, spotted the second British Catalina. It was twenty
miles west-north-west of Panjang Island in the Gulf of
Siam. The time was 0950 hrs.[5]

The Malaya Force was then sixty miles west of that
position. It was coming up to Point G, the rendezvous in
the Gulf of Siam, where the convoy would disperse and
the deception manoeuvre towards Bangkok would cease.
Ōgata judged that the Catalina would sight the convoy
within thirty minutes. He slipped in underneath the
Catalina, opening fire as he did so. Up to that moment, it
seemed not to have seen him, but joined battle at once.

So began the first air combat of the Pacific War – in fact
the first exchange of fire between British and Japanese.

Ōgata was attempting to lure the Catalina eastwards,
away from the convoy, and he succeeded. These Zero sea
reconnaissance aircraft were nicknamed '*geta-baki*' by the
Japanese – 'planes with clogs on' – but they were handy
all-purpose machines which could act as bombers with
a single 250 kilogram bomb, as night reconnaissance
aircraft, or as anti-submarine patrol planes. They were
armed with a 7.7-mm gun. The Catalina had three such
machine-guns, and Ōgata was not sure whether he could
shoot it down on his own. The issue became academic
when ten Japanese fighters arrived. Twenty-five minutes
elapsed between Ōgata's sighting and the shooting down
of the Catalina, but no message was received in Singapore.

The Malaya Force reached Point G without further
incident at 1030 hrs and the ships began to split up:

For Kota Bharu: (Takumi Force)	cruiser *Sendai,* 19 Destroyer Division, three minesweepers, three transports
For Singora, Patani: (25 Army HQ, 5 Division)	12 and 20 Destroyer Divisions, five minesweepers, seventeen transports

For Nakhorn: (Uno Force)	coastal vessel *Shumshu*, three transports
For Bandon and Chumphorn: (Uno Force)	cruiser *Kashii*, two transports
For Prachuab: (Uno Force)	one transport

The landings in Thailand were assumed to be fairly straightforward. Kota Bharu was the problem. It was the only landing in British territory, and had two newly completed aerodromes close by which would have to be taken by any large Japanese force pushing south from Thailand. These airfields constituted one corner of the airbase network on the Thai-Malaya border: Kota Bharu – Sungei Patani – Alor Star. Given the short range of Japanese Army aircraft the capture of this network was vital for 25 Army's operations across the border. The possibility had to be considered of British attacks by air, by torpedo bombers, and by submarines, and as the extent of this threat could not be gauged beforehand, the Tokyo Agreement between Army and Navy had specifically left consideration of Kota Bharu to the commander on the spot – in the event, Admiral Ozawa. He had to decide whether the landing should be simultaneous with those in Thailand, or on D-plus-one.

Ozawa went over these considerations:

i   His planes had not sighted the British Fleet on 7 December off the coast of Malaya. They had seen submarines, but all on the surface. He assumed the British knew the outline of his convoy, but since he had not yet been attacked he judged they had not resolved to open hostilities.

ii He did not know what moves the British Fleet had made from Singapore from 5 December onwards, but all the evidence pointed to the fact that it had not sortied to attack.

iii The British Army at Kota Bharu would be expecting a landing and would have prepared accordingly. But he thought there would be no other source of resistance and it would be possible to land. The main body of the escort could prepare for a counter-attack by the British Fleet off Kota Bharu.

Weighing these up, Ozawa finally opted for a simultaneous landing at Kota Bharu and his flagship *Chōkai* closed the transport *Ryūjō* to signal Yamashita: 'Execute landing as expected. Simultaneous landing Kota Bharu.'[6]

The Kota Bharu force knew it was in for the toughest resistance, and tension mounted as it steered down the coast of Thailand. Then, at 1630 hours, one of the escort ships, *Uranami*, spotted a merchant ship. Another Norwegian! She was a 1,350-ton merchantman, about 120 miles north of Kota Bharu. The ship was boarded and the Japanese, suspecting she was carrying out intelligence tasks for the British, made the crew take to the boats and scuttled her.

About three hours later, when the escort was about sixty miles from Kota Bharu, a Blenheim bomber appeared. The time was 1925 hours on 7 December. To prevent it making contact with the transports, the destroyer *Uranami* opened fire and the Blenheim made off. Nonetheless, the Japanese assumed that the Norwegian ship and the Blenheim had reported back, so they dismissed any lingering possibility of a surprise landing. It would be opposed now, without a doubt.

They were right. The Blenheim reported sighting what appeared to be a cruiser and a transport vessel 110 miles north of Kota Bharu at 1900 hours (2030 hours Japanese time). Four ships, possibly destroyers, were seen at 2000 hours making south, forty miles north of Patani. The signal reached Brooke-Popham at 2100 hours* (an excessively long interval). He called on Percival, and they went together to see Layton.

* His despatch (para. 98) reports a *Hudson* sighting of *three* ships heading south past Singora. Percival (*War in Malaya* pp.109-10) speaks of receiving a little before 2000 hrs – though he is not sure of the exact time – the news that a Hudson had sighted *four* Japanese vessels at 1848 hrs. They looked like destroyers, steaming south about seventy miles off Singora. *Another* Hudson, he says, had been fired on by a Japanese cruiser at 1750 hrs. Percival recalls notification as being at 2030 hrs.

On 6 December, Percival had been amazed that Matador had not been ordered on the first sighting, until he heard Brooke-Popham explain about the other element in the convoy steaming into the Gulf of Siam, with the implication that the ships were not aimed at Singora after all. That implication ceased to matter when the sighting of the vessels moving south off Singora was reported, particularly since one of them had fired on the British reconnaissance aircraft.

At that moment, Percival later wrote, the problem ceased to be political and became strategical.[7] He was in no doubt himself that this was an invasion force. If it were strategically advantageous, then Matador should be ordered then and there.

Percival was no longer sure it *was* advantageous. The required conditions – twenty-four hours' notice of Japanese presence and rapid movement of British forces – no longer existed. If bound for Singora, the enemy convoy could reach it by midnight. The leading troops of 11 Indian Division, assuming they met no opposition, could be there by 2 am on the 8th, at the earliest. So there was no longer any question of denying the port to the Japanese. There would simply be an encounter battle, in circumstances less favourable to 11 Division than if it were in its own positions. He therefore told Brooke-Popham that he considered Matador inadvisable.[8]

At the Naval Base, they found the Commander-in-Chief, Eastern Fleet, Admiral Sir Tom Phillips, back from Manila where he had been conferring with Admiral Hart, C-in-C of the US Asiatic Fleet. After fresh consultations, at half past ten that evening, Brooke-Popham finally decided Matador was not on, and the decision was signalled to London, where the Chiefs of Staff were still debating whether a force should be sent into Thailand or not. Thailand's neutrality should not be violated, they decided, unless the Japanese had done it first (which was itself a denial of the possibility of Matador).

The first part of the signal read:

The Approach to Malaya: To Matador or not to Matador?

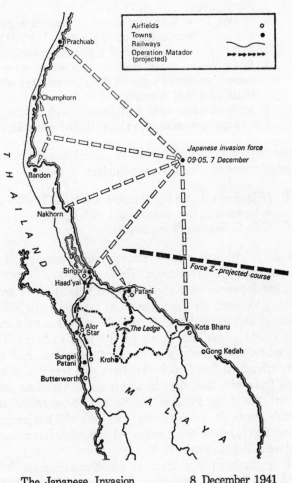

The Japanese Invasion

8 December 1941

Map labels: Prachuab · Chumphorn · THAILAND · Bandon · Nakhorn · Singora · Haad'yai · Patani · Alor Star · The Ledge · Sungei Patani · Kroh · Butterworth · MALAYA · Kota Bharu · Gong Kedah · Japanese invasion force 09·05, 7 December · Force Z - projected course

Legend: Airfields ○ · Towns ● · Railways · Operation Matador (projected)

A. Have decided not to operate MATADOR for the following reasons: -
   1. Conditions for reconnaissance were very bad and there can be no real certainty that ships seen were an expedition.
   2. If expedition is in fact aimed at Singora region it can reach there before we can arrive. MATADOR is designed only to forestall a Japanese expedition.
   3. If conclusion drawn from reconnaissance prove incorrect we should incur all the disadvantages of first breaking THAI neutrality.
   4. Japanese movements are consistent with a deliberate attempt to induce us to violate THAI neutrality.

The second and shorter part of the signal reveals the state of puzzlement in which Brooke-Popham worked:

B. If Japanese do land in southern KRA ISTHMUS is it to be assumed that we are at war with Japan.
C. C-in-C. Eastern Fleet, concurs.[9]

His despatch gives a more circumstantial account of his reasons than the signal could. There could be no certainty that the Japanese were about to open hostilities, he wrote (para. 98), 'and on more than one occasion the British Minister to Thailand had stressed the serious consequence that would ensue should we be the first to break Thai neutrality.' So Crosby's letters and telegrams had had their effect. In fact Brooke-Popham had received a telegram from him that day, in which he said he had interviewed the Thai Foreign Minister. Crosby urged that British forces should not occupy an inch of Thai territory unless the Japanese went in first. Irreparable harm would be done if Britain made the first aggression.[10]

'It is pertinent to record,' Brooke-Popham adds, 'that, until the Japanese had committed some definite act of hostility against the United States, the Dutch or ourselves, permission had not been given to attack a Japanese expedition at sea.'[11]

This final observation is incomprehensible, since he had evidence by that time that the Japanese convoy, whatever its destination, had in fact opened fire on a British aircraft. How hostile can you get?

To be more certain, Brooke-Popham requested a dawn air reconnaissance of the Singora area on the 8th; and yet the weary, rain-sodden troops of 11 Indian Division, who had been standing to since the afternoon of the 6th in a tropical downpour, were not stood down. At 2330 hrs, Heath was told to be ready to operate Matador on the morning of the 8th.

Time had run out. At 2355 hrs on 7 December 1941, Takumi Force was anchoring off Kota Bharu. Less than two hours later, the first landing craft would leave the ships. The invasion of Malaya was on.

JAPAN'S INTELLIGENCE ACTIVITIES IN MALAYA

The Japanese knew pretty well what was awaiting them, thanks to their intelligence service in the Peninsula. Even before Major Arisue called for an intensification of Japan's intelligence activities in Malaya in 1936, Japanese businessmen had settled in the larger towns, and even in smaller ones the barber and photographer might well prove to be Japanese. Japanese business interests owned rubber estates and tin mines and transported the products directly back to Japan in their own merchant ships, which gave the crews of those ships a good knowledge of many parts of the Malayan coast. Sometimes they pretended to be Chinese, like the Chinese photographer at Sungei Patani who was on friendly terms with many troops of the 11th Indian Division and turned out to be Major Harada of the Japanese Army. He was caught making for the Thai border on the outbreak of war.[12]

But from the beginning of 1941 this effort was stepped up considerably, as a result of the activities of Taiwan Army Unit No 82, the Research Department of the Japanese Army on Taiwan, which had taken over the task of reconnoitring all the enemy territories which were to be invaded in the Southern Regions. The brains behind the intelligence operation into Malaya was Colonel Tsuji Masanobu, who christened the unit 'the *doro nawa* unit', or 'robber-rope unit'. The term implies a criticism of the attitude of mind which catches a thief and then has to find a rope to bind him with. The implication is that 82 Unit was asked to do far too much too quickly.

Allocated the absurdly small sum of 20,000 yen (about £1,200), the unit was told to accumulate, in six months, the latest intelligence on military formations, equipment, weapons, medicine, supply, and geographical information (the Japanese army – like the British – was very badly off for maps of Malaya) as well as to devise administrative machinery for occupied territory. Some of the best reports were sent back by a young staff officer, Asaeda, whom Tsuji sent into southern Thailand and northern Malaya, in disguise.

Asaeda told Tsuji that it would be difficult to disembark at Singora and Patani during the winter months because of the north-east monsoon. He had learnt that the local fishing boats did not put out because of the nine-foot high waves, and these might cause losses during a mass landing. On the other hand, the Thai coast hardly seemed to be defended at all. There were wire entanglements, but no pillboxes. The airfields at Singora and Patani were very poor indeed, compared with those the British had built at Kota Bharu and Alor Star. It would be essential to control the British airfields as soon as possible. The road from Patani into Malaya, which led through Betong to the Upper Perak Valley, was not very good for motor transport, but a single column, with an infantry regiment as nucleus, should be able to make use of it.[13]

Tsuji decided to have a look himself in October 1941. He left Saigon at dawn one morning in a military reconnaissance aircraft, and reached Kota Bharu two hours later at a height of 18,000 feet. He had to drop to 900 feet before he could do any worthwhile observation, but even a cursory glance showed what a threat the Kota Bharu airfield represented to the proposed landing just a few miles away, across the Thai border. Tsuji made the trip twice, and the second time went on as far as Alor Star in north-western Malaya. No attempt at interception was made by the RAF, and he flew on without hindrance over Sungei Patani and Taiping. He was back in Saigon before noon, having to rely on his memory because none of the film he took came out.[14]

Tsuji had agents in Singapore itself, and the picture they presented was as follows:

   i The Johore side of the Island was defenceless.
  ii The RAF was rumoured to be reinforcing, but most of the rumours were propaganda, aimed at bluffing the Japanese into overestimating British air strength.
 iii The land and air reinforcements in Kedah were real.
 iv The armed forces in Malaya as a whole were reckoned at 80,000 men, of whom half were British.[15]

VII

The Japanese Landings

25 Army's original plan for the landing at Kota Bharu envisaged the start of operations as midnight on 7/8 December. In its view, the success or failure of all the operations in the Southern Regions depended on the success of the Malaya landings, and to ensure their success the Army wanted to start disembarking halfway through the night of 7/8 December, and to have completed the operation by dawn on the 8th.

The Navy opposed this plan. It claimed that the success not just of one operation but of the entire war depended on the surprise attack on Pearl Harbour. Nothing should put the secrecy of this operation at hazard. If battle commenced elsewhere before Pearl Harbour, then the surprise attack would collapse 'like a bubble on water'.

To thrash out a compromise between these two views, a conference between Army and Navy was held in Tokyo in November, at the Military Academy. The Navy was represented by the C-in-C Combined Fleet, Admiral Yamamoto, his chief of staff, Admiral Ugaki, and the C-in-C Second Fleet, Admiral Kondō; the Army by the C-in-C Southern Army, Field-Marshal Terauchi and his chief of staff, General Tsukada. The conference started on 8 November and took three days. The deadlock was broken by the Navy revealing for the first time to the Southern Army chiefs the plan for the attack on Pearl Harbour. This was the first time it had been discussed outside a small circle. The Army saw the point, and agreed to make the Kota Bharu landings after midnight on 7/8 December, the landing time, 1.30 am (Japan time) being chosen with the expected beginning of the Pearl Harbour raid in mind.[1]

When the landing units arrived off the anchorage at Kota Bharu there was cloud, but visibility was fair. Lights could be seen on shore, and the harbour light at Tumpat was visible. Then, as the transports cast anchor, all the lights on shore went out. The Japanese took it that the British had seen them anchor.

Kota Bharu was defended in strength by Brigadier (later Major-General) B. W. Key's 8 Brigade, reinforced by units from 22 Brigade, under command of 9 Indian Division (Barstow). Key had Indian Mountain Artillery and a regiment of Field Artillery to back his beach defences. The beaches themselves – wired, mined and pillboxed – were criss-crossed by creeks and streams. There were no mangrove swamps but groves of coconut palms and thickets of nipah palm. The north-east monsoon blew the sand into high banks. A strong east wind was blowing as the first wave began to lower the boats, and the heavy swell made some of them capsize, tipping the Japanese infantry into the water. In spite of this, by 0135 hours the first wave was soon speeding ashore in twenty landing craft. Shortly after 0200 hours, the watchers on the ships saw signals near the landing points. At the same time, shots were heard, flares went up, and the struggle for Kota Bharu began. It was the first land battle of the Pacific war (the signal to attack Hawaii was sent later at 0319 hrs).[2]

The second wave was delayed. Some of the landing craft of the first wave returned to the ships at 0330, when British aircraft came over. For an hour, they repeated low-level bombing and strafing attacks over the Japanese convoy. The escort commander was afraid that he would sustain too much damage if he did not withdraw and proposed to do so for one hour, cancelling the third landing wave. The Army strongly resisted this, on the grounds that it was vital to reinforce, at all costs, the infantry which had already gone ashore. Finally there was an agreement to withdraw at 0630 hrs and preparations for the third wave went ahead.

At 0500 hours, four more British aircraft came into the attack. The escorts shot down one of them, but one of the transports, the *Awaji-San Maru*, received a direct hit and fire broke out aboard. The situation which the escort commander, Hashimoto, had feared, was fast becoming a reality. In the turmoil, the unit's third wave did not set out together as the first and second had, and there was a chaotic to-and-fro of landing craft, made worse by the arrival of British aircraft again at 0600 hours.

In the three British air attacks, the *Awaji-San Maru* received three direct hits and could not be moved. The *Ayato-San Maru* received three hits, and suffered heavy casualties – sixty dead, seventy wounded, and seven derricks smashed. She had a hole a yard deep and two yards across, above the water-line. The *Sakura Maru* received two hits, and had three dead and sixteen wounded. She was holed in the first hold, and suffered considerable damage.

The British then sent over five torpedo bombers, which turned their attention from the transports to the escorts. Under this attack – during which two Hudsons were shot down – Hashimoto interrupted the disembarkation, took 396 men off the *Awaji-San Maru* and ordered it to withdraw. It lay off shore at Patani until noon. Without help from Japanese aircraft this opposed landing suffered very heavy casualties. The damage inflicted by a handful of Hudsons and old Wildebeeste aircraft stationed at Kota Bharu is a clear indication of what might have happened if the RAF in Malaya had been reinforced to the 336 aircraft promised for the end of 1941 by the Chiefs of Staff. Heavier, more persistent and wider-ranging attacks might well have destroyed the Japanese invasion fleet, or at any rate a portion of it large enough to tip the scale in favour of the British Army defenders in North Malaya. As it was . . .

Enough of Takumi Force got ashore to push back the Indian troops of 8 Brigade from the beach defences. Japanese infiltration then began to sow confusion in Key's rear. At 1930 hours, a rumour went round the airfield at Kota Bharu that the Japanese had reached the perimeter. The station commander asked permission to evacuate it, and the planes were flown off to Kuantan. Someone quite unauthorized – not the station commander – gave orders that the denial scheme was to be put into effect, the airfield buildings were set ablaze, and the ground staff were evacuated down the railway to Kuala Krai. It was too late to rectify the situation when the rumour was shown to be false.[3] Takumi Force followed up, and occupied the airfield halfway through the night of 8/9 December. The town of Kota Bharu was taken on the 9th, and two days later Key decided to abandon the other two airfields, Machang and Gong Kedah, which had already been abandoned by the ground staffs, who had not troubled to carry out demolitions. The runways were left intact for the Japanese. In spite of heavy losses, 18 Division's Takumi Force had got its foothold in Malaya, at the cost of one transport sunk (the *Awaji-San Maru*), 179 dead and 314 wounded.

Further north, in Thailand, the invasion was far smoother. 143 Infantry Regiment of 55 Division – Uno Force – was soon ashore at a number of points in the Kra Isthmus. Meeting little resistance, it reached Victoria Point in Burma and took the airfield.

The main body of 5 Division and 25 Army Headquarters came ashore at Singora and Patani in heavy seas with no casualty more severe than a staff officer's sprained ankle. The defence trench along the sea-coast was empty. In theory, once the first landing party was ashore, it should have been met by a Japanese Army officer, Major Osone, who was working as a clerk at the consulate in Singora. Osone was nowhere in sight, so Colonel Tsuji and an interpreter made off to the consulate. The Japanese consul, Katsuno, who gave every evidence of having been drinking freely, sleepily opened his gate. Behind him, rubbing his eyes, appeared the figure of Major Osone. He should have had plans for the seizure of motor transport and how to deal with the Thai gendarmerie, but it turned out the plans had never been forwarded from Saigon.* With

---

* Poor Osone had not even known the time of the landings. This had been notified to him in a coded telegram, the cipher for which was contained in a letter, which he received with instructions to burn it after use. In his eagerness to preserve security, he had burned the letter first, and was unable to decipher the telegram when it arrived (Tsuji, *Singapore: The Japanese Version*, p.88).

Katsuno, and an orderly carrying a folded silk square filled with 100,000 Thai *bahts*, Tsuji made his way to the police station. The Thai police fired on their car, putting out their headlights and wounding Tsuji in the arm. They abandoned the car and retreated.[4] As soon as enough infantry were ashore, Tsuji reported to Yamashita, who gave orders to crush resistance by the Thai gendarmerie at once. This was quickly done, and the airfield captured, in spite of sporadic shelling by the Thai Army, which continued to resist until noon on 8 December. Japanese fighter aircraft began to pour into the landing strips. Originally, a Japanese force dressed in Thai uniform was to cross the frontier into Malaya, but the tumult in Singora made this concealment impossible. The men changed back into their Japanese army kit, and the advance formation of 5 Division, led by three medium tanks, was soon on its way to the border. The Japanese had succeeded, in a matter of hours, in putting 12,000 men ashore in Thailand, with five tanks and nearly 400 vehicles.

VIII

The Campaign

I THE DEFENCE OF NORTHERN MALAYA – JITRA, GURUN, KAMPAR

It is impossible to follow what happened in Northern Malaya unless the theory behind the endless retreats is understood. The British troops were not intended to fight a battle of annihilation. They were fighting in north Malaya, but they were not supposed to defend it to the last man. They formed part of the long-range defence of Singapore, and sooner or later would be needed on the island. They were to defend the aerodromes. If they were driven from the aerodromes, or the positions defending them, then they had to retreat to the next position southwards, imposing delay on the Japanese by careful demolitions, and conserving their own strength. These demands naturally made the British commanders fearful at all times of being surrounded and cut off, and hence liable to retreat before it became absolutely imperative to do so. It left the initiative firmly in the hands of the Japanese. And, of course, all the initial moves were dogged by the indecisiveness over Matador.

There was an ancillary operation to Matador which would have been feasible as a temporary measure: the movement of a force from Kroh into Thailand along the road to Patani, reaching the position called The Ledge – it was, in effect, only a stretch of road – the purpose being to block one possible Japanese route into Malaya. A small force called Krohcol (3/16 Punjab Regiment) under Lieutenant-Colonel Moorehead was to carry out this move. Here too, though, there were needless delays.

Heath had been told to keep the Matador troops ready to move on the morning of the 8th, depending on the results of a dawn air reconnaissance over the Gulf of Siam. Brooke-Popham had told Percival that London had permitted him to violate Thai territory, provided Kota Bharu in Malaya was attacked. Unfortunately, he added the rider 'Do not act'.[1] The air reconnaissance over Singora and Patani on the 8th clearly revealed the extent of the Japanese landings, and this was known at Kota Bharu at 9.15 am. Unaware of this three-quarters of an hour later, Percival attended the Straits Settlements Legislative Council in Singapore and reported the situation. He usually attended these sittings: it was a way of keeping in touch with the political direction of Malaya. Unfortunately it meant he missed an important telephone call from Brooke-Popham about the dawn reconnaissance. Percival was back at Malaya Command at 11 am, and learned then that sanction had been given to enter Thailand. He telephoned Heath to occupy defensive positions on the Singora and Kroh-Patani roads. He did not make a note of the time he telephoned, but remembered it as shortly after he returned from the Legislative Council meeting. The Official History puts the time at 11.30 am and adds

> For some reason which cannot be ascertained, the gist of these orders was not passed immediately to III Corps on the telephone and it was not till shortly after 1 p.m. that Heath received them. To make quite certain that he was free to enter Siam he spoke on the phone to Percival at about 1.10 p.m. At 1.30 p.m. he ordered 11th Division to adopt the alternative plan . . .[2]

This puts the gap of time at a crucial two hours between Percival and Heath on top of the time wasted in deliberation over Matador after the sighting. In a letter to Professor J. R. M. (later Sir James) Butler (7 January 1962) Percival says the gap occurred between III Corps and 11th Indian Division and gives the hair-raising explanation of inadequate lines:

> What happened between 3 Corps and 11 Indian Div. I do not know, but I would point out once again that there was only the one civil trunk telephone line, which we all had

to use, and the Services only had limited privileges on it.
It was not to be expected, therefore, that calls would go
through very rapidly.[3]

Whatever the reason for the delay, the upshot was that
Krohcol received orders to move at 1.30 pm, four hours
after the dawn reconnaissance had confirmed that the Japanese were pouring into Singora and Patani in force.

The change-over from the offensive to a defensive pos-
ture had its effect on the troops of 11 Division. They had
been keyed up for weeks expecting to advance into Thailand to seize the port of Singora. They had been ready to
move since the afternoon of 6 December, soaked through
and through in the tropical rain. Now they were merely
to delay the Japanese, who had already taken the initiative
from them by landing, almost unopposed, on the east coast.

It had been hoped that the Thais would at any rate remain neutral, if the British crossed into Thailand to repel
the invader. Instead, as Krohcol went over the border at 3
pm, it was fired on by a Thai post manned by troops with
light automatics. Road-blocks and snipers delayed the advance so successfully that by nightfall Krohcol was only
three miles inside Thailand.

Further west, things were going even worse.

JITRA

11 Indian Division (Murray-Lyon) had two brigades – 6
and 15 – covering the Jitra position. This was a village
about six miles south of the Thai frontier, and ten miles
north of the British airfield at Alor Star. Situated on the
main road running south, just north of the point where it
was joined by the road from Kangar in the province of
Perlis, the position had been selected before war broke out,
largely because it covered the Alor Star airfield and the
group of airfields to the south; but it had not been properly prepared, the site was waterlogged, and 11 Indian
Division still retained stores in readiness for an advance
of the two forward brigades, 15 to the right, 6 to the left,
into Thailand. When Matador was cancelled, the troops

had to erect barbed-wire barriers, lay anti-tank mines and fresh telephone cables. 15 Brigade (1st Leicester, 2/9 Jat, 1/14 Punjab) held a 6,000-yard line from the jungle-clad hills east of Jitra, through ricefields now well under water, the main roads, and rubber plantations. From these to the sea ten miles to the west the front – mainly swamp – was covered by 6 Brigade (2 East Surrey, 2/16 Punjab, 1/8 Punjab). Three Gurkha battalions of 28 Brigade were to act as reserve. The infantry were supported by two batteries of 155 Field Regiment, Royal Artillery, 22 Mountain Regiment (part), Indian Artillery, and part of 80 Anti-Tank Regiment, Royal Artillery.

When the Japanese crossed the border, they pushed back the Punjabis who withdrew south. Orders came from Division to 15 Brigade to hold the Japanese north of Jitra until dawn on 12 December. The Brigade sent all its Punjabis forward to Changlun, and put 2/1 Gurkhas, which had been detached from 28 Brigade, into Asun. The Japanese broke the Changlun position on the morning of the 11th, during which the Punjabis lost their two anti-tank guns. 15 Brigade's commander wished to withdraw the Punjabis further south through the Gurkhas at Asun, but was told by Division to hold an intermediate point at Nangka, about five miles south of Changlun. The Punjabis were withdrawing through the persistent heavy rain in the afternoon of the 11th, when Japanese medium tanks and lorried infantry tore down the road behind them, through them, and on top of the anti-tank battery, which was not ready for the onslaught and could not put its guns into action in time.

The leading tank was hit after the column rushed the Asun bridge, and the road was then blocked. The British made unsuccessful attempts to blow the bridge, but the Japanese were not to be stopped. They looped round the Gurkhas and attacked from the front at the same time, clearing the road for the continued advance of their tanks. Some of the Punjabis and some Gurkhas rejoined the division later, but this action put paid to them as fighting units.

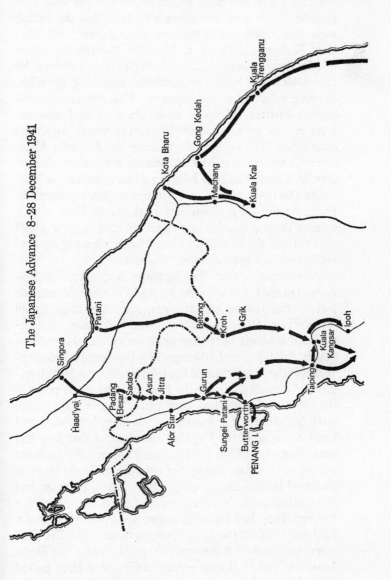

The Japanese Advance 8–28 December 1941

While this was happening, 6 Brigade was ordered to evacuate Perlis and bring its battalions into the main Jitra position, in spite of the Sultan's protests that the British were abandoning him in violation of their treaty. The road from Kodiang, in Perlis, to Jitra, led through the village of Mannggoi, where there was a bridge over a stream. An officer blew the bridge prematurely, mistaking the withdrawing brigade for the Japanese. This left most of the brigade carriers, transport, mountain guns, and anti-tank guns on the wrong side of the stream, where they were abandoned. The 15 Brigade commander (Brigadier K. A. Garrett) was missing, and 28 Brigade commander (Brigadier W. Carpendale) was told to assume command at Jitra.

On the night of the 11th, Japanese infantry began to penetrate the Jat position east of the road. Next, a tank column came down the road, lights blazing, right through the centre of the British position. The two front tanks were hit by anti-tank guns and spun to a halt.

False reports that the Japanese had occupied high ground in the hills east of the Jat position made Carpendale fear he was risking encirclement, and he brought up all his reserves. His men were rain-sodden, weary, and bewildered by their own changes of order and the suddenness of the Japanese blitzkrieg. The Japanese had been appalled at the destruction of the road wrought by British engineers' demolitions near the frontier, where one point of the main road south had been turned into a huge trench sixty feet deep and a hundred yards long; but their rapid brushing aside of the Punjabis and the fact that they had seen ten guns with muzzles pointing towards the Japanese but standing unmanned by the roadside while the gunners sheltered in the jungle nearby, showed them that they had little to fear from the enemy troops.[4] On his own initiative Colonel Tsuji had collected a group of three tanks and a field gun to join up with the leading elements of 5 Division, when he received a message, dropped from a low-flying Japanese 'plane: 'Large enemy mechanized force passed Changlun moving north noon today'. The detachment he caught up with was commanded by Lieutenant-Colonel

Saeki Shizuo and it was to occupy a position as far forward as possible to cover the disembarkment at Singora. Saeki took the tanks Tsuji had brought up, and with a strength of about 300 men – the 5 Division Reconnaissance Unit – decided to meet the British column coming up from Changlun: it could cause great havoc if it went any distance along the road to Singora. The result of the first engagement was the capture of a marked British map, which showed in detail the British defence dispositions round Changlun and Jitra.

On the evening of the 11th, Japanese patrols reconnoitred the advance positions of 11 Indian Division. One of these, led by a Second-Lieutenant Oto, had gone right into the Indian lines and reported back that there were wire entanglements, but they had gaps, and the Indians were not yet in position. A night attack should succeed in breaking through.

On the basis of this report, Saeki sent in a night attack, which was met by a heavy concentration of artillery – forty or fifty guns, Tsuji thought. The Japanese fought bitterly during the night to make some headway into the Indian lines, but by morning Saeki's ten tanks were still standing on the road waiting for the order which would allow them to pass through, and being shelled by British artillery. Shortly after noon, the Japanese artillery regimental commander was pressed to put his guns into position. Japanese shells began to pour into the British lines. At sunset, a report came to Japanese HQ that the British units were pulling out of their positions, and the Japanese moved forward until they were face to face with what they knew was the Jitra line. The British left behind fifty field guns, fifty heavy machine-guns, and 300 trucks and armoured cars. The Japanese found enough ammunition and food to keep a division going for three months; all this for a loss of fewer than thirty men. 3,000 Indian troops surrendered to the Saeki Detachment, after taking to the jungle in despair.

The Japanese attack, in the abstract, was reckless. If they had weighed up the disproportion of their numbers with what they knew was the British force defending Jitra, the sensible thing would have been to wait until the main body of 5 Division had disembarked and was ready to follow Saeki. Oto's report that the British line was vulnerable was disproved by the concentrated British shelling which followed the Japanese attack. But then that attack, backed by their own artillery, began to gather momentum, and their assault tanks carried them through. The Jitra line was meant to be held by a division for three months. It was cut through by a few hundred Japanese troops in fifteen hours.

Tragically, the airfield at Alor Star, which the Jitra position was covering, was evacuated by the RAF ground staff at the start of the battle, and its hangars and petrol tanks were set ablaze. The sight of this, visible from the road to Gurkhas moving up to reinforce their brigade, can hardly have been encouraging for morale. The RAF did not notify their intention to HQ 11 Division, and the runways were not properly destroyed.

On the road south from Patani, the Japanese found Siamese resistance less persistent, and moved seventy-eight miles along that road inland before they came into contact with Krohcol, which they pushed back. Along both the roads from the landing points at Singora and Patani, 5 Division was now pouring into North Malaya. Neither Murray-Lyon nor Heath were timid men. But Murray-Lyon had been told often enough that he was to keep his division in being as the defence of northern Malaya, and he therefore sought permission to withdraw its battered brigades from Jitra to Gurun, thirty miles south. The request went right to the top. Heath was in Singapore, and it was put to Percival, who put it to the Far East War Council. The verdict was that the demoralization of troops and civilians implied by a withdrawal from Jitra was unacceptable. He would have to fight his battle there. The fact that Krohcol was unlikely to hold up the Japanese coming from Patani, and the panic he found among his transport on returning to his HQ, made Murray-Lyon repeat his request for a withdrawal behind the River Kedah. This was at 7.30 pm on 12 December, Heath still being with Percival at Malaya Command HQ in Singapore. After discussion with Percival, Heath told Murray-Lyon his task was to fight for North Kedah, that he should use effective obstacles to hold up the Japanese and obtain scope for British artillery. In phoning the message, III Corps HQ gave Murray-Lyon permission to withdraw from the Jitra position.

His men began to move after midnight on the 12th, a distance of fifteen miles to Alor Star. They were tired and shaken, orders went astray, equipment was lost, the fear of enemy tanks made some units take to the forest, others tried to make it down the coast and were shipwrecked – one party even ended up in Sumatra. Guns and lorries were abandoned. It was a disaster.

GURUN

After the catastrophe at Jitra, another delaying action was attempted by 11 Division at Gurun, thirty miles to the south. The position was suitable for defence, astride the road and railway running between the slopes of Kedah Peak and the jungle to the east. But it needed reinforcing, and the civilian labour hired to construct defence works had evaporated upon the news of the British retreat, and the tired troops of 11 Indian Division had to erect defence works themselves. The road bridge over the River Kedah was blown, but the railway bridge remained stubbornly intact, and the defenders were astonished to see not merely lorried infantry but Japanese tanks appear in front of their positions almost as soon as they had dug in on the afternoon of 14 December. A tank was hit by anti-tank fire and the remainder withdrew, but the infantry came on and began to break through 1/8 Punjab astride the main road.

That same afternoon Heath met Murray-Lyon at a point four miles south of the battle, and the divisional commander represented to him that the policy of short retreats and piecemeal defence was courting disaster. Murray-Lyon already feared for his rear communications. An advance through Betong and Kroh could cut into the west coast north of Penang, or move down the Perak River on Taiping and Ipoh. Either way, his communications would be severed.

Heath accepted that, in theory, a long retreat to carefully prepared positions was preferable to a series of small delaying actions and the inevitable withdrawal, but he told Murray-Lyon that his immediate task was to hold Gurun. The roads to Kroh and Grik would be held by 12 Brigade, so his rear was covered.

A Japanese night attack a few hours later destroyed 6 Brigade's defences north of Gurun. Brigade HQ itself was annihilated.

The Punjabis' battalion commander believed the East Surreys on his right hand had been overrun, so he withdrew his men west along a lateral road, hoping to rejoin the brigade later, further south. This move left the road completely open, but the position was sealed by 28 Brigade and reserves from 15 Brigade. Murray-Lyon visited the forward positions the following morning, realized the situation was hopeless, and ordered a further withdrawal southward. Keeping the Japanese at bay by using his artillery, he pulled his division back beyond the Muda River on 16 December. Within four days it was pushed further and further south to Taiping, leaving Penang uncovered. Georgetown had been bombed on 11 December, and as the defences had no anti-aircraft guns whatever, no resistance was possible. Many of the city's installations were destroyed, and the European population was evacuated; but the radio station and many small craft in the harbour fell intact into the hands of the Japanese. Elsewhere in north-west Malaya stocks of high-octane petrol were captured. The Japanese soon repaired the airfield runways, and by 20 December they had effective use of the airfields in north-west Malaya.

11 Indian Division had a face-lift. On 24 December, Brigadier Paris replaced Murray-Lyon, and as all three brigade commanders were out of action in hospital, new ones were appointed. The higher command structure was changed, too. On 23 December Brooke-Popham was relieved as C-in-C Far East by Lieutenant-General Sir

Henry Pownall, whose appointment only lasted until the entire command structure was altered by the creation of American-British-Dutch-Australian Command under the supreme command of General Wavell on 5 January 1942, when Pownall became his Chief-of-Staff. The upshot of the battle for Malaya was unaffected by these changes. The Japanese were in Taiping the day Pownall took over, and five days later had taken Ipoh. Heath's next serious attempt to stop them was at Kampar.

KAMPAR

The position was roughly halfway between Penang and Kuala Lumpur and thought to be the strongest in Malaya. It lay in rich tin-mining country, crisscrossed with streams but far more open than the mountainous jungles of northern Malaya, and suitable for artillery, an arm in which the British still had superiority. The main road and railway south from Ipoh ran past a steep jungle-clad hill, nine miles by six, rising to 4,000 feet, with a road looping round either side. This 'rocky bastion' was to be occupied by the merged 6 and 15 Brigades, while 12 and 8 Brigades fought delaying actions north of Ipoh and on the Blanja front to enable Ipoh to be evacuated.

12 Brigade inflicted heavy losses on the Japanese ten miles north of Ipoh at Chemor, on 26/27 December. All troops had left Ipoh by 26 December, with as many stores as could be taken, the rest being destroyed. Almost the last to leave were the telephone operators – Chinese and Eurasian girls – who stuck to their posts to keep open the military telephone traffic until they were ordered to leave. Paris decided to fall back behind Ipoh on the night of 27/28 December, 28 Brigade being ordered to move into position at Kampar and 12 Brigade to delay the Japanese approach.

Some respite was hoped for, but none was forthcoming. The Japanese were on to them on 29 December. 12 Brigade was told to withdraw through the Kampar position and to act as reserve at Bidor, but the Japanese kept close behind them with tanks. Rescued by the armoured cars of the Argyll and Sutherland Highlanders, the brigade managed to cross the Kampar River and the bridge was blown. Not that this stopped the Japanese, for the river proved to be easily fordable. By the time 12 Brigade pulled into the reserve position at Bidor, it was beaten to a frazzle. It had fought for two weeks without a break. In the constant withdrawals it had lost nearly all its armoured vehicles and over 500 men.

Percival's purpose at this stage was perfectly consistent. He had been told that reinforcements were on their way to Singapore and would arrive during the early part of January: an Indian infantry brigade, the British 18 Division, re-routed from the Middle East, and fifty Hurricane fighters with their crews. One brigade of 18 Division was coming ahead in large American liners and it was vital to keep Japanese aircraft away from the convoys. If Percival got hold of fifty Hurricanes it might redress the balance in the air. Japanese aircraft operating not only from northern Malaya, but from aerodromes at Kuantan on the east coast and Kuala Lumpur, would pose a grave threat to the convoys. Central Malaya must be held as far forward as possible while the ships arrived in Singapore and were turned round. This was timed for 13-15 January.

Kampar could be by-passed with some difficulty, through the loop-road to the east through Sahum. Westward, the sea was twenty miles away at Telok Anson, where the River Perak filtered through marshes to the Straits of Malacca. So the British could expect to hold what was in effect a very narrow front, only turnable by seaborne landings. Paris was ordered to hold the Kampar position as long as possible, and in any case not to retreat south beyond the road junction at Kuala Kubu without permission.

28 Brigade was to prevent the Kampar position being turned along the loop road to the east. 12 Brigade found its rest period shortlived and was told to cover Telok Anson. The position was naturally strong, but it needed building up. This was where the defence system began to go wrong. Coolies had been employed to help 6/15 Brigade in defence works, but on Christmas Eve Japanese aircraft

bombed them, and in a day the coolies had fled, leaving the depleted and exhausted 6/15 Brigade to dig gun pits, put up wire entanglements and clear fields of fire.

The Japanese probed the loop-road through Sahum. 28 Brigade, using Gurkhas and 155 Field Regiment, repulsed this attack on 31 December. The country was perfect Gurkha terrain, scrub hillside.

Early on New Year's Day, 1942, the Japanese attacked the main Kampar position. Fighting was heavy, particularly on the right flank, where the 'British Battalion' (the amalgamated remnants of the Leicesters and East Surreys) was positioned. Some points were lost, then retaken in counter-attacks. By the end of 1 January the British positions were still firmly held.

On the 2nd, the Japanese began to attack the hillside positions east of the main road. The British Battalion was hard-pressed, and the situation was only saved by repeated charges by 1/8 Punjab which went through two sets of Japanese lines, and a third, by which time the unit was down to thirty men. The company commander, Captain Graham, who led the charges, was mortally wounded, having both his legs blown off by mortar fire.

The Japanese pressure on Kampar continued, and Paris judged that 6/15 Brigade was unlikely to be able to hold it much longer. At nine in the evening of 2 January, 6/15 Brigade started to pull back. Screened by 28 Brigade, they extricated themselves from the Japanese, and moved into the Tapah Bidor area south of the main position.

Percival attributed the withdrawal to 'the influence of events elsewhere'.[5] What were these events?

The Japanese were not relying exclusively on a frontal assault on Kampar, merely doubled with a probing of the loop. Given the effectiveness of their air cover, there was another way. West of Kampar, at Telok Anson, the River Perak ran through marshes to the coast. A few miles further south lay the mouth of the River Bernam. Telok Anson was covered by an Independent Company and a squadron of 3 Indian Cavalry. Long distance patrols reported Japanese in Lumut, further up the west coast, on 28 December.

They were assembling a flotilla of forty motor boats which had been used in the Singora landings, brought across to Alor Star by road and rail, and finally re-assembled at Lumut at the mouth of the Perak River. Three days later, British air reconnaissance spotted small steamers moving south from Lumut, towing barges. British aircraft machine-gunned them, one being shot down by the Japanese, who returned the fire. At 9 am the following day (1 January) a river patrol saw a tug with four barges in tow at the mouth of the River Perak. The motor launch patrol did not engage them, but reported they were stationary, and appeared to be stuck on a sandbank. The launch called for an air-strike or a naval patrol, but Japanese air cover prevented any intervention. 'Unfortunately' wrote Percival later 'neither the navy nor the air force was able to take advantage of this unique opportunity.'[6] Churchill could not understand this. Control of the western coast had passed to the Japanese Army, which did not have even one naval vessel there. The failure was a blot on the past history of the British Navy. Why did not the Navy oppose the enemy advance with destroyers, submarines or aeroplanes?[7] The Japanese were puzzled too. That was precisely the opposition they thought they were risking.[8] Admiral Pound told Churchill that lack of air cover prevented the Navy using ships, and the failure of the scorched-earth policy in Penang meant the Japanese could use small boats left behind by the British. These were hardly adequate reasons.

At 7.30 in the evening of 1 January, Japanese seaborne troops landed at Utan Melintang on the River Bernam. This could have represented a direct threat to the road to Kampar, because launches could carry troops up river to Rantan Panjang, whence tracks led to the main road. The Japanese units were parties of 11 Infantry Regiment of 5 Division and were in fact only staying there overnight. British patrols attacked them, and were driven back on Telok Anson. At dawn the following day a battalion landed at Telok Anson from another direction, having been brought down the River Perak by boat.

To meet the threat to Kampar's flank presented by these

forces, 12 Brigade was brought out of rest at Bidor and sent to Telok Anson. The Independent Company and the 3 Indian Cavalry Squadron, after offering some resistance to Japanese in Changkat Jong, withdrew through 12 Brigade. The Japanese came on, and by two in the afternoon were fighting 12 Brigade forward units. The commander of 12 Brigade (Brigadier I. Stewart, former battalion commander of the 2nd Battalion, Argyll and Sutherland Highlanders) estimated he was under attack at regimental strength (a Japanese regiment is the equivalent of a British brigade in numbers) and reported he could not guarantee to keep the main road open for more than twenty-four hours.

The withdrawal from Kampar was ordered as a result of this report.

II THE SINKING OF FORCE Z

Before the First World War, even if there had been no Anglo-Japanese Alliance, a British Fleet large enough to dominate the Japanese Fleet could be maintained permanently in Far Eastern seas. Under that umbrella Britain's commerce with the East could thrive unhindered. The First World War changed all that. Japan emerged from it as the world's third largest naval power. Britain's economy could no longer maintain a fleet either at Hong Kong or at Singapore permanently. This realization dominated the thinking about the new naval base at Singapore, which clearly had problems even before its construction was begun.

If a fleet could not be kept permanently in the Far East, the role of the base was to remain open to receive a fleet from European waters; and the defence of the base was linked with the period of time it would take that fleet to arrive in the Indian Ocean or the South China Sea. Initially, it was assumed that important units of the Royal Navy could be in the Far East in forty-eight days, but that assumption was based on another: that the Navy should not be involved elsewhere. By 1941, the Royal

Navy was engaged in a mortal struggle with the Germans in the Atlantic, a struggle which ultimately was won by a hair's breadth. The time by which elements of the British Fleet could be in the East was lengthened, first to seventy days, then to 180 days. Each prolongation implied greater stress on the other two arms, Royal Air Force and Army.

Then politics began to overtake the purely strategic considerations. It never seems to have occurred to Churchill, during 1940 and most of 1941, that the Japanese were seriously intending to make war on the British Empire. He was convinced they were too heavily involved in China to risk further military adventures. To all intents and purposes the making of British policy in the Far East, at least as far as relations with Japan were concerned, was left to the Americans, with Great Britain and the Netherlands East Indies acquiescing in their decisions. By the summer of 1941, the USA and Japan had reached the stage of head-on confrontation. It was no longer possible to be so sanguine about relations between Japan and Britain, and with an eye to the Japanese naval authorities in the first place, and to Japan's foreign policy in the second, it was decided by the Defence Committee in London, on 17 October 1941, that the presence of one modern capital ship in Far Eastern waters would act as a deterrent.

The old battle cruiser *Repulse,* which had been built as long ago as 1916, was already in the Indian Ocean. She had six 15-inch guns and could do 29 knots. The First Sea Lord, Admiral Sir Dudley Pound, proposed that when she arrived in Durban early in October – she had been escorting troop transports to the Middle East – she should be sent on to Ceylon. Even this addition to the East Indies Station was not conceived willingly. Pound believed it meant weakening Britain's naval strength in the Atlantic, where the war against Germany would be decided. He and his Vice-Chief of Naval Staff, Vice-Admiral (later Admiral) Sir Tom Phillips, thought that the kind of force that could be spared for the East would be the First World War battleships *Barham* or *Valiant*, then in the Eastern

Mediterranean, to be augmented by four of the obsolescent Royal Sovereign class battleships by the end of 1941,
with the old aircraft-carrier *Eagle.* It was not expected that
this second or third eleven would match up to Japan's ten
modernized capital ships and as many carriers. But Pound
and Phillips counted on the presence of the US Pacific
Fleet at Pearl Harbour – with its nine battleships and three
carriers – to be the real deterrent. The purpose of the proposed British force would be to face Japan with the unpalatable alternative of giving a hypothetical invasion convoy adequate defence against the British battle fleet, and
thereby leave her home islands uncovered to a possible
American attack from Hawaii; or to maintain protection of
the home islands and leave her convoys to their fate.

Given the factors as they saw them, Pound and Phillips
had made a sensible proposal. Churchill was unconvinced.
He did not see the Japanese fleet's plans in this way. If
war did break out, the real risk would be to British trade.
Japanese battle cruisers might attempt sorties against British trade routes.

Here the Germans and Italians took a hand. In the last
week of November, 1941, *Barham* was sunk by a U-boat.
Three weeks later Italian 'human torpedo' attacks put
Queen Elizabeth and *Valiant* out of commission. The question of sending *Barham* or *Valiant* to the East no longer
arose. Both Churchill and his Foreign Secretary, Anthony
Eden, were convinced that only a battleship with the prestige of the King George V class would have the political
effect on Japan which they required. *Prince of Wales* had
recently been completed. She had ten 14-inch guns and
could make the same speed as *Repulse.* Again most un-
willingly, Pound agreed that *Prince of Wales* might make
for Capetown. Once she was there, they could make further
decisions on her future movements. *Prince of Wales* left
the Clyde on 25 October 1941, accompanied by two destroyers, *Express* and *Electra.* The small force, designated
'Force Z', was under the command of Sir Tom Phillips,
who was promoted to acting Admiral, with Rear-Admiral
Palliser as chief of staff.

Force Z received fresh orders on 11 November 1941, four days before Cape Town was reached. *Prince of Wales* was to rendezvous with *Repulse*, at Ceylon, and they were then to proceed together to Singapore. It seems that the intervention of Sir Earle Page, the special Australian envoy, had played a part in this. He was the Australian Minister for Commerce, and had been sent to London to urge the sending of reinforcements to the Far East. Page attended a meeting of the War Cabinet on 5 November and pointed out that nine months had passed since the air requirement for the defence of Malaya had been put at 336 aircraft, and there were still only 136 front line aircraft available. Churchill replied that there was no alternative, given the need to retain an air nucleus at home and supply Russia and the Middle East. Sending Force Z to the Far East was intended to offset the shortage of aircraft, but Page was not reassured, nor was the Australian war cabinet, which wanted Singapore to receive the promised air reinforcement too.[9] Another Commonwealth Prime Minister was not too happy about Force Z, either. Phillips flew to see Smuts, the South African Prime Minister, while *Prince of Wales* was in Cape Town. On 18 November Smuts wired to Churchill his concern about the division of the future Allied naval strength between Hawaii and Singapore, each of the two fleets stationed in these places being separately inferior to the Japanese Navy: 'If the Japanese are really nippy there is here opening for a first-class disaster.'[10] His prescience amply compensates for the pun.

Ten days later Force Z was in Colombo. Phillips flew to Singapore, leaving Captain Tennant to take the fleet into harbour. The two battleships had four destroyers with them, but a most important component was missing. In theory, Force Z should have had its own air cover provided by the carrier *Indomitable*. But, with the ill-luck that was to characterize the Force's short career, *Indomitable* ran aground in Jamaica and had to be docked for repairs. Perhaps another carrier should have been detailed to replace her, but *Ark Royal* was sunk by a U-boat off Gibraltar on 14 November and the decision was taken that no carrier could therefore be spared. So, without air cover, Force Z arrived in Singapore on 2 December. It was received with rapture. The entire population derived comfort and confidence from the presence of the great ships.

But how vulnerable they were became evident when news came through of Pearl Harbour. The role of Force Z was by no means clear when war broke out. Tom Phillips proposed the fleet should make for Port Darwin in Australia. The suggestion was also made that they should go to Hawaii to join the remnants of the US Pacific Fleet, 'a proud gesture', wrote Winston Churchill, which would 'knit the English-speaking world together'.[11] Alternatively they could, he thought, roam among the Pacific islands and act 'like rogue elephants'.

In the upshot, they were to do none of these things. The meeting of the Defence Committee in London which discussed the issue came to no conclusion and broke off at 1 am on Wednesday 10 December – 8.30 am in Singapore. A final decision was to be taken the next day.

Admiral Phillips and the Japanese together took the decision out of London's hands. Not unnaturally, Phillips had been unwilling to sail out of Malayan waters to the comparative safety of Port Darwin while British troops were engaged with the Japanese in northern Malaya. He decided to sail north to intercept the Japanese convoys and sink their transports. If he could achieve surprise, and provided he were given fighter cover by the RAF, he thought he could wreak havoc among the invasion fleet, since no major modern Japanese warships had been sighted in it. *Prince of Wales* and *Repulse*, with destroyer escort, sailed from Singapore at 5.35 pm on 8 December.

The signals that passed between Pulford and Phillips at this time are of some importance. Before sailing, Phillips asked Pulford for:

a) reconnaissance 100 miles north of his Force during daylight on 9 December;

b) 100 miles reconnaissance with Singora as mid-point 10 miles from the coast, starting at first light on 10 December;

The Sinking of Force Z   10 December 1941

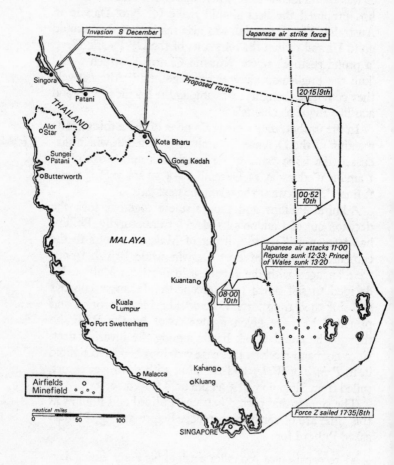

Invasion 8 December

Singora

Patani

THAILAND

Alor
Star

Sungei
Patani

Butterworth

Kota Bharu

Gong Kedah

Proposed route

Japanese air strike force

20·15/9th

00·52
10th

Japanese air attacks 11·00
Repulse sunk 12·33; Prince
of Wales sunk 13·20

MALAYA

Kuantan

08·00
10th

Kuala
Lumpur

Port Swettenham

Kahang

Kluang

Malacca

Airfields   o
Minefield   o o o o

nautical miles
0   50   100

Force Z sailed 17·35/8th

SINGAPORE

   c) fighter protection off Singora at daylight on 10 December.[12]

The arrangement was that Pulford would look into these questions and give the answer to Palliser, Phillips's chief-of-staff, who was to remain behind in Singapore. In the event, Pulford signalled from Changi Signal Station as the fleet moved out of Singapore: 'Regret fighter protection impossible'.[13]

The signal was amplified to Palliser who notified Phillips: Pulford could not provide a), hoped to be able to provide b), and could NOT repeat NOT provide c).[14] This news was bad enough. But Phillips also lost the advantage of surprise, which in his mind would have been some substitute for air cover. A Japanese submarine spotted the ships on the afternoon of 9 December and signalled their position. Planes of 22 Air Flotilla, from Saigon and Thudaumot in Indo-China, made a sortie against them but failed to find them and returned to base. Phillips was sure he had been sighted and decided to return to Singapore. He changed course at 8.15 pm on 9 December. Just before midnight, Palliser signalled from Singapore: 'Enemy reported landing Kuantan, latitude 3°50' North.'[15] Palliser gave no indication of the reliability of the report, but Phillips was well aware that a road ran inland from Kuantan across central Malaya. If the Japanese seized it, they could cut the British lines of communication neatly in two, far to the south of where the fighting was then. Kuantan was 400 miles away from the enemy-occupied airfields in French Indo-China and the risk must have seemed worth taking. Phillips seems to have assumed that Palliser knew he would act on the report. It has been supposed that he also assumed air cover would be available for Force Z at Kuantan, though this is by no means certain. At any rate, he did not signal to Singapore his change of course, since he did not want to break wireless silence and thereby reveal his position to the Japanese.

At no time *while he was at sea* did Phillips ask for air cover. This fact, together with the fact that he never notified Singapore of his change of course to Kuantan, surely needs some explanation. It may lie in the form of signal which Pulford sent as Force Z was leaving harbour. It will be remembered that what Phillips had asked for was quite precise: 'Fighter protection off Singora at daylight 10 December'. Now the answering signal from the RAF received on board *Prince of Wales* read: 'Fighter protection on Wednesday 10th will not be possible'.[16] Not until five years later was the possible significance of the wording scrutinized. The signal was found by Air-Vice-Marshal Maltby when he was making investigations for the writing of his despatch on the air operations of the Malaya campaign. He wrote to Brooke-Popham (30 April 1946):

> You will notice that this wording makes no mention of Singora and recipients might read into it that no fighter defence could be made *anywhere* [my italics] on 10th December which, of course, was not the intention.[17]

Very naturally, Maltby concluded that a contention might be made that Phillips did not risk breaking wireless silence to ask for fighter cover over Kuantan since he had been led to believe, by the terms of the signal, that it was useless to ask for fighter cover anywhere; when, in fact, Pulford's intention had been merely to say he could not have it over Singora.

The apparently trivial omission of the mention of Singora *may* have made the whole difference to Phillips's assessment of the worthwhileness of asking for fighter cover at Kuantan. Indirectly, therefore, as Maltby suspected, it may have led to the events off Kuantan. It is interesting that Maltby's speculations are not echoed by any of the later historians, who all quote the signal.

The report of the Kuantan landings was false and Singapore did nothing to provide fighter cover, since there was no reason to suppose any was needed. A Japanese submarine sighted the battleships with their destroyer escorts in the early hours of 10 December and radioed Phillips's position to French Indo-China.[18] The Japanese signal traffic does not seem to have been intercepted. 22 Air Flotilla sent out thirty bombers and fifty torpedo bombers at 6 am on the 10th, to seek out and destroy the British ships. Fanning out over the South China Sea, the Japanese aircraft flew south, almost as far as Singapore itself, 150 miles south of Kuantan, without sighting the ships. There was considerable broken cloud and the Japanese pilots were flying at around 9,000 feet. Having seen nothing, the Japanese planes made for home. Suddenly the cloud broke over the fleet and the Japanese saw them, destroyers first, then the big ships.

High level bombers made the first run-in just after 11 am, followed by the torpedo bombers. *Repulse* was hit, but her captain's superb handling enabled her to dodge the next wave of attack and she went to the help of *Prince of Wales*, which had been severely damaged by two hits. *Repulse* was then hit again but kept on firing her anti-aircraft guns at the Japanese, while four torpedoes found *Prince of Wales* in rapid succession. When *Repulse's* steering was damaged the torpedo bombers came in again to finish her off. She rolled over at 12.33 pm and 796 officers and men – including her commander, Captain Tennant – were picked up by the escort destroyers, out of a total complement of 1,309. *Prince of Wales* – she had been termed 'unsinkable', which seems a fatal challenge to destiny – was slowly steaming north, unable to steer, settling in the water and listing to port. But she was still afloat, and this very fact was a source of great concern to Rear-Admiral Matsunaga, who commanded 22 Air Flotilla in Saigon. His staff had forcibly to restrain him from flying out himself to give the *coup de grâce*.[19] His impulse was reasonable. The Japanese ships and aircraft, far from wishing to avoid battle with Force Z, had been actively hunting it for days. If it were not destroyed, the whole of the Japanese army's campaign in Malaya would have been in jeopardy. Matsunaga's intervention was not required. *Prince of Wales* turned turtle and sank at 1.20 pm, taking Admiral Sir Tom Phillips to the bottom with her.

It would be surprising if the Admiral had not been criticized for his handling of the situation. Compton Mackenzie in *Eastern Epic* answers Phillips's critics in one respect by saying that, unless he filled his bunkers with oil and sailed away westward, he was bound to become involved in action of this kind.[20] The US Pacific Fleet was, for the time being, out of the war. Their air force in the Philippines had been destroyed. No help could come to Malaya or the Netherlands East Indies from that source. Phillips could have escaped back into the Indian Ocean or have stayed on in Singapore waiting to be bombed in the harbour by Japanese aircraft. He chose to use his ships to intervene in Malayan waters to help the army.

Evidence has been adduced above to show it is possible Phillips may have thought it futile to hope for air cover. Against this is the evidence given by the Official Historian of the war at sea, Captain S. W. Roskill, who refers to one of Phillips's staff officers who spent most of the night of 9/10 December with him. This officer is not named, but according to what he must be presumed to have told Roskill, Phillips did assume that Palliser, once he had sent the message about Kuantan, would automatically take it for granted that Phillips would act on the signal; in turn, that would imply Palliser would arrange fighter cover over Kuantan.[21] Such cover was, of course, perfectly possible, as events showed: when *Repulse* signalled she was being attacked, fighters left Sembawang at 12.15 and were over the scene just an hour later, in time to see the destroyers picking up the survivors.

Another element in the story remains puzzling. The Kuantan message was the result of misinformation. There was no such landing, and Phillips verified this on the spot. 'Actually the report of the Kuantan landing was false' writes Roskill, 'and Singapore took no action to anticipate the squadron arriving there at dawn on the 10th.'[22] That can only mean it was known in Singapore that the report was false in time not to send aircraft. Why was Phillips not informed the report was false? None of the accounts records Palliser, or anyone else, notifying Force Z to this effect. Nor do they say at what time Singapore – or which authority in Singapore – learned of the true facts at Kuantan. In *Main Fleet to Singapore,* Captain Russell Grenfell writes that Palliser only discovered the report was false *after Prince of Wales* and *Repulse* had been sunk. The delay was due to 'all the early confusion of the invasion'.[23] Given the importance of the Kuantan signal, the reason seems a little thin.

It is quite clear that Phillips knew of the risks from the Indo-China based aircraft. Brooke-Popham had signalled information that an estimated fifty to sixty Japanese bombers were using the airfields of southern Indo-China. In his despatch he says he does not know whether that information was ever received,[24] but Grenfell makes it clear that it was, having been reported by Palliser at 11 pm on 9 December, together with news that British airfields in Northern Malaya had been evacuated.[25] Without going so far as Captain Geoffrey Bennett* who implies that Phillips's lack of battle command experience may have been a contributing factor[26] – he had spent much time on the staff – it is feasible to suggest that Phillips's own ideas on sea-power may have played a part in his decision.

In this particular instance, he does seem to have set store by adequate fighter cover, since he mentioned to Captain Bell, the Captain of the Fleet, that he thought Pulford did not realize the importance he (Phillips) attached to fighter cover over Singora; and this made him contact Pulford again to stress it further.[27]

But in *general* terms, the evidence about his attitude to the relations between sea and air-power goes the other way. Marshal of the Royal Air Force Sir John Slessor – then a Group-Captain and Director of Plans – worked with him in the Joint Planning Committee just before the war. He describes Phillips as a splendid Naval officer and a staff officer of exceptional calibre. But, he adds, 'it was perhaps the one defect of his outstanding qualities that he was quite irrational on the subject of air-power in relation to navies . . . we had to have a sort of pact not to discuss aircraft versus ships except when our duty made it inevitable

* *The Loss of the Prince of Wales and Repulse,* London, Ian Allan, 1973.

in committee – when there was usually a row. Tom re-
solutely and sometimes violently rejected the idea that an
aeroplane could be any real threat to a man-of-war.'[28]

That confidence, expressed so vigorously while Britain
was fighting the Germans in Norway in 1940, may have
become over-confidence in *Prince of Wales* – even though
he knew she was not fully efficient[29] – and may have made
Phillips refrain from asking for fighter cover while at sea.
He may have been too afraid of breaking wireless silence
for security reasons. He may have been misled by the terms
of Pulford's signal. Certainly the information sent later
by Palliser about the evacuation of aerodromes in northern
Malaya adds colour to this, and also the additional news
that the C-in-C Far East was concentrating aircraft on
Singapore. We shall never know.

The upshot, on the other hand, was only too clear. If
we except the Japanese preponderance in aircraft carriers,
it could be calculated that the Allied fleets (American,
British, Dutch, Australian, New Zealand, Free French)
operating in the Pacific area were roughly equal in strength
to the Japanese fleet when war broke out. Less than three
days later, by the afternoon of 10 December 1941, the
Japanese fleet was mistress of the seas from Hawaii to
Ceylon.

III THE DEFENCE OF CENTRAL MALAYA – THE SLIM RIVER BATTLE

Kampar was a hard-fought engagement on good defensive
ground, and the position might have held much longer had
it not been turned from the mouth of the River Perak.

The position to which the exhausted British forces fell
back was far inferior, and led 11 Indian Division into the
greatest disaster since Jitra. It was perhaps the mainland
campaign's decisive engagement. When the Japanese pen-
etrated the Slim River position, the British had definitely
lost North Malaya and the largest city in Malaya, Kuala
Lumpur, lay open to the Japanese.

As in the earlier battle, the cause of the débâcle lay not

in Japanese air superiority nor in their ability to outflank and infiltrate: it lay in the use of tanks. The British were taken by surprise by the appearance of 12-ton medium tanks, and never recovered.

The position consisted of a stretch of road between Songkai and Trolak, with rubber plantations on either side, and, behind the rubber, thick jungle. This was 12 Brigade's area. Beyond Trolak, the road turns east at Slim River to the Slim River Bridge, where it turns south again. Up to this point was 28 Brigade's area. The battalions which made up the two brigades were down to three poorly armed companies each. No battalion had more than two anti-tank rifles. Some had none.

Unlike the Kampar position, the country offered little chance of effective artillery action but, to block the narrow jungle corridor through which the road ran, 12 Brigade had been supplied with large concrete cylinders. These and other defences could only be put in position at night, because of the constant harassment of Japanese aircraft. The exhausted soldiers of 12 Brigade found the deathly silence of the dense jungle unnerving, since all that broke it was the sudden roar of Japanese aircraft, and the blanket bombing which followed. The leading battalion saw its casualties mount under the bombing without being able to retaliate. 28 Brigade was five miles behind them, resting in harbours at Slim River Village.

The Japanese first probed down the railway line on the afternoon of 5 January, and were repulsed. Just after midnight they came on again, down both the railway and road corridors, and probed the British positions throughout the following day. Then, in the early hours of 7 January, the nature of the battle changed completely.

The Japanese put in a column of tanks, intersected with infantry. This was not their original intention. Colonel Andō, the commander of Andō Force which made the attack (the nucleus being his own 42 Infantry Regiment), summoned his battalion commanders at 15.30 hours on the 6th and told them that part of the infantry would go through the jungle on the left, and make for Trolak; the

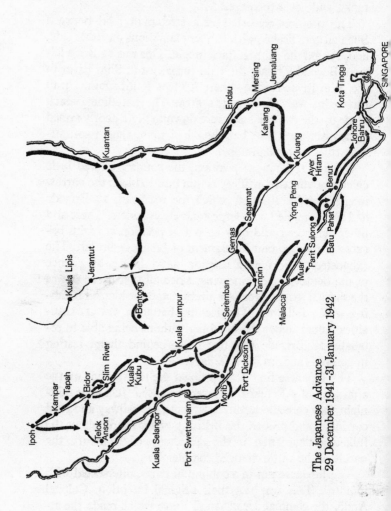

The Japanese Advance
29 December 1941-31 January 1942.

major part of the force would attack the following day with tanks in support. Major Shimada, the commander of one of the tank companies, pleaded with Andō to let a tank attack go in at night and make a breakthrough. 'What can tanks do by themselves in the jungle?' Andō answered. 'They're dumb, deaf and blind, they'll just be going straight into the mouth of the enemy. Tanks have one role: to serve as armour for the infantry.' Shimada begged him to let him try. If the tank attack failed, he could still go through with his infantry assault. Finally Andō gave in, and let Shimada's seventeen medium tanks and three light tanks move first, with an infantry company of eighty men and a twenty-man strong engineering section.[30]

Shimada told the tanks to go at five miles an hour, with six yards between them, and a total black-out. Protected by the infantry, the engineer section had been moving the tank obstacles. In bright moonlight, the tanks went through one wire obstacle, then a second. They were 200 yards from the British when flares went up on all sides, and the tanks became targets for British artillery. The sixth tank came out of line, and stopped dead. The other nineteen went right through the British positions and fired at the artillery positions 200 yards further on among the rubber. The tank gunners couldn't see the enemy guns, but even though they fired at random they saw lorries and petrol dumps explode. Darkness came down again as they moved on.

Over a mile from Trolak, they saw the lights of lorries. British infantry, 300 yards ahead. Still advancing, the tank-men saw two British officers in a stopped car, and soldiers marching behind the lorries. The tanks opened up with everything, and tore into the column, which melted into the jungle. Major Winkfield of the 2/1st Gurkha Rifles, moving with his men to take up positions in the Cluny Estate in the early morning, had gone about a mile along the road when he sensed a feeling of unease behind him, which he couldn't understand. The battle sounded closer than he'd anticipated, but they were still miles behind where they thought the front was. His men kept marching faster, and looking back, and he told them to maintain distance. 'The next thing I knew', he later recalled, 'was a gun and machine-gun blazing in my ear; a bullet grazed my leg, and I dived into a ditch as a tank bore down upon me. It had passed through half my battalion without my realizing that anything was amiss.'[31]

The battalion disintegrated. The following day, the major, four Gurkha officers and twenty other ranks mustered. All the rest had died in the jungle or had been taken prisoner by the Japanese.

The tanks moved on again. The bridge over the Slim River should have been blown, but the engineers had not been warned of the armoured breakthrough, and the Japanese took the bridge intact. Anti-tank guns might have stopped them, but none were available. The division had 1,400 anti-tank mines, but the brigade was only allotted twenty-four of these. A troop of 16 Light Anti-Aircraft Battery tried to deal with the situation by depressing the barrels of their guns – the German 88-mm anti-aircraft guns had wreaked havoc among British armour in the Western Desert by the same tactic – but the troop was overrun.

Nothing seemed to stop the Japanese tanks. By the time a halt was called, with every shell and every round fired, Shimada's armour had cut through nineteen miles of 11 Indian Division's territory. They could not have gone as far as they did if the bridges had been blown. But although charges had been laid, blowing the bridges would have cut off large bodies of British and Indian troops who were still fighting behind the Japanese tanks. The leading Japanese tank commander, Second-Lieutenant Watanabe, on one occasion leaped from his tank and hacked the demolition fuse wire in two with his sword. In another case he tore it apart with machine-gun fire. In this way the Japanese tanks crossed five bridges, every one of them intact.

Even so, if the supporting brigade had been warned in time, the Japanese need never have got beyond Trolak. Partly owing to lack of telephone cable, the troops in the rear were not warned of the approach of the tanks and were

taken completely by surprise. But they should not have
been. There is some evidence that in the afternoon before
the attack was put in, a Malay boy was questioned at an
artillery observation post who said he had seen Japanese
troops forming up, *with many tanks*. The post reported this
to Brigade HQ, where it was received with scepticism.[32]
Chinese and Tamil labourers reported the presence of
tanks to Division, and the news was passed to 12 Brigade
but not, for some reason, to 28 Brigade. Wherever the fault
lay, the result was plain: as fighting forces, two brigades
of 11 Division had, for the time being, almost ceased to
exist.

IV THE DEFENCE OF SOUTHERN MALAYA – THE BATTLE FOR JOHORE

With northern and central Malaya in enemy hands, Percival decided to cut his losses and to make a substantial
withdrawal to what he hoped would be a more defensible
line in Johore. This involved abandoning the provinces of
Selangor, Negri Sembilan and Malacca without a fight.
It also involved fighting in an area where there were more
roads, which allowed the enemy to use his tanks more
fully. But the risk had to be accepted in the hope of halt-
ing the piecemeal withdrawal, and making a stand in
Northern Johore, on a line running from Muar on the west
coast, via Mount Ophir, to Segamat, and on to Mersing
on the east coast, with a forward position at Gemas. It was
an opportunity to give some relief to 11 Indian Division,
too. Percival intended to switch the major role from the
Indians to the Australians, who had not so far been
brought into the battle.

The Australian commander, Lieutenant-General Gordon Bennett, was not impressed by the leadership shown in
III Corps so far, and in his view many units with British
officers in them lacked the aggressive spirit, often throughout entire formations. For this reason, he wanted to fight
his own battle. He proposed two alternatives: either he
should command all the forces in Johore, once the with-

drawal had taken place; or the Australians now on the east coast should be transferred to the west, while III Corps looked after east Johore. Percival would do neither. He would not accept the administrative chaos which would, he felt sure, follow from a too rapid welding together of III Corps with the Australians; and he felt it was asking for trouble to switch the Australians from one side of Malaya to the other while operations were in progress. It has since been pointed out that the Australians could in fact move fast enough to remove any risk involved. When the 2/19 Battalion, the only unit to be released from 22 Australian Brigade for service on the west of Malaya, was relieved at Jemaluang, it was in action at Bakri, a distance of one hundred miles, in under five hours, to the amazement of Percival's staff.[33]

At Segamat, on 5 January, there was a conference of commanders, Percival, Heath and Bennett. The Japanese were to be held at Kuala Lumpur and Port Swettenham until the middle of the month, and then the Imperial forces were to fall back on the Muar River. If the Japanese were held north of Johore, 18 British Division would arrive in time to strengthen the front. It was not out of the question – at the time – that further Australian elements might then be landed, which would force the Japanese onto the defensive, while the Indians were moved from Malaya to reinforce the Netherlands East Indies.

It was seen, quite rightly, that there was no point in trying to use any of the area between Kuala Lumpur and Gemas as a defence belt. All the roads into Johore, except the coast road, ran through Tampin, and as the Japanese could use coastal landings, there seemed to be little to prevent them cutting in behind III Corps into Tampin and blocking the retreat of the entire Corps. Muar was the best place to stand, particularly since no bridges crossed it along its lower reaches. To strengthen III Corps in holding the western position, Bennett agreed, but it must have been with great reluctance, to 27 Australian Brigade coming under Heath's command. The disaster at Slim River smashed the chance of organizing these shifts with time

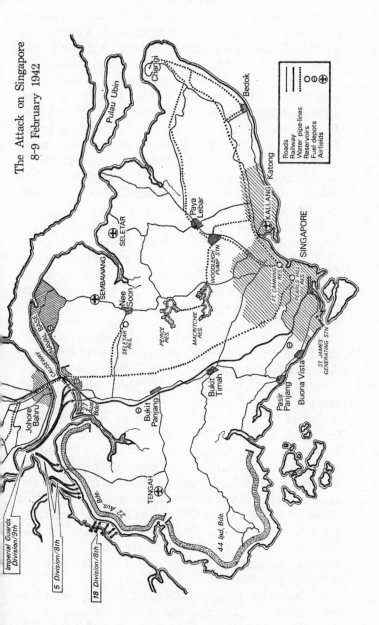

The Attack on Singapore
8-9 February 1942

Roads
Railway
Water pipe-lines
Reservoirs
Fuel depots
Airfields

Pulau Ubin

Changi

Bedok

SELETAR

Paya Lebar

KALLANG Katong

WOODLEIGH PUMP STN.

SEMBAWANG

Nee Soon

FT. CANNING RES.
PEARL'S HILL RES.

SINGAPORE

SELETAR RES.

PEIRCE RES.

MACRITCHIE RES.

ST. JAMES GENERATING STN.

Buona Vista

CAUSEWAY NAVAL BASE

Bukit Timah

Pasir Panjang

Johore Bahru

27 Aus. Bde.

Bukit Panjang

Imperial Guards Division/9th

5 Division/8th

18 Division/8th

TENGAH

22 Aus. Bde.

4.4 Ind. Bde.

to spare. As a result of it, 12 Brigade's three battalions now had the equivalent of a company each, a battalion of 28 Brigade had been destroyed and the other two halved. Guns and transport had been lost. The sight of these forces compelled Wavell, on 7 January, to agree to let Percival withdraw to Johore at once. Gordon Bennett was to assemble an Australian brigade around Segamat. 45 Indian Brigade would come under him and so would 9 Indian Division (8 and 22 Indian Brigades) as soon as it reached Johore. III Corps would withdraw into positions behind them, and be responsible for a line Endau-Kluang-Batu Pahat. It would have 22 Australian Brigade under command, on the east coast.

This lateral division was Wavell's idea, whereas Percival preferred the longitudinal division of the country, with the Australians on the east and III Corps on the west. But III Corps was not in a fit condition to continue resistance to a thrust from the two Japanese divisions (5th and Imperial Guards) now operating down the trunk road and the west coast. In the event, Gordon Bennett was unable to control the widely separated points of Muar and Segamat, and Percival reverted to his own plan later. This is one of the many instances of too frequent changes of command structures and commander which bedevilled the British performance.

One of the new formations given to Bennett's 'Westforce' was 45 Indian Brigade (Brigadier H. C. Duncan). Reports on 44, 45 and 46 Indian Brigades – the latter a reinforcement to Burma – all stressed the rawness of the recruits, some of them under eighteen, with only a few months' training, and the battalions milked of their best Viceroy's Commissioned Officers and NCOs to form training companies in India. Many of the British officers had had very brief contact with their men and were not as fluent in the language as regulars – a situation with disastrous implications.

11 Indian Division, which had received the worst battering from the Japanese, was to take advantage of the Australian take-over by resting in southern Johore, while

12 Brigade moved to the Island to re-form. Paris, the most recent commander of 11 Indian Division, was put in command of 12 Brigade, Percival giving as his reason for the transfer that Key, the commander of 8 Brigade, was an Indian Army officer and therefore more likely to be successful in pulling 11 Indian Division together. On 13 January, American liners brought reinforcements into Singapore, in spite of an eighty-strong bomber raid by the Japanese. 53 Brigade of 18 British Division was landed, with two anti-aircraft regiments and an anti-tank regiment, plus fifty-one crated Hurricanes, and twenty-four pilots. 53 Brigade should have been allowed to train and acclimatize itself, but there was no time for normal delay, and it was flung into the battle almost at once, after being at sea for nearly three months. The division as a whole would not be deployed until mid-February, Percival thought, and he was convinced – wrongly – that the Japanese now had five divisions against him.[34]

The Japanese entered Kuala Lumpur on the evening of 11 January and set up GHQ 5 Division there on the 12th. They took over not merely a city, but vast stores. Petrol and oil stocks had been fired, but food, maps and ordnance were left for the Japanese to take over. 11 Indian Division reached the bottleneck at Tampin on the 13th, and withdrew through Westforce to the area Kluang-Rengam the next night. Meanwhile the Japanese rested their 5 Division in the Seremban area, while the Imperial Guards concentrated in Malacca. Yamashita intended this division to move down the coast while 5 Division continued on down the trunk road. The rest of 18 Division was to be landed on the east coast. Endau was first thought of, but then Singora was chosen as the safer port. On 14 January, a Japanese force was on the move again: Mukaide Force, consisting of a battalion of infantry on bicycles, and a tank regiment with artillery and engineers.

Bennett had devised a way of dealing with them. Ambush was the answer. 700 yards of the trunk road west of Gemas, east of a bridge over a small river, was the site selected. On either side of the road was a company of 2/30

Australian Battalion, with a field battery covering the road west. The bridge was ready for demolition. Mukaide Force came along the road on the 14th, and after twenty minutes had elapsed, and many Japanese had crossed, the bridge was blown. The Japanese sustained many casualties and would have had more had artillery been used; but the telephone wires were visible and had been cut. Nonetheless, the trap worked. Undeterred, the Japanese attacked Gemas the next day, but were thrown back by the Australians. Then the pressure increased, and 2/30 Battalion was withdrawn to Batu Anam that night.

While the Australians were inflicting casualties on the Japanese in the central sector, 45 Brigade, holding Muar, was attacked by the Imperial Guards Division. The Japanese cut behind the position by sea landings and a force crossed the river east of Muar on the night of 16 January. They blocked the road Muar-Bakri, cutting the communications of 45 Brigade's two forward battalions. One of these was wiped out trying to break through and the other managed to withdraw on Bakri with heavy losses. The piercing of Westforce's left flank in this way left the way open to Yong Peng, the junction of the road to Segamat. If the Japanese pushed on beyond Bakri to Yong Peng, the Australians would be trapped along the trunk road. A conference of commanders showed that none were keen to abandon the Segamat position after the Australians had shown the success of vigorous offensive action against the Japanese. So Bennett sent 2/29 Australian Battalion to reinforce the Muar area. The arrival of 53 Brigade, sent to east Johore, enabled another Australian battalion to be released from there and sent across to the west coast. Westforce's rear, the area Yong Peng – Batu Pahat – Ayer Hitam, was taken over by III Corps. But the front was soon to give. Further Japanese landings were made between Muar and Batu Pahat, and they attacked and secured a defile along the road between Bakri and Yong Peng held by a battalion of 53 Brigade. It proved impossible to dislodge them. Bennett had now to pull Westforce out of the Segamat area while its exit to south Johore – at Yong

Peng – was still open. Japanese air mastery made day-time movement impossible, and it was estimated that four nights would be needed to move Westforce past Yong Peng. From Bakri, where it had re-formed, 45 Brigade was therefore ordered to recapture Muar. A three-pronged attack was to be made, but one of the prongs – the coastal attack – was cut to pieces, and the attack was cancelled by midnight on 17 January. The Japanese then put in a determined effort to take Bakri, and though Australian artillery destroyed several of their tanks, their infantry infiltrated and set up road blocks. The threat to Yong Peng had greatly increased. After a 'phone call between Percival and Bennett, the Muar area was taken out of Bennett's hands and put under III Corps, so that the Australian could concentrate on removing Westforce safely from Segamat.

Percival held a conference on the 19th. 53 Brigade was to hold the defile at Bukit Pelandok, east of Batu Pahat, and 45 Brigade was to be withdrawn the next day to a position west of Yong Peng, while Westforce fell back on Labis. 53 Brigade in fact consisted merely of the 6th Norfolks, and they were forced back from the defile by the Japanese, whom counter-attacks failed to dislodge. 45 Brigade began to withdraw, fighting its way through one Japanese roadblock after another. Brigadier Duncan was killed, and the force was then taken over by the Australian battalion commander, Lieutenant-Colonel C. G. W. Anderson of 2/29 Battalion, who finally had to destroy his guns and vehicles and take to the jungle. Ultimately, of the 4,000 men who had made up the force in the Muar area, less than 1,000 rejoined. The Japanese massacred the wounded who were left behind. But 45 Brigade had not wasted its tragic effort. Its resistance held up the Imperial Guards Division for close on a week, and enabled Westforce to withdraw from the Segamat area through Yong Peng in time to avoid encirclement.

The next line was ninety miles across, from one side of Malaya to the other, Mersing to Batu Pahat, through Kluang and Ayer Hitam. This was southern Johore, III Indian Corps' area, and Heath now took command, controlling Eastforce in Jemaluang and Kahang (22 Australian Brigade) and Westforce (Australians plus 9 Indian Division) holding Kluang and Ayer Hitam, through which the road and railway passed to Singapore. 11 Division was to hold Batu Pahat and the west coast road, with the help of 53 Brigade as soon as Westforce released it. No unit was to retreat from this line without Percival's permission, since it was still hoped to deny airfields in the area to the Japanese, and to enable further reinforcements to reach Singapore; and in fact on 22 and 24 January, 44 Indian Brigade (7,000 men) landed, and nearly 2,000 Australians. They were not much use. The Indians were raw and untrained, and Brigadier Sir John Smyth describes the Australians as so undisciplined as to be 'a liability to their own side'.

At Batu Pahat, Brigadier B. Challen in command of 6/15 Brigade reported on 25 January that he could not hold the town much longer. Key agreed with him, and a request to withdraw went up through Heath to Percival. Challen was ordered to withdraw, much against Percival's will, because he knew this uncovered Kluang and Ayer Hitam, and he ordered Westforce to pull out that night.

Challen's brigade left Batu Pahat during 25/26 January, only to find the way to Benut and the south blocked at Sengarang. A column tried to break through from 53 Brigade to relieve them and was wiped out. Challen realized he would not make it down the road, destroyed his vehicles and artillery, split his brigade into two groups, and told them to trek across country to Benut, twenty miles south. One group, about 1,000 strong, succeeded. Another, with Challen himself, was held up by an unfordable river, and Challen was captured. What remnants were left – about 2,700 – were finally evacuated by gunboat.

In east Johore, the Australians repeated their ambush success. In the Nithsdale Estate, ten miles out of Mersing, they prepared a 'fire box' with rifle companies disposed on either side, and field artillery firing down the centre. On the night of 26/27 January, a Japanese force which had landed at Endau entered this box and its leading battalion was practically wiped out, the rest returning in disorder to Mersing. But such actions could not reverse the general trend, and on the same day Wavell authorized Percival to carry out the last stages of the retreat to the Island. Eastforce had little difficulty, and arrived at the bridgehead at Johore Bahru, opposite Singapore, on 30 January. On the west, disasters multiplied: 9 Indian Division, which had withdrawn right from Kota Bharu down through the railway via Kuala Lipis, kept on moving down the line, while 22 Australian Brigade withdrew along the trunk road. But for twenty miles of this route, road and railway run far apart until they join at Kulai. So 9 Division's guns and vehicles, going by road, were separated from the men, who moved down the railway. 22 Brigade was to provide a rearguard, retreating through 8 Brigade's positions, both of them leap-frogging southward in this sequence.

Then communications went wrong. Against orders, a railway bridge was prematurely blown. It took the railway telegraph line with it, thus ensuring that the various units could not contact each other: their wireless sets were in the vehicles, going down by road. When 8 Brigade took up a position too remote from 22 Brigade, the Japanese managed to slip in between them, without Major-General A. E. Barstow, the GOC 9 Indian Division, being aware that this had happened. Attempting to contact the forward Brigade, after visiting the rear one, Barstow was caught in Japanese fire and killed. With his force short of ammunition, and cut off from other units, 22 Brigade's commander, Brigadier G. W. A. Painter, decided to take to the jungle, carrying his wounded. After a calvary of four nights' bitter slogging through unspeakable conditions, Painter surrendered his men to the Japanese on 1 February, the day after he was supposed to be across the causeway into the Island. Only a few survivors managed to reach the shore and were picked up by Royal Navy rescue boats.

In the retreat through Johore, 45 Indian Brigade had been smashed to pieces, and 22 Indian Brigade captured or killed almost to a man. Several thousand men fewer than it had planned to be by the end of January, III Corps

passed across into the Island. At eight in the morning of 31
January, the pipers of the Argylls played the last troops of
the bridgehead across the Causeway. As the strains of
Jennie's Black E'en died away, the Causeway was blown.
After the explosion, it was seen that a hole seventy yards
long had been blown in the structure. The Japanese would
not be able to cross on foot. At any rate, not at high tide.
At low tide, the break turned out to be only four foot
deep . . .[35]

V THE BATTLE FOR THE ISLAND

The Causeway linking Johore with Singapore Island was
blown at 0815 hours on 31 January 1942. To some British
troops the *fait accompli* gave fresh courage. Told they were
to prepare for twelve months' siege, they felt the mere
imposing of delay was over, and the chance for a real fight
had arrived. Those troops who saw the Naval Base got a
different impression: half-eaten meals lay rotting on the
table, looters had scattered papers everywhere on their way
to the godowns, which were crammed with mountains of
tinned food of every description. There were 180,000 tons
of ammunition, from 15-inch shells to .303 armour-pierc-
ing bullets – there for the taking. Then the oil tanks, one
by one, were attacked by low-flying Japanese aircraft and
their smoke pillared the sky.

Percival's decision to withdraw into the Island implied,
as he knew, the abandonment of the last reason for the
Army's presence in Malaya: the protection of the Naval
Base. It was a choice between that and risking the loss of
all the forces still left in Johore, where the Japanese had
cut the communications of forward detachments and had
landed a fresh force at Endau on the east coast, in spite of
RAF and naval attacks to sink the convoy and its escorts.
Fourteen aircraft were lost, which put paid finally to the
possibility of RAF help in the battle for the Island. Save
for one fighter squadron, the whole of the RAF was withdrawn to the Netherlands East Indies on 30 January.

Reinforcements arrived: 44 Indian Brigade (7,000 men)

and 2/4 Australian MG Battalion, with nearly 2,000 other Australians. The Indians and most of the Australians were raw, and some of the Australians had only a few weeks' training. 53 Brigade of 18 Division had already arrived and took part in the fight for Johore. The rest of 18 Division, which had been en route to the Middle East from October 1941 and had been re-routed, arrived, together with a light tank squadron from India, the only tanks Percival had in the whole campaign. The tanks needed overhaul, and large quantities of the Division's equipment and weapons went down in the *Empress of Britain*, the casualty of the convoy.

The population of Singapore was 550,000, but it had been swollen with refugees and reinforcements to close on 1,000,000 by the end of January 1942.

Percival had no idea how the Japanese would come at him. He envisaged the possibility of sea-borne landings on either tip of the Island combined with crossings of the Johore Straits; also of an airborne landing of the kind which had been so successful in Crete a few months before. To meet these threats he had 85,000 men, including an administrative tail of 15,000.[36] In infantry terms, he had seventeen Indian battalions, thirteen British, six Australian and two Malay. This was a sizeable force for one small island, but numbers were deceptive. A large proportion were either battered as a result of the mainland defeats or newly landed, untrained, from the ships. There was enough food for three months and economies had ensured that the Island could manage with its own water supply once the Japanese controlled the pipe from Johore. Seventeen million gallons a day were available from reservoirs. There was ample ammunition, save for field guns, which had 1,500 rounds apiece. He divided the Island into four zones: one surrounding the city, held by two Malay battalions and the Straits Settlements Volunteer Force; a north-east area including Changi, Seletar and the Naval Base, defended by III Corps (11 Indian Division, now strengthened with 8 Brigade from the disbanded 9 Indian Division, and 18 Division); a western area defended by 8 Australian Division (22 and 27 Brigades, with 44 Indian Brigade on their southern flank). A reserve area, including the reservoirs, was held by the command reserve, 12 Indian Brigade. There were airfields at Sembawang and Seletar in the north, Kallang east of the City, and Tengah in the west.

One major problem that faced Percival was to assess the direction of the Japanese attack. There is a great discrepancy in the accounts of his opinions on this. In his Despatch, his appreciation of the topography of the Island and the approaches to it through the state of Johore led to an indication of a western crossing:

> The comparative narrowness of the western channel of the Johore Straits and the fact that the main west coast land communications led to that front made it appear probable that the main Japanese attack would develop from the west.[37]

But this did not exclude other possibilities:

> There was also the possibility of an approach via the Malacca Straits to the south-west sector of Singapore Island. Another possible avenue of approach which could not be neglected was from Kota Tinggi via the River Johore leading to Tekong Island and the Changi area.[38]

Later in the Despatch he affirms the preponderant role of the western approach in his thinking:

> I expected the attack to develop from the west, combined perhaps with a sea-borne attack via the Straits of Malacca. I thought it probable that another force would come down the Johore River to attack either Tekong Island or Changi.
>
> If a direct sea-borne attack was undertaken this would probably be directed against the south coast east of Singapore Town while the objectives of an air-borne attack would probably be the aerodromes.[39]

In other words, Percival considered almost every approach as having some feasibility, and felt he had to keep troops in reserve for every one of them. It was a question of how to parcel out what he had. His book, *The War in*

Malaya, published a year later (1949), confirms the statement in the Despatch:

> As regards the attack from the mainland, everything pointed to this developing from the west as the main communications down which the Japanese were advancing led to that part of the front. I thought it very likely that, combined with this, the Japanese would make a sea-borne attack via the Straits of Malacca, as they now clearly had plenty of their special landing-craft on that coast. There was also a possibility that the force which was advancing from Mersing would come down the Johore River to attack either Tekong Island or the Changi area.[40]

This seems to make it pretty clear, and Lieutenant-Colonel Ashmore adds a confirmatory detail. He attended a conference at which Heath and the divisional commanders were present;

> The G.O.C. (Percival) presided, and had in front of him a large scale map of the Island. He spoke at length regarding the location of the force on the Island. I well remember his short appreciation of the probable Japanese plan of attack. The G.O.C. did in fact point to a place on the map and turning to the Commander of the Australian Imperial Forces (Gordon Bennett), he said, 'I think this is the most probable place for the enemy attack.' No one was under any illusions that the attack would come from the South or seawards. Actually when the attack did come the enemy had selected the exact spot pointed out by the G.O.C.[41]

As if to clinch the matter, Colonel Harrison, the GSO 1 of 11 Indian Division, records that Brigadier Paris, whose duties included the preliminary defence plans for the Island, declared

> Personally I am convinced that the Jap will land on the west coast. That's been his strategy right through and he won't give it up now.

He added, for good measure, 'I give Singapore a fortnight'[42] (Smyth, *Percival and the Tragedy of Singapore,* p.218).

Unfortunately, the records do not all tell the same story. When Wavell visited Singapore on 20 January 1942, he

discussed the defence of the Island with Percival, and expressed the view that if the battle for Johore were lost,
the freshest troops should be placed on the north-west
side of the Island. That was where the Japanese would
attack. Percival, on the contrary, was convinced that the
north-*east* coast was the dangerous area, according to
Wavell's biographer.[43] Conveniently adding weight to
Percival's view, the Japanese Imperial Guards staged a
deception manoeuvre on the north-east side, by taking
Pulau Ubin, the island to the east of the naval base, in the
Straits, which Percival had reluctantly decided to leave
undefended save for a few patrols. On 8 February, Percival
wired to Wavell: 'Present indications show main enemy
strength north of Pulau Ubin'[44] (Connell, p.151).

The signal was sent in the early hours of the 8th, and at
noon on that day the Japanese artillery opened up at the
eastern end of the Johore Straits, and was answered by
British heavy guns firing from Changi. Was this not an
indication of preparations for a north-east landing?
Wavell's Despatch (written in August 1942, published in
1948) echoes these indications:

> I had instructed General Percival to place the fresh 18th
> Division on the front most likely to be attacked and the
> 8th Australian Division in the next most dangerous sector,
> keeping the Indian troops as far as possible in reserve for
> reinforcement and counter-attack. He estimated that the
> Japanese were most likely to attack in the north-east of the
> island and placed the 18th Division there. He put the
> Australians in the north-west.[45]

Given this total discrepancy in the Despatches and
memoirs, do Percival's actual troop dispositions show the
way his mind was working? Wavell suggested to him on
20 January 1942, that the newly arrived British 18 Division should be allocated to that part of the Island most
likely to be attacked. For Wavell, this meant the north-
west coast. 8 Australian Division – reduced to a strength
of under two brigades after the losses in Johore – should
be given the next most dangerous spot, with the tired and
battered Indian 9 and 11 Divisions to be re-formed as a

central reserve. Percival did in fact place 18 Division on the north-*east* side, because it was there that he expected the Japanese to attack. This is quite clearly put forward by General S. Woodburn Kirby in his *Singapore: The Chain of Disaster*[46] (p.221), who also provides an explanation of the inconsistency between Wavell's and Percival's accounts. 'In a letter to the author written after the war', General Kirby affirms, 'General Percival admitted that the statement in his book, *The War in Malaya*, to the effect that he expected the Japanese attack to be made in the north-west was incorrect and based on hindsight'[47] (*ibid.*, p.221, n.1).

So, in this point at any rate, Percival and his biographer are in error, and Wavell and his biographer are right (Ashmore's recollection is, after all, based only on a finger pointing to a map, and may well have been coloured by the actual landings). Yet it was not the erroneous predictions of the landings which proved fatal, but the manner of dealing with them. Percival conceived of two quite different counters: he could try and stop the Japanese coming ashore or destroy them on the beaches if they got a foothold. Alternatively, he could hold the seventy-mile long coast-line thinly and withdraw the bulk of his forces inland to build up a huge reserve with which to fight an encounter battle on the Island. There were drawbacks to both courses. The first really required enough men to cover the entire coast-line. The second required a bigger area of manoeuvre than was available in front of Singapore City.[48] In addition, even at this late stage, Percival did not consider that his role was to defend Singapore Island or the city as such. He was there to defend the Naval Base, which was on the north shore, while dumps and airfields were scattered round the Island. Once the Japanese managed to get a foothold, some of these points would certainly be captured. In addition, Percival was always sensitive about the effects of his decisions on the morale of both troops and civilians. If he adopted the second alternative, withdrawing the bulk of his troops to a favourable site for an encounter battle, that would entail allowing the

Japanese to land, and a successful enemy landing would be bad for morale. He therefore opted for the first course, meeting the Japanese on the beaches.[49]

It is easy, and futile, to criticize Percival from the vantage point of hindsight, and accuse him of having predicted the wrong landing place. Where he *is* blameworthy, though, is in having repeated on the Island the same parcelling-out tactics which had been used on the mainland. There, he had had no choice: his dispositions were dictated by the siting of the airfields, against his own better judgement. This factor no longer applied. Yet he repeated what was in effect a formula for defeat, and it produced the same result that it had at Jitra. Out of an overall numerical inferiority, the Japanese contrived to have a local superiority at the point of assault, at their crossing points, which guaranteed their success.

With the onset of the siege, the rift between civil and military authorities came to the surface. Some of the soldiers, but not all, said that this had already been evident in the lack of preparations for air-raids, and the inadequate provision of civil labour for defence works. The vicissitudes of Brigadier Ivan Simson, Chief Engineer, Malaya Command, are the best illustration of this. At a meeting of the War Council presided over by Duff Cooper on 30 December 1941, Simson was made Director-General of Civil Defence. Percival told him the next day that he would still retain his duties as Chief Engineer.

Duff Cooper gave Simson full authority to organize civil defence in Johore and on the Island. Twenty-four hours later Sir Shenton Thomas, the Governor, cancelled these instructions. He told Simson his area was the Island only, and that even there he was to act within existing regulations. If anyone challenged his decisions, the dispute was to be referred to the Malayan Legal Department.[50] It was the perfect peacetime civil service answer.

Conflict of this kind induced Duff Cooper, on his return to England (Wavell's appointment as Supreme Commander made Duff Cooper's post superfluous) to wire the Secretary of State for the Colonies (Lord Moyne) that a state of siege should be declared and a Military Governor appointed, who should be the Fortress Commander, Major-General Keith Simmons. The Colonial Secretary and the Secretary for Chinese Affairs should go. He sent a copy to Wavell, but Moyne wired Wavell on 13 January that he thought the Governor, Sir Shenton Thomas, was '*not* blameworthy'.[51] Wavell agreed, provided the Colonial Secretary were changed. He would insist on Simson's proposals being sanctioned under martial law.

But the same day (14 January) on his return from Washington, Churchill saw Duff Cooper's signal, and wired to Wavell his agreement with it. However, in the upshot, the unwillingness of Wavell, Pownall and Layton, to back a change of governor left Thomas where he was.[52] Meanwhile Wavell's attention had also had to focus on the Philippines. He had at first demurred at taking over this responsibility, since communications were tenuous and uncertain; but the Americans insisted and he set about supplying MacArthur from Port Darwin and bombing targets he named, from the Netherlands East Indies. His purpose in the Philippines was very similar to what he envisaged for Malaya: the retention of a foothold in north Mindanao which would enable reinforcements and supplies to be brought in. After which the enemy would slowly be driven back.

He had to notify Churchill that Singapore's defence prospects landward were bleak. Little defensive work had been done, on the theory that an enemy seaward could be stopped by fortress cannon, and an enemy landward could be held in Johore or further north. The fortress cannon had all-round traverse, but their flat trajectory made them useless for counter-battery work. They could not dominate siege guns set up by an enemy in Johore. This was news to Churchill. 'The possibility of Singapore having no landward defences,' he later wrote, 'no more entered my mind than that of a battleship being launched without a bottom'.[53]

The need for defences on the Island was pointed out to Percival on 26 December 1941. The route was roundabout but the message was clear. At Ipoh, on 24 December, Heath had told Simson, the Chief Engineer, that the troops of III Corps could not go on indefinitely digging, fighting, then retreating. He needed successive lines of defence made before he was forced back on Johore. Percival received Heath's message with the answer 'Defences are bad for the morale of troops and civilians'.[54] He had issued orders on 23 December to Simmons, Fortress Commander, to reconnoitre the north shores of the Island and he apparently failed to acquaint his Chief Engineer with this order.[55]

When Wavell visited him on 20 January 1942, and suggested that the freshest troops – 18 Division – should hold the north-west coast where it seemed most likely the Japanese would attack, Percival is said to have replied that the north-east coast was the danger area. This seems odd in view of Percival's estimate (in his Despatch and book) that he assumed the likeliest place was on the west coast.[56] Since Percival was the man on the spot, Wavell eventually left him the choice and signalled the Chiefs of Staff what he had done, while pointing out how grave the situation in Johore was. A characteristic signal arrived from Churchill on 21 January:

> I want to make it absolutely clear that I expect every inch of ground to be defended, every scrap of material or defences to be blown to pieces to prevent capture by the enemy, and no question of surrender to be entertained until after protracted fighting among the ruins of Singapore city.[57]

THE CROSSING

To keep their moves secret, the Japanese evacuated all inhabitants from a twelve-miles-wide strip round the Straits. Within a week they completed an artillery survey of the Island, revising their maps. Everything up to the heights of Bukit Timah could be seen from 25 Army HQ in the Sultan's palace at Johore Bahru, which was also an artillery observation post. So conspicuous was it the British never thought the Japanese would use it, and it was never shelled directly. The Japanese artillery set about destroying the oil tanks on the north shores of the Island. Yamashita had been told by a German general of the possibility of setting fire to a water surface by flooding it with oil and then igniting it. His staff thought the strong tide and current in the Johore Strait would make this impracticable but it was decided to reduce the British oil stocks by shelling, just in case. The Japanese 18 Division artillery was to be sited at the water's edge and the guns sighted low to guard against British naval vessels interfering with the crossing.[58]

An elaborate deception was planned. The Imperial Guards Division was to occupy Ubin Island on the north-east on 7 February. On the 8th, all the Imperial Guards' thirty-six field guns, with twelve infantry guns and four heavy guns shelled Changi. The guns were in rubber plantations and invisible from the air, so when the British began to fire back very little damage was done. The same night, 5 and 18 Divisions came out of the jungles in Johore and made for the water's edge on the north-west. Colonel Tsuji assumes that it was the deception manoeuvre of the Imperial Guards behind and on Ubin that led Percival to put III Corps on the north-east front, using two divisions.[59] In fact, Percival seems to have had it in mind to do this long before Nishimura made his move. But the Imperial Guards' move confirmed the likelihood of a major attack on the north-east. 'Present indications,' he wired to Wavell, as we have seen, early on 8 February, 'show main enemy strength north of Pulau Ubin.'[60]

Each Japanese division had fifty small motorboats and one hundred collapsible launches for the crossing, all carried on the shoulders of the troops from the jungle rendezvous to the water's edge, several miles distant. When the assembly was complete, at 11 pm, all the Japanese artillery opened fire, along the whole length of the Straits, 440 guns using 200 rounds per gun. The first wave of 4,000 men crossed from the north-west at midnight. Minutes later, blue flares went up on 5 Division front, signalling the success of the crossing. By dawn on 9 February, the entire infantry of both 5 and 18 Divisions, and part of the artillery, were ashore.

The crossing front was that of 8 Australian Division (22 and 27 Brigades) which also had under command 44 Indian Infantry Brigade in its southern sector, with three regiments of field artillery, three anti-tank batteries and a machine-gun battalion. This area contained the first Japanese objective, Tengah airfield. The broad Kranji River was the boundary between 27 Brigade and 22 Brigade, which had fought on the east coast of Johore and was reckoned to have the freshest troops on the Island. 44 Brigade was attacked on its front on the River Bireh but the attack was successfully repulsed. 22 Brigade bore the main brunt of the Japanese onslaught. The Japanese shelling destroyed beach lights, beach guns, machine-guns and all the lines to forward posts, which delayed requests for artillery support until it was too late. Bennett reinforced 22 Brigade with another Australian battalion and Percival moved his command reserve, the weak 12 Indian Brigade, to the western area, but to no effect. By the small hours of 9 February, all 22 Brigade's surviving forward troops had to make their way back to their battalion perimeters. From where the River Kranji bit deep into Singapore Island on the north, to the Jurong Road, a shorter defence line was established, on which 22 Brigade fell back. The left flank was covered by 44 Indian Brigade. There were large dumps of food and petrol between this Jurong Line and Bukit Timah village, which Percival had to ensure did not fall into Japanese hands. Having moved 6/15 Brigade, his new command reserve, into Bennett's area as further reinforcements, Percival returned to his HQ in Singapore City to plan the defence of a new perimeter, which should include the Kallang aerodrome east of the city, the Bukit Timah depots, and the MacRitchie and Pierce reservoirs vital for his water supply. Japanese infiltrations split the Australians up, and they came back in penny packets, under heavy Japanese shelling and bombing from the air. By nightfall the Japanese had taken Tengah airfield and Yamashita set up 25 Army HQ in a rubber plantation north of Tengah that same night.

The Navy and the RAF did what little they could to

stem the flow of Japanese reinforcements. Three patrol boats ran the gauntlet up the west side of the Johore Straits almost to the Causeway, sinking landing craft, and Hurricane patrols carried out raids during 9 February until Pulford withdrew them to Sumatra, the Island airfields having become untenable.

On the evening of 9 February, it was the turn of 29 Australian Brigade, holding the western sector between the River Kranji and the Causeway. At 7.30 pm the Japanese Imperial Guards came ashore, after losing many landing craft, and pushed the Australians back, leaving 11 Indian Division with its left flank exposed.

Wavell visited Singapore again on 10 February. It was a day of disasters. The house in which he, Percival and Gordon Bennett met was shelled. In the afternoon they learned that the Australians had been forced back from the Jurong Line and later still that the Japanese were nearing Bukit Timah village. Percival promptly ordered the petrol depot to be destroyed. It burnt for days.

From London Churchill wired the next day: '. . . defenders must greatly outnumber Japanese forces . . . and in a well contested battle they should destroy them. There now must be at this stage no thought of saving troops or sparing the population. The battle must be fought to the bitter end at all costs . . . Commanders and senior officers should die with their troops.'[61] Wavell dictated a message to Percival along similar lines, 'a wounding exhortation' as Percival's biographer calls it.[62]

Meanwhile, on Tengah airfield, Yamashita planned his move down the road to Bukit Timah. This 600-foot high position dominated the Island. From it he could control Singapore's water.

Another decision faced him on the morning of 10 February. He had originally planned to use the Imperial Guards as the second line of the Singapore assault from the west, but their commander, Lieutenant-General Nishimura, had protested so violently that he had agreed to let the division take part on an even footing with 5 and 18 Divisions. After the feint behind Ubin, the Imperial

Guards were to move west and come across just west of the causeway. Yamashita was breakfasting in his tent at Tengah when a staff officer burst in and told him an entire Guards regiment had been incinerated by burning oil as they crossed. Yamashita went pale. Then another officer arrived, and when he was questioned it turned out that the report was inaccurate, the result of a misunderstanding. Nishimura had accepted an engineer's report without troubling to verify it. Tsuji said to Yamashita: 'We can take Singapore with 5 and 18 Divisions,' and Yamashita turned to the Guards staff officer: 'Go to your divisional commander and tell him the Guards division can do what it pleases in this battle.'[63]

What Tsuji had said about the 5 and 18 Divisions was entirely in keeping with their generals' views. In spite of being wounded during the crossing, Mutaguchi of 18 Division wanted to push ahead at once even though the Japanese had as yet no heavy artillery on the Island. A night attack without artillery support was agreed. By dawn on the 11th, a message came from 18 Division to say that Bukit Timah had been taken, and 5 Division confirmed this. It was *Kigensetsu* (the anniversary day of the founding of the Japanese Empire) and Tsuji had hoped the campaign would be over by then. To hasten its end, a surrender appeal to Percival was dropped by a Japanese reconnaissance aircraft. Percival notified Wavell he had received it, but added he could send no answer, and it would in any case have been 'No.'

Yamashita still needed his heavy guns and tanks, but the Guards had not yet reopened the Causeway. 5 and 18 Division's onslaught was running out of impetus, which left the Guards as his prime cover at this stage. They were told to advance east of the reservoirs and hit the British on the left flank as they made the counter-attack on Bukit Timah which Yamashita expected. But the Guards would not be hurried. 5 Division attacked the reservoir sector on 12 February, and found it bitterly defended, but by this time tanks and heavy artillery were coming across the Straits. The Guards moved round north of the reservoirs

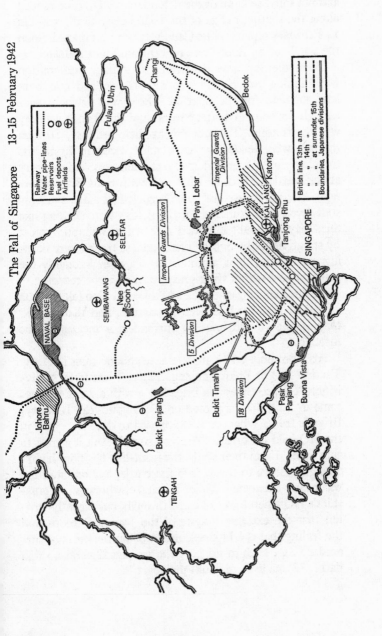

The Fall of Singapore   13-15 February 1942

Railway
Water pipe-lines
Reservoirs
Fuel depots
Airfields

British line, 13th a.m.
"   "   14th "
"   "   at surrender, 15th
Boundaries, Japanese divisions

Pulau Ubin

Changi

Bedok

Imperial Guards Division

Paya Lebar

KALLANG

Katong

Tanjong Rhu

SINGAPORE

SELETAR

Imperial Guards Division

Nee Soon

SEMBAWANG

NAVAL BASE

5 Division

Johore Bahru

Bukit Panjang

Bukit Timah

18 Division

Pasir Panjang

Buona Vista

TENGAH

and out into the flank of the defenders. 18 Division moved along the southern edge of the Island close to the sea. On 14 February repairs to the Causeway were completed. Soon the whole of 25 Army was concentrated on the Island.

Then the Japanese discovered that their ammunition was running out. Barely 100 rounds per field gun were left, and less for the heavies. There was nowhere near enough for counter-battery work, and the British artillery was devastating. To supplement their artillery, 16-inch mortars were loaded on carts and placed in front line trenches, firing a round every ten minutes. An infantry attack was launched, and halted by a furious British barrage. At 4 pm it eased off. The barrage had made 25 Army staff revise their thinking: if the British were shelling like this, they no doubt intended a fight for Singapore street by street, house by house. The Japanese troops were nearing exhaustion, their ammunition likewise. Suddenly the prize, almost within their grasp, seemed to be receding.

At this moment, when the staff of 5 Division felt that the appeal to Percival had been premature, and that instead *they* might be the ones to surrender, a message came through.

At 2 pm on 15 February, the telephone rang in Army Tactical HQ at Bukit Panjang. The call was from 5 Division. 'A peace envoy – a brigadier – with a white flag has come in from the main road on the Sugiura [21 Infantry] Brigade front. What are we supposed to do?' Everyone in the HQ held his breath. 'Are you sure?' 'Isn't it a trick to gain time?' From their angle, the front-line positions hadn't a single reserve to throw into the battle, and ammunition was nearly exhausted. Major Kunitake, who was in Yamashita's HQ when that call came through, has recently written that the extreme fatigue of the Japanese troops and the feeling that the Japanese might be on the brink of surrender ('. . . kochira no hō ga te wo agetai kurai no toki datta . . .') made them doubt their ears.[64]

VI SURRENDER

Looking back, it is hard not to think of the final surrender as inevitable. It did not seem so at the time. Once the troops had withdrawn from the mainland, there was real determination to hold the Island. 'My impression at this time,' wrote Colonel Ashmore, 'was that everyone was full of determination to hold the Island. There was no lack of morale on the 1st February when the Causeway was blown and the Island settled down to a siege.' Even ten days later, the mood still held: 'Until the 11th February I am sure there was no idea that the Fortress would not hold out. It was unpleasant, the shelling and the bombing had increased a great deal but everyone felt we were giving as good as we got in so far as shelling was concerned.'[65]

On the very eve of the surrender, Shenton-Thomas noted in his diary that heavy shelling had been going on all afternoon, but Percival had spoken to him and told him the position was no worse than the previous day, 'and therefore we would carry on'.[66] In between that encounter with the Governor and the following morning, Percival was compelled to change his mind.

Firstly, his own will to resist was not supported by his subordinate commanders. Heath in particular was positively insolent. It was at Heath's suggestion that a conference of corps and divisional commanders was called at Fort Canning on Friday 13 February. Percival kept a note of this conference, and the two which followed, and which determined the fate of the garrison. Heath opened the conference by saying the Japanese had driven them down the Peninsula for 500 miles and he did not see how they could be stopped, when they were within three miles of the centre of Singapore City, which was under close range artillery fire and heavy air attack. The troops were exhausted and dispirited, and he did not see any use in continuing the struggle. Gordon Bennett agreed entirely with Heath. Percival answered that to stop fighting now would be contrary to the orders he had received from Wavell, Commander-in-Chief of the South-West Pacific Area. He hoped to organize a counter-attack shortly, he added, to which Heath replied, 'You have already tried one counter-attack and it was a complete failure. You have no fresh troops available for a counter-attack. I do not think a counter-attack has the least chance of success.'[67]

All commanders present agreed with this view, and Heath urged again that the only possible course was immediate surrender. Percival answered:

> There are other things to consider. I have my honour to consider and there is also the question of what posterity will think of us if we surrender this large Army and valuable fortress.

Heath's retort was quick and cruel:

> You need not bother about your honour. You lost that a long time ago up in the North.[68]

The Conference broke up after Percival had told all his commanders that he could not accept the proposal to surrender and they would go on fighting for as long as they could.

He repeated that statement the following morning at a conference at the Singapore Club with Shenton-Thomas and Jones's successor as Colonial Secretary, Hugh Fraser. Percival had just left a discussion on the water situation with Simson, the Chairman of the Municipal Commissioners and the Municipal Water Engineer. Shenton-Thomas said he had been informed of the serious water situation, and could not face the prospect of Singapore with its large Asiatic population being left without water. It would lead to riots of the worst kind and possibly to attacks on the European population. There were many bodies putrefying in the streets, and this could lead to disease and pestilence. He advocated immediate surrender.

Percival replied, as he had to his commanders, that he intended going on fighting as long as he could; but he was prepared to discuss the issue of surrender if this should be necessary. A day later, at 9.30 in the morning of 15 February – Sunday – Percival held his last conference, at Fort Canning.

He had already received administrative and water reports. He asked the formation commanders for news from their fronts. There had been no change since the previous day, apart from infiltration on 18 Division's front. Percival then said the administrative situation was less satisfactory than the military one. Two pumping stations were still pumping water, but there was a very heavy wastage from broken mains and pipes. The supply in the Fort Canning Reservoir, in a single day, had gone down from 12,000,000 gallons to 2,000,000. Simson 'gave the whole thing another 24 hours'.[69] The food reserves under the Army's control were reduced to two days. The large reserves at the Bukit Timah and race-course depots were now in Japanese hands. There were adequate reserves of small arms ammunition (4 million rounds in the Fort Canning magazine) but all the 25-pounder ammunition had been issued and there were only 200 boxes of Bofors ammunition left. The only petrol which remained was now in vehicle tanks.

After this survey, he went round the commanders asking for their views. Heath was as brusque as he had been on the 13th:

'In my opinion there is only one possible course to adopt and that is to do what you ought to have done two days ago, namely to surrender immediately.'[70] He stressed the seriousness of a situation in which Indian troops would be without water, and pointed out that the Bofors shortage meant Japanese aircraft could come and go as they liked. There was no ground for thinking they could resist another determined Japanese attack. To sacrifice countless lives by a failure to appreciate the true situation would be an act of extreme folly. Percival should surrender immediately. On behalf of the Australians, Gordon Bennett concurred.

'The Commander-in-Chief's orders are,' Percival declared, 'that we should continue the struggle at all costs and without consideration to what may happen to the civil population. It is our duty to continue fighting as long as we can.' Testily, Heath broke in: 'How can **General** Wavell command this battle from Java?'[71]

At this point, there is a curious conflict of evidence. Percival notes that he himself then proposed a counter-attack to recapture the food depots at Bukit Timah and asked if it were not possible to do this. Gordon Bennett asked him how he thought he would maintain his troops if he got them there? 'It is quite impracticable.'[72] Heath and the other commanders agreed that it was out of the question to counter-attack. Major Cyril Wild, who attended the conference as GSO (III) of III Corps and later acted as Percival's interpreter with the Japanese, took notes also, and he recalls Gordon Bennett proposing a counter-attack when the actual details of the surrender were being discussed:

> Some minutes later, when details of the surrender were being discussed, Major General Gordon Bennett, GOC 8th Aust Div, remarked 'How about a combined counter-attack to recapture Bukit Timah?' This remark came so late, and was by then so irrelevant, that I formed the impression at the time that it was made not as a serious contribution to the discussion but as something to quote afterwards. It was received in silence and the discussion proceeded.*[73]

The upshot was the same. Percival said that in view of the critical water situation and the unsatisfactory administrative situation generally, he reluctantly accepted the advice of the senior officers present to capitulate.

A similar discrepancy in the records affects the timing of the cease-fire. A deputation to arrange for the surrender parley, consisting of Brigadier Newbigging, the Deputy Adjutant-General, Fraser, the Colonial Secretary, and Major Wild, as interpreter, was to leave at once for the Japanese lines. Heath asked that ample time be given for the parleys and for orders to be communicated to the

---

* And cf. Percival's comment on Gordon Bennett, in MS notes on certain senior commanders among the Percival Papers: 'At the Command Conferences on the 13th and 15th January Gordon Bennett was emphatic that his troops were exhausted and quite incapable of a counter-attack effort. On both occasions he supported Gen. Heath in the recommendation that there should be an immediate surrender.'

forward troops. The earliest time for a safe cease-fire, in his view, was 2000 hours (GMT). It was objected that it would be dark by then, which would cause difficulties. Percival finally decided to request a cessation of hostilities from 16.30 hrs* but made it clear that fighting should continue until definite orders for a formal cease-fire were issued.

Wild says that Percival selected 1600 hours as the cease-fire time, in spite of Heath's objections.[74] III Indian Corps acted on this and instructed 18 Division and 11 Indian Division to cease fire at that time. At 1700 hrs a staff officer came from Fort Canning to Heath to say that Percival had *not* ordered a cease-fire and Heath promptly countermanded his instructions. Wild had himself asked Brigadier Newbigging to send III Corps precise instructions about the time of the cease-fire. Newbigging said such orders had already been sent. When Wild returned to the Cathay Building, where III Corps HQ was situated, he found Heath and his staff under the impression that the first time, 1600 hours, was still valid, no change having been notified. Wild promised to see definite orders were sent to III Corps before he left for Bukit Timah and the Japanese with General Percival.

Let Wild take up the story:

> I got back to Fort Canning shortly after 1600 hrs. Gen. Percival was seated at his desk and Brig. Torrance, the Brigadier General Staff and Brig. Newbigging were standing beside it. They had been awaiting my return. I at once told Brig. Newbigging, in the hearing of the others, that III Corps were still without definite orders regarding the time of cease-fire and I asked that such orders should be sent to them. I received no reply whatever.

> No one else was speaking, and it appeared to me that Brig. Newbigging had chosen to ignore my question. As a last resort I appealed directly to Gen. Percival, who had got up and was standing behind his desk with his head bent forward. I said 'If I may express an opinion myself, it is that we should not cease fighting until after you have seen the Japanese Commander at Bukit Timah.'

---

* That he was unsure of the *exact* time is shown by the figure 1600 hrs, followed by a query, in his notes on the conference.

I believe I added, and I know I thought, that even if the
Japanese were annoyed when we met them at our not having ceased fire, this would be nothing in comparison with
the risk of total disaster which we ran if our men disarmed
themselves before the terms of the truce or the capitulation
were decided. Again my remarks were received in total
silence.

This was only broken when Gen. Percival (I think it was)
said 'We ought to go', and he and the two Brigadiers walked
out of the room and down to the two cars which were awaiting us. I had no choice but to follow them.[75]

Wild's anger and mortification are betrayed in the paragraph which follows:

Astonishing though this may sound, it was not altogether so
to me, as I had become inured during the past week to
seeing Gen. Percival's painful inability to give a decision,
and on three occasions to make any reply whatever, when
points of operational importance were referred to him,
particularly by my Corps Commander [Heath].

The delegation went to the Ford Factory, down the
Bukit Timah Road. Percival was never given a copy of the
surrender terms, he says in his book, and the record of the
brief exchange between him and Yamashita is given in the
first volume of the Japanese Official History, from the
records of Lieutenant-Colonel Sugita, an English-speaking
staff officer from 25 Army HQ. When Yamashita took his
seat opposite Percival, he asked:

Have you seen our terms, which were handed over to the
peace envoy?
Percival: Yes.
Yamashita: Further details are given in an annexed sheet.
                (This was placed within Percival's reach.)
                I want everything carried out in accordance
                with this. (Percival briefly glanced through
                the contents of the annexe. A pause).
Percival: There are disturbances in Singapore City. As
                there are non-combatants in the city, I should
                like to keep 1,000 men under arms.
Yamashita: The Japanese army will be stationed there,

	and will maintain order. So you need have no worry on that score.
Percival:	The British army is familiar with the situation in Singapore. I should like to keep 1,000 armed men.
Yamashita:	The Japanese Army will look after that, you need no longer concern yourself with it.
Percival:	Looting is taking place inside the city. And there are non-combatants.
Yamashita:	Non-combatants will be protected by the spirit of *Bushido*. So everything will be all right.
Percival:	If there is a vacuum, there will be chaos in the city, and looting. Outbreaks of looting and rioting are undesirable, whether from the British or the Japanese point of view. For the purpose of maintaining order, it is desirable that 1,000 men should be permitted to retain their arms.
Yamashita:	As the Japanese Army is continuing its assault on the city, an attack is likely to go forward tonight.
Percival:	I should like to ask you to postpone any night attack.
Yamashita:	The attack will go forward, if we cannot come to an agreement.
Percival:	I would like you to postpone it.

Yamashita then repeated what he had said.

| Percival: | Because of the rioting in Singapore, I would like 1,000 men left with their arms. |

Yamashita then turned to a staff officer: What time is the night attack scheduled for?

Staff Officer (Colonel Ikeya): Eight o'clock.

| Percival: | If there is a night attack, you put me in a difficult situation.[76] |

It seems from later evidence that by this time in the parley Yamashita was sure Percival was playing for time. He felt the British had a trick or two up their sleeve, and were perhaps entering into negotiations only to delay the Japanese final assault. Journalists' accounts of the parley gave it a certain notoriety at the time, because Yamashita was depicted as having banged the table with his fist at this point and generally to have bullied Percival. According to the staff officer who spoke English on the Japanese side (Colonel Sugita), Percival had come with the intention of surrendering (as is indeed clear from Percival's notes on his own Conference) but wished to scrutinize the Japanese terms carefully and to make his own views plain before he put his signature to any document. Yamashita, on the other hand, considered all details as trivial and wanted to postpone discussion of them, once the main point of surrender was conceded. His attitude was: first decide whether you are going to surrender unconditionally or not. (Though in the surrender terms first shown to the British, Sugita records, the phrase 'unconditional surrender' did not occur).[77] Yamashita seems to have reasoned that if he sanctioned the stationing of armed British troops in Singapore, as requested by Percival to keep order, that sanction would indicate that an unconditional surrender had not taken place. This explains the banging on the table and the brusque exchange which terminated the parley:

Yamashita :	The time for the night attack is drawing near. Is the British Army going to surrender or not? Answer YES OR NO. (*He used the English words*).
Percival :	Yes. But I would like the retention of 1,000* armed men sanctioned.
Yamashita :	Very well.[78]

In order to avoid any risk of misunderstanding by the British, Yamashita forbade Japanese troop movements on the night of the 15th, but he ordered his air force units to keep a look-out for any attempts by the British to escape by sea.

It will be noted that Sugita's record contains no reference to the time of the cease-fire, which had been the subject of heated discussion between Percival and Heath. Major Wild, who was, as he says himself, obsessed by the

* In his Despatch (Para. 581 (e)), Percival records this figure as '100 men' but this is clearly a misprint. The Official History (p.414) correctly gives '1,000 men'.

thought of ensuring that the troops of 11 Indian Division and 18 Division were not over-run by a treacherous Japanese attack as a result of having disarmed themselves prematurely, took note of what Yamashita said about the proposed night attack.

When Yamashita asked Percival at what time he would cease hostilities, Percival put forward the suggestion of 2200 hours (2330 hours Tokyo time). Yamashita made the counter-proposal of 2030 hours. This was not a capricious haggling over a trivial detail. Percival gave way when Yamashita said that if he insisted on 2200 hours he (Percival) and Sir Shenton-Thomas would have to come out as hostages. Percival then consented to the time of 2030 hours, much to Yamashita's relief. 'I can now tell you frankly,' he said, 'that my assault on Singapore was timed to begin at midnight (Tokyo time) tonight. If you had declined to cease fighting until 2330 hours (Tokyo time) I should only have had thirty minutes in which to stop the advance and might not have been able to halt it everywhere. As it is, I shall have time to order my forces to stand fast'.[79]

The two generals rose, and shook hands. Yamashita looked at the thin body and pale face of the defeated British general. He could see Percival was under great strain, and as they were shaking hands he wanted to say one last word of sympathy to him, but could not find the appropriate English phrase; and the kind of thing he wished to say was not for the ears of an interpreter. So he said nothing.[80]

After Percival and Brigadier Torrance had returned to Singapore, Wild stayed behind at Bukit Timah for a while with Brigadier Newbigging. He took the opportunity to cast a quick glance at a Japanese staff-officer's chinagraphed map of the operations on Singapore Island. From the blue-pencil marks he could see that the spear-head of the attack was to have thrust east of the Bukit Timah Road, across the Golf Course and Mount Pleasant. The sector was covered by 18 Division on a total front of 17,000 yards and many of the troops were badly shaken. The Japanese had medium tanks and 6-inch guns. Wild later wrote:

In all these circumstances few acquainted with the situation can doubt that had the attack gone in that night it would have broken clean through to the sea, splitting the garrison in two. The half-million citizens of Singapore would then have shared the fate of those of Nanking and Hangchow. As it was, Yamashita never allowed these three Divisions to enter the city after the capitulation.'[81]

The following morning, Major-General Key, with his GSO 1, Colonel Harrison, visited the headquarters of the Japanese Imperial Guards Division to obtain instructions on the surrender of his troops of 11 Indian Division. He was received very courteously by Lieutenant-General Nishimura's Chief of Staff. Their conversation was conducted in French. After they had gone through the formal details, the Chief of Staff decided to impress Key. He called for a map of the Pacific and spread it out on the table. 'We have captured Malaya and Singapore,' he said, indicating each place on the map. 'We will shortly have conquered Burma, Sumatra, Java and the Philippines. We do not want India. We do not want Australia. It is time for your Empire to compromise. What else can you do?'

'What will we do?' answered Key. He cupped his hand round Sumatra, Java, then the Philippines on the map, swept it northwards and covered Japan. 'We will drive you back. We will occupy your country. That is what we will do.'[82]

IX

What Went Wrong?

More than thirty years have passed since the surrender of
Singapore, and recriminations and accusations have never
really ceased. The British troops have been accused of
being unprepared and unable to adapt to circumstances.
The Australians have been described as courageous in battle but squalid in defeat. The Indians have been called
under-trained and their officers resentful over race discrimination in the clubs of Malaya.

The Japanese were both thoroughly trained and quick
to improvise, fiercely brave and bitterly cruel. They knew
British strategic plans in general and some tactical dispositions in detail. They were numerically inferior, but
produced local superiority where it counted. Their crush-
ing mastery of the air was the direct result of the fall of
France in 1940, which left French Indo-China vulnerable
to them. As a result, North Malaya came within range of
land-based aircraft, and the British Eastern Fleet within
range of land-based torpedo-bombers.

The British Command was dogged by false priorities.
The Army was there to defend the Naval Base, but that
defence was based on a chain of aerodromes. So the Army
was parcelled out into penny packets with brigades covering groups of airfields and was not used as a mass of manoeuvre to defeat the Japanese Army. And in order to con-
serve itself for the last-ditch defence of Singapore Island,
there was imposed upon it the most demoralising policy
of planned withdrawals, destroying bridges as it went. How
could it be possible both to stand and fight and at the same
time work on the principle of fighting another day? So they
became a prey to Japanese infiltration, in constant fear
of their communications and lines of retreat being cut.
The British failed to use the Malays because many officers
believed they were not a martial race. They failed to use

the Chinese because they were afraid of arming Chinese Communists. Their commanders, from the very top down to brigade level, were frequently changed in the course of the brief campaign. The Japanese higher command remained intact. Percival, the British Army commander, on whom fell the onerous burden of an impossible battle and a humiliating capitulation, was a skilful, knowledgeable and compassionate soldier, and a man of outstanding physical courage. But the circumstances called for a leadership that went beyond bravery and competence.

There was, too, a clear difference as far as the British were concerned, between fighting for their country's very life – the situation after Dunkirk – and fighting for their country's property – the situation in the Far East after December 1941.

In contrast, Japan saw herself as fighting for her very existence, for without the oil of the Indies her factories would grind to a halt and she would die. She also saw herself as the vanguard of the rest of Asia against the old colonial usurper. On both counts, the morale of her troops was high, and their purpose clear.

Even so, the British need never have been defeated. What Churchill rightly termed 'the worst disaster and largest capitulation in British history' need never have happened. Singapore and Malaya could have been saved, by better pre-war planning, by a timely truce to internecine warfare between the services, by adequate wartime reinforcements in planes and tanks, by more decisive leadership on the spot and a true historical perspective at the centre of power, in London, in the two decades before.

YAMASHITA

It is possible to summarize very briefly the reasons why Britain lost Malaya. If we omit the rather tendentious hints of Wavell, the Supreme Commander, that the troops were lazy and cowardly, these reasons can be put as follows. They underestimated their enemy. Their intelligence was poor. Their dispositions were wrong. Their training was inferior. They had no tanks. They did not have enough aircraft.

It is interesting to see what the enemy commander thought. When he was posted to Manchuria later in the war, Yamashita jotted down a few notes on the Malayan operations.[1] Firstly, he had been mistaken about the actual moment when the British would be compelled to surrender. Before the campaign began, he thought they would do so once he reached the Johore Causeway. Once he had to fight his way on to the Island, he then thought that they would surrender when he had taken Bukit Timah. In practice, it was necessary to exert pressure on the perimeter of Singapore City itself before Percival capitulated.

He thought he had under-estimated the British forces by a figure of 20,000 to 30,000. (This makes an interesting contrast with the constant *over*-estimate of Japanese numbers by the British, not merely during the campaign but in post-war accounts. Both Percival and Compton Mackenzie speak of five Japanese divisions. But the Japanese took Malaya and Singapore with three divisions, no more).[2]

Once on the Island, he saw that he had wrongly estimated what Percival would do. In spite of the Imperial Guards deception manoeuvre on Pulau Ubin, Yamashita expected the main British force to be distributed west of the causeway. In fact, it lay on the east. He had, too, expected the main resistance to be made on the line between the Jurong and Kranji rivers, which represented a sensible shortening of the front to defend. In fact, it was at the water's edge.

In this lay the success of his crossing. The deception manoeuvre must have been effective, he thought. He hit the enemy's weak points. Heavy artillery fire made them withdraw from the water's edge. And plenty of crossing material was available.

Once the Japanese were established on the Island, Yamashita attributed the British surrender to the fact that shelling and bombing had reached the city streets, 18 Division was on the heights by the south shore and 5 Division in control of the water sources, and there was a shortage of food and water. He also adds that the Australian and Indian troops were unreliable. On the other hand, Percival had incomprehensibly delayed the switch of his offensive power from the east side of the Island to the west. He could have done this before the Japanese occupied high ground, ie between 10 and 13 February. The Japanese were running short of ammunition and could not have prevented the switch.[3]

Yamashita's puzzlement at the British failure to transfer forces across the Island in these vital days was shared by Colonel Ashmore in his report on the campaign, writtten in 1942:

> Knowing the Japanese mentally to some small extent I, among others, felt the very vital need to inflict a reverse however small on this party which had landed. Could they have been driven back by sheer weight of numbers, we had the men, they would in all probability have delayed any further assault for some days or even weeks. This time would have been of the utmost value to our forces. Why no full scale counter-attack ever took place I cannot say. A check to the enemy at this stage might well have changed the whole course of events. It will be said that it was unwise to withdraw British troops from the Eastern area – I agree, but it was surely a gamble worth taking at such a time. The result could certainly have been no worse than the ultimate one.[4]

PERCIVAL

Percival changed his views on the reasons for the Japanese victory, with the passage of time. At the height of the battle for the Island he wired home an appreciation: Japanese success was due primarily to superior training, previous war experience, discipline and morale. The Japanese had a strong offensive spirit. They were tough. He did *not* think air superiority and the fact that they used tanks were determining factors.

In correspondence with Professor J. R. M. Butler, author of the series *Grand Strategy* (II) in the official histories, Percival claimed that this appreciation of 13

February 1942 'was intended to give the authorities at home a line as to what they should expect in other theatres of operations in the Far East, especially Burma. It was NOT a considered opinion of the reasons for the Japanese success. It is now my considered opinion, after a study of all the available evidence, that the Japanese air and sea superiority, and the fact that they had tanks while we had none, were decisive factors.'[5]

This view is reflected in his despatch:

> The Japanese, in commenting on the Malayan campaign, have attributed their success to their pre-war operations, to the fact that this campaign was the centre of interest throughout their whole Army, to the fact that their commanders, senior staff officers and troops were specially selected, and to the fact that their land operations were closely supported by their Navy and by their Army and Navy Air Forces.
>
> Other important factors in their success were undoubtedly:-
> (a) The great superiority, both as regards the quantity and quality of their machines, of the Japanese Air Force;
> (b) The freedom of manoeuvre conferred on the Japanese Army, and conversely the crippling effect of the very present threat to our own communications and bases, resulting from the Japanese strategical naval supremacy off the east coast of Malaya and, to a lesser degree, from their tactical supremacy off the west coast also;
> (c) The inclusion in the Japanese Army of a strong modern armoured component, while we on our side had to rely on armoured cars and Bren gun carriers.[6]

In the following year, 1949, he published his book *The War In Malaya*, in which a number of explanations for British weakness in face of the enemy are adduced; though it should be added that in this book – as throughout the campaign – Percival vastly over-estimated the number of Japanese facing him. He claims they employed a minimum of 150,000 men, and that by the end of the campaign there were 'over 100,000 Japanese troops on Singapore Island

and in South Malaya'.[7] (In fact, as we have seen, there were at no time more than three divisions in the campaign.) These factors were:

(a) British air forces had less than a quarter of the planes available to the Japanese. The latter had complete superiority at sea after *Prince of Wales* and *Repulse* were sunk.

(b) British failure to modify pre-war strategy, which was based on a British fleet being available for the Far East whenever required. After 1939, this condition was impossible of fulfilment.

(c) Army dispositions were dictated by the pattern of airfields throughout Malaya – widely dispersed, and doubly vulnerable when the air forces to man the airfields did not arrive.

(d) His strategy was a fighting withdrawal, with the purpose of a final concentration in South Malaya, where he hoped the main battle would be fought.

Lack of strength in the navy and air forces defeated this strategy. The army had to bear the whole brunt of the retreat, threatened in its rear all the time by the enemy's sea-borne thrusts, and no match for an enemy having air superiority. In addition, Japanese tanks forced them to give up obstacle after obstacle and more ground than they would have done.

(e) Considerations of morale were, of course, important too. The British soldier could not live off the country as the Japanese did, because he was not ruthless with the local inhabitants and because pre-war stress on troops' welfare had pampered the soldier.

(f) The psychological effect on untried troops of being flung into a losing battle was catastrophic. Other psychological damage was caused by the RAF's evacuation of aerodromes without adequate denials to the enemy by demolitions: 'We were therefore faced with the problem, not of holding them for the use of our own air force, but of holding them to deny their use to the enemy air force.'[8]

(g) Among the junior leaders, experienced officers were few. In the Indian Army, replacement officers had inadequate knowledge of the troops and their language. In the Australian, the nucleus of officers trained in the art of war was very small. This weakness in leadership puts emphasis on *esprit de corps* and regimental tradition. There had been a pre-war tendency to undervalue the latter, but Percival's experience was that units with a strong regimental tradition 'gave of their best in circumstances which might well have dismayed even the bravest.'[9]

GORDON BENNETT

Gordon Bennett gave his account of the campaign in *Why Singapore Fell* (Sydney 1944). But he had already given to the Australian Government an analysis of where the faults lay, and the substance of this was communicated to the War Office in London early in April 1942.[10]

Gordon Bennett's first purpose was to lay the blame on the Indian Army. The prime cause of the failure of the campaign, he said, lay in the low morale of the Indian troops. The reason for this was that Eastern races were less able to withstand the strain of modern war, and their officers had not attempted to counter this by a deliberate building up of morale. Troops were often quartered in rubber plantations, never saw sunlight, were homesick and lacked entertainment.

Another cause was the lack of offensive spirit and the 'retreat complex' with which many commanders and senior officers were imbued. 'A spirit of resignation prevailed.'[11] Our own offensives were checked by the slightest enemy opposition and many withdrawals took place without enemy pressure. In short, there was a lack of spirit among the junior officers. Some staff work was poor, and he singled Ordnance and III Indian Corps out in this respect. Many officers were simply inefficient. Those who were not were hampered by the British administrative system. Operations reflected this, there was lack of system in obtaining and disseminating information.

The quality and quantity of air support was inadequate. Far too many aircraft were lost on aerodromes. Adequate air support could have protected the navy and thus Japanese coastal landings could have been obstructed. In addition, the Japanese ability to make a perfect reconnaissance of our defence positions on Singapore Island immediately before their assault would have been prevented.

Wishful thinking that the Japanese would never attack and an under-estimation of the enemy also hit morale when the attack came.

18 British Division was of poor quality.

Tactically, Gordon Bennett criticized the British retention of 1918 textbook methods. In 1918, the British method of attack was to pound a position heavily with artillery until the opposition was reduced, then to advance under an artillery barrage. In his view, this method had been obsolete since 1939 but a large conservative element among British officers adhered to it. Likewise, their beach-defence systems consisted of a long thin line of posts along a beach, without depth. The modern perimeter system of defence on a shorter flank was preferable.

He contrasted the British training, 'too much emphasis on barrack square',[12] with the Japanese insistence on jungle patrols; and unsuitable British equipment with the Japanese light automatics and light mortars, and the fact that they had no artillery except what was captured. (This latter, incidentally, was untrue.) The British were too mechanically minded and too reliant on excessive amounts of transport. The Japanese infantry were suitably clothed, travelled light, and used bicycles. 18 British Division, on the other hand, went into battle with full equipment, with the result that the troops were worn out in a few hours.

On the general strategy of the campaign, Bennett agreed that to defend Singapore Island from distant positions was sound. He thought Matador unsound, however, because there were insufficient troops to carry it out.

The strategy implied a fighting withdrawal, but Bennett says this must have meant that the retreat which began on 7 December would end on the Island. This in turn meant that defences should have been prepared there at once, whereas when troops arrived on the Island on 30 January no defences were ready except those which had been prepared before the war.

Bennett's report gave a full account of the defence of the Island and concluded with a summary of the attitude of the civil population. Many Chinese guerrillas were passed behind the enemy lines during the mainland operations, and he said it had been reported that as many as a thousand were still fighting in northern Malaya when operations ceased, though transmitter sets had not been left behind the enemy lines. Not one case of fifth-column activities was reported in Australian-held areas, though the natives showed 'disinterestedness'[13] [*sic*] in the war. On the other hand, a Malay regiment in contact with the Australians fought as well as Indian troops, and the Singapore Chinese showed great stoicism under bombing.

BROOKE-POPHAM

This report was passed on for comment to Brooke-Popham, who agreed with some of its criticisms. On the morale of Indian Army units:

> The fighting qualities of the Indian Regiments [he wrote] certainly varied; one of the main reasons why some did not do so well as had been expected was the fact that they had a very small number of experienced British officers. There would be two or three at the top with perhaps 15 years' service and then a long gap till one came to officers who had only joined up since September 1939. Then there was but a small leaven of men in the ranks with previous war experience. The Regiments in Kedah and Kelantan had to buy their own experience under these conditions and had to take the first shock against an enemy who adopted two or three novel forms of tactics.[14]

He added that Key's 8 Indian Brigade had done well at Kota Bharu, and Bennett probably had not seen the Indian regiments of III Corps until they had retreated for 200 miles or more. He also doubted the assertion about the inability of Eastern races to withstand the strains of modern war. Libya and Abyssinia did not bear this out. Nor would he admit that a lack of offensive spirit was characteristic of the troops in Malaya as a whole. Since the object was to avoid war with Japan, the enemy was bound to have the initiative at the start.

The 'retreat complex' was not an attitude of mind but the practical result of certain factors. The weakness of total strength meant that there were limits to reinforcements available for Kedah, because Johore and Singapore could not be reduced below a definite point. Lack of good communications prevented the troops in Kelantan being reinforced at all. Since we could not afford the *loss* of these troops, then retreat became necessary:

> This was a disheartening experience at the start, especially for the Indian troops; further the memories of France, May-June 1940 and of Greece may have had some influence in making them think that a retreat was the natural result of any campaign. To this extent the criticism of a retreat complex is justified . . .[15]

On the subject of transmitter sets and stay-behind parties, his judgement conflicts with the opinions expressed in Percival's letter to Spencer Chapman.[16] He knew it was planned to leave sets behind, but did not know if the sets ever became available:

> I feel the whole subject of left behind parties should have been organised earlier and more thoroughly. It was part of the duties of the O.M. section of the Ministry of Economic Warfare under Mr Killery; the inadequacy of the arrangements is in no way due to lack of keenness on the part of him or his staff, but partly to inexperience of those responsible and partly to a peculiar mistrust of the O.M. activities which was manifest in many places including Malaya Command and the Malaya civil administration.* My own G.H.Q. should have pushed the matter more forcefully.[17]

Brooke-Popham took upon himself some of the blame for lack of defences on the north shore of the Island. He had issued orders for a position to be prepared in northern

* In his Despatch,[21] Percival was more outspoken on these matters: In the summer of 1941 a Branch of the Ministry of Economic Warfare was started in Singapore. It suffered from an excess of secrecy and from a lack of knowledge on the part of the gentlemen responsible as to how to set about the work. Thus valuable time was lost.

Johore before he handed over command (ie by the end of
December 1941). At that time it was still hoped to hold
Kuala Lumpur. He agreed that more should have been
done during January on Singapore Island and in fact more
should have been done before war broke out:

> It was a problem of morale and man hours. I was always
> on my guard against the fortress complex and against too
> much reliance on water obstacles, barbed wire and pill-boxes
> and insisted on the principle that troops must make their
> own field works and obstacles, wherever practicable. General
> Percival rightly pointed out to me that all barbed wire in
> Malaya had to be replaced about every six months and that
> we might reach a stage when most of the Army would be
> employed on renewing wire.[18]

Gordon Bennett had slipped in a note criticizing the Governor, saying that he was adversely criticized in some
quarters 'justifiably or not'.[19] Brooke-Popham took up this
point, and what he says bears comparison with Shenton-
Thomas's own justification of his stewardship. He had
found Shenton-Thomas always ready to help, anxious to
reach a decision and determined to set an example. He had
the faults of these virtues. He would agree to suggestions
without argument and only later realize the difficulties in
execution. He let members of his personal staff go to duties
connected with the war, with the result that long before
December 1941, he was overburdened with detail.[20]

As far as the RAF was concerned, Brooke-Popham's reply was that it had been found very difficult to put an aerodrome out of action for more than two or three days. In
this connection, the former C-in-C Far East seems to
have mellowed since 1941. On 24 December 1941, he
sent what can only be described as a rocket to the AOC,
Pulford, with instructions to pass it on to all units. Far
from finding excuses for inadequate demolitions, it is very
critical of the RAF:

> During the last fortnight it has been necessary to order the
> evacuation of several RAF aerodromes. It has come to my
> notice that in some cases the process has been badly carried
> out. This has been due largely to failure on the part of those

responsible to organise in advance and to set a proper example of leadership.

There have been many cases of gallantry and devotion to duty on the part of individual officers and airmen, but there have also been instances where aerodromes appear to have been abandoned in a state approaching panic. Stores that will assist the enemy in his further advance have been left behind, material that is urgently required has been abandoned and a general state of chaos has been evident.

This is utterly opposed to all the traditions of the air force formed over a period of 30 years. It is the duty of every commander, whatever may be his rank, to remember his first duty it towards the officers and men who are under his command; his second duty is to see that the aeroplanes or other material for which he is responsible is safeguarded, moved, or if no other course is possible, rendered useless to the enemy. After he is satisfied on all these points, then and only then is he at liberty to think of his own safety and comfort.

In the majority of cases the bombing of aerodromes has been on a far smaller scale than that suffered calmly by women and children in London and other towns in England, and aerodromes have usually been vacated whilst still well out of range of enemy land forces. Several of the moves back were carried out in a regular and orderly manner; there is no reason why they should not all have been.

Let us hope that there will be no further need for withdrawal, but whether this be so or not, I look to everyone to play his part, not only in ensuring that there is no ground whatever for criticism of RAF movements in future, but that we in MALAYA add our full share to the high reputation being gained by the Air Forces of the Empire elsewhere.[22]

As a footnote to Gordon Bennett's criticism of the low morale of the Indian troops, some British comments on the Australians might be interesting.

The Australians' disregard of the barrack square had mildly pained Brooke-Popham when he visited them in March 1941. 'Of course they have a different standard to us as regards smartness,' he wrote to Ismay, 'and their quarter guard turning out to do a general salute would hardly satisfy a Sergeant Major from Caterham. Then again, they are sparing in the use of the word "Sir", but so long as one remembers the attitude of mind on such matters they are absolutely grand.'[23] He had, though, the good sense to realize that the attitude of the Australians was not that preparing for war was an incident in normal peace routine, but a practical reality 'which is at present the sole aim and object of their life'.[24] They were training hard and finding solutions to the problems of living in the jungle. He was also taken by surprise by the background of some of them:

> I spoke to a dispenser in a casualty clearing station and found that he was a sort of managing director of a big firm of chemists and druggists with many branches in Sydney and Melbourne. A disreputable looking individual inadequately dressed in a greasy pair of shorts and working in a mobile repair shop gave me a discourse on the physiological effect of ultra violet rays from an electric welding arc. I asked an aged corporal whether he had ever been to Malaya before and he replied that the last time he visited Singapore was as A.D.C. to Lord Roberts. I found out later that he had commanded a Brigade in 1918.[25]

These men were the same who successfully used ambush tactics against the Japanese in Johore. It was their reinforcements who went to pieces. Colonel Ashmore is almost apoplectic in his recollections of their breakdown during the Singapore fighting:

> The A.I.F. had by this time [10 and 11 February] definitely cracked and the roads leading from the West were littered with Australian soldiers in all degrees of demoralization. Considerable looting of private houses, including my own, took place by these men in search of liquor. The docks were full of them and quite a large number managed to get away. The reason for this 'crack' is difficult to understand as the A.I.F. had fought extremely well in Johore and at the battle of Gemas but there is no doubt whatever that something failed. I am of the opinion that it was largely due to lack of discipline. Where discipline is weak it takes very little for a panic to set in ...

The state of discipline among the A.I.F. was appalling, no one ever saluted, no one ever made any attempt at drill or correct turn-out. Half-naked Australian soldiers roamed the streets at all hours of the day. Venereal disease, which I always consider is a matter of discipline, had a far too high incidence among all types of troops. Lack of discipline was, I feel, a minor contributory cause to the loss of Malaya. The crack in the A.I.F. morale after the landing of February was in no small measure due to the strange absence of discipline in the A.I.F. I myself saw five Australian soldiers, naked except for a pair of dirty shorts, no boots or socks, lying and sprawling in the gutter of one of the main thoroughfares leading west from Singapore on February 10th. They had their rifles and were drinking from bottles. Such a spectacle reduced any confidence and respect the native population may still have retained for the white soldiers . . .

The British soldier may have lacked some discipline but he with his Indian brother at least retained their self-respect and courage.[26]

PLAYFAIR

It will be noted that Brooke-Popham refers disparagingly to 'safety and comfort'. The comfort of the civil population in Malaya is a constant theme in the various military apologias.

Percival refers to it several times in his Despatch. Many of the European civilians had, after many prosperous years in Malaya, 'lapsed into an easier routine'. The standard of living was exceptionally high, as a result of the natural wealth of the country and the climatic conditions; possibly, he adds, 'too high for the maintenance of a virile European population.'[27] Freedom from strife over long years had bred a feeling of security. The Asiatic population was enjoying the benefits of British rule and had been so long immune from danger that they found it difficult to appreciate its reality and to believe their lives might be disturbed.

Major-General I.S.O. Playfair (Chief of Staff, Far East, from July 1941 to January 1942) was even more outspoken in a secret paper he wrote a year after the fall of Singapore, 'Some Personal Reflections on the Malayan Campaign':

Most of the British population of Malaya were there to make as much money out of the country as they could. They counted the days to the time when they would leave. Their social and economic structures were highly artificial. They strongly opposed the introduction of an Income Tax in 1940. They had no natural patriotic feelings for Malaya and not enough was done to help them change their outlook. This is not to say that there were no generous or patriotic individuals; that would be quite untrue. But it must be remembered that H.M. Government had laid down that the primary duty of civilians was to earn dollar exchange by producing as much rubber and tin as possible, and civilians can hardly be blamed for doing as they were told.

. . . The holders of the principal Government offices had been for 30 years or more in the enervating climate of Malaya, a country which was untouched by the 1914-18 war. It was not easy for them to acquire a war-mentality.[28]

The climate of Malaya is something Playfair returned to when assessing its affects, military as well as civil:

I had served in Malaya twice before and knew it to be a place where, for various reasons, the tempers of busy people became easily frayed; where it seemed more natural to take offence than to 'laugh it off' and where criticism was more common than discretion. The lack of a change-of-air station had something to do with this. The hill stations (Fraser's Hill and Cameron's Highlands) were so small as to be negligible. Splendid holiday resorts existed in Sumatra and Java, but these were expensive. When I reached Singapore in June, 1941, I was shocked to find so many tired people, longing for a change, working long hours, and out of touch with the war. I got the impression that some of them were already drawing on their reserves of moral and nervous energy . . .

A cable was sent to the War Office asking for a systematic change-over of personnel with fresh officers and men who had had first-hand experience of modern war. Evidently this was not possible.[29]

WAVELL

The theme recurs in Wavell's comments. One of them unspoken, or rather unreported, is perhaps more eloquent than the rest. When the future Field-Marshal Slim received his first appointment as Corps Commander from Wavell, in India in 1942, he asked him why Singapore had fallen as it did. 'He looked at me steadily for a moment and then told me.'[30]

We need little imagination to reconstruct the sense of what passed between Slim and Wavell. John Connell's biography describes how disturbed Wavell had been by what he had seen in Malaya – British, Indian and Australian troops outfought by Japanese skill and boldness. He drafted a note on what he had deduced and sent it to Percival, concluding:

> As in all other warfare, in thick or open country, in Asia or Europe, in advance or retreat, in attack or defence, the leadership of the officer and the fighting spirit of the soldier – the determination to beat the other man whatever happens – is the deciding factor. There are three principal factors in all fighting – good equipment, tactical skill and guts. But the greatest of these is *guts*.[31]

In a telegram to Churchill (11 February 1942) Wavell made the point again. Percival did not have as many troops on the Island as Churchill believed, he said, but he should have 'quite enough to deal with the enemy who have landed if the troops can be made to act with sufficient vigour and determination.'[32] When the surrender was an accomplished fact, Wavell looked back on the atmosphere of Malaya. That was the root cause of the Army's inability to hold out long enough for him to rally the rest of his command, long enough to bring in enough reinforcements. He had wanted only a month, but the Malayan front had crumpled in his hands:

> The trouble goes a long way back; climate, the atmosphere of the country (the whole of Malaya has been asleep for at least two hundred years), lack of vigour in our peacetime training, the cumbersomeness of our tactics and equipment, and the real difficulty of finding an answer to the very skilful and bold tactics of the Japanese in this jungle fighting.
> But the real trouble is that for the time being we have lost a good deal of our hardness and fighting spirit . . .[33]

It may be imagined that Percival would object to this picture. When Wavell's statements were incorporated into the draft of the Official History (J. R. M. Butler, *Grand Strategy*, III) the draft was shown to Percival who was very forthright about Wavell:

It must be pointed out that Wavell at the time he sent these messages, was a disappointed man. He had recently been relieved of his command in the Middle East and given the, at that time, non-active command in India. The further failure in ABDA (although he never really had a chance there) obviously endangered his future career. He therefore resorted, as commanders have frequently done, to blaming his subordinates. Although he certainly saw as much as he could for himself while he was in Malaya, yet a great deal of his information was second-hand, in many cases from unreliable sources. Further, as C-in-C India he obviously had to speak as well as he could of the troops. Thus, 'most of the troops fought well until reduced in numbers by casualties' and 'Indian troops counter-attacked with great dash on many occasions.' I am afraid I cannot agree with these statements. Many of the Indian troops, especially the 44th and 45th Brigades, and the Australian reinforcements were quite lost in those conditions. As regards Indian counter-attacks, there was a good one at Kampar and another at Kluang, and local ones elsewhere, but generally speaking it was difficult to get Indian troops to take offensive action. Further, in Wavell's report there is no mention of British troops except the 18th Division. Those which had a chance were much better than many of the others.

. . . I think I am right in saying that Wavel had never been in the Far East before, so that his opinions were based on two months' experience there and what other people told him. And who were those other people? Mostly disgruntled people who had made good their escape from Singapore – some with permission and some without it. Many of them had only a restricted knowledge of Malaya and its problems. Where, for instance, did Wavell get his information about 'lack of vigour in our peace-time training' or about pre-war 'complacency'?

I am prepared to claim that I know far more about these things than Wavell ever did.[34]

X

Who Was to Blame?

(i) THE SIMSON CASE

Ivan Simson was a sapper brigadier and Chief Engineer of Malaya Command. He took over the job four months before the Japanese invasion and, under Percival, was responsible for military engineering requirements in Malaya and British Borneo. When he returned from captivity in 1945 he wrote a number of accounts of his experiences, and attempted to have them represented in the various official histories. His failure to do this made him publish his own version, which he did with some reluctance, in 1970, though the draft had been completed many years earlier: *Singapore, Too Little, Too Late.*

Simson's main charge is against the civilian authorities in Malaya, particularly the governor, Sir Shenton-Thomas. But some of his criticisms transcend personalities. I would like to look at three of the areas in which his comments bear on crucial matters: defence against tanks, water supply, and civil defence. Much against his will, Simson had been given responsibility for civil defence in addition to his chores as Chief Engineer, on 31 December 1941, by a decision of the War Council under the presidency of Duff Cooper. Simson's unwillingness stemmed from his awareness that at this date the likelihood of Singapore Island being invested was very great and under siege conditions a Chief Engineer was second in importance only to the GOC. His work would be cut out.

Simson had left England without written orders describing his appointment, and the letter from the Chief of the Imperial General Staff to Percival confirming its details never arrived. In the circumstances, all he could do was appeal to Percival to retain him in his purely military functions and allow him to get on with constructing the military defence works which still remained to be done, and which might make a considerable difference to the outcome of the future battle. Percival refused his plea, and told him he would have to have both appointments, Chief Engineer and Director-General Civil Defence.

Duff Cooper's idea was that Simson should have plenary powers to deal with the problems that would arise, both on the Island and in neighbouring Johore. But Shenton-Thomas provided the first snag. Simson called on him the day after the War Council had met, and was astonished to be told that he considered Duff Cooper's terms of reference for the Director-Generalship illegal as far as Johore was concerned. Not only that, they might annoy the Sultan. As Governor-General he therefore limited Simson's civil defence powers to Singapore Island and added that if Simson's orders were challenged he must refer the matter for decision to the Malayan Legal Department. Simson's fury at the insistence on bureaucratic procedures needs no imagination. He was sure the Governor was still mentally living in a pre-war era: how else could he have stayed away from Singapore on leave for eight crucial months in 1940?[*][1]

---

* On Simson, Shenton-Thomas commented later as follows: 'His appointment was pressed on the War Council by Duff Cooper. Percival . . . did *not* consent. He told me that neither he nor General Pownall had been in favour and that he had written to Duff Cooper to say so. He was informed by telephone that his view could not be accepted. I was never consulted at all though I was away from Singapore for only 3 days . . . I gave Simson a fair wind. In notifying the Colonial Secretary I said "He is assured of your support and mine, and I know that all who are engaged in the civil defence at Singapore will give him theirs."

'. . . Simson was not "made responsible through the Minister to the Far East War Council" as Percival states. Duff Cooper's original order was that "he will report through the Governor to the War Council." My amended order, approved by Duff Cooper was "Simson will be responsible solely to the Governor who will include his activities in the report which His Excellency makes periodically to the War Council. The appointment is designed to ensure unified control, with centralisation of all civil defence measures under one authority."

'. . . My recollection is that the Defence Regulations gave me authority to provide for every sort of contingency, and if Simson had found any loophole he had only to ask me to stop it.

But Simson is justifiably harsh on Percival also. After reconnoitring a number of defence positions in Malaya, Simson had an interview with Percival in October 1941 to put a number of propositions for strengthening fortifications:

    i. Anti-tank and machine-gun positions in depth across roads and railways at as many natural defiles as possible, to prevent the kind of deep tank penetration that had won the Battle of France for the Germans in 1940. Mine chambers to be built for all main bridges, and every position to have flank protection (ambush positions, anti-personnel mines).

    ii. Round Johore Bahru, to keep the Singapore naval base out of shell range, a ring of permanent defences.

(It is an interesting comment on the changing philosophies of defence expenditure at Singapore that Simson discovered machine-gun pill-boxes in the jungle near Kota Tinggi, at intervals of a mile or two. He suggested this line be developed as the defence line for Johore, but did not know how the pill-boxes had got there. Neither did

---

On the complexities of the Johore situation: 'It had been decided that priority of labour should be given to the Air Force "for the construction of new air strips in southern Johore" and it was thought that a landing might be attempted at Mersing in the South-eastern corner . . . All available transport, and all available labour, was required for military use in the State. I told the Sultan this on January 20th. For this reason, appeals for help would similarly have been fruitless. Simson could have made them himself, or have asked me to make them.

'. . . Simson came to see me several times after his appointment, and before long he was made a member of the War Council. I do not recall that he ever commented on the terms laid down for his office. If he had complained, the War Council would unquestionably have been consulted. There is no such reference in the minutes.

'. . . I wish to record that Simson gave all the help he could and was very useful. He was naturally reluctant to take on the work, and here I quote my diary dated January 7th, 1942, "Discussed Passive Defence with Simson. He realises now that his job is not to uproot the whole organisation and create a new one (which Duff Cooper and Bisseker led him to believe was necessary) but to strengthen and improve it where desirable." I think he would agree, that he and I were in perfectly friendly terms throughout.'
(Shenton Thomas, paras. 125-131).

Percival, neither did his Brigadier General Staff. It later turned out that General Dobbie had had them built in 1939, and his successor, General Bond, had stopped them. £60,000 had been allotted by the War Office for the work, and only £23,000 of it spent.[2] This is a clear indication that the responsibility for events in Malaya needs spreading very widely indeed.)

    iii. North shore of Singapore Island: defences in depth, including trenches, pill-boxes, mines, petrol fire-traps, floating barbed wire, methods of illuminating stretches of water, with the principal idea behind all this that the water surface and the shore should be the main killing ground of the invader.

All the heavy work was to be carried out while peace conditions still prevailed, the minor works being left until actual hostilities clearly showed the enemy's line of advance.

Simson describes the response:

There were very many questions by the GOC and BGS and it was clear to me that they were really interested in the historical examples quoted and the defensive suggestions for Malaya and Singapore. I had great hopes that some defences at least would now be ordered or that reference to the War Office would be made on their instructions to me; *but finally General Percival decided to take no action at all* [*My italics*]. He would give me no reason. I was very disappointed of course and gave much thought later to what his reasons might be for no defences.[3]

Simson imagined that Percival might have thought war was not coming, or that there was no need to depart from General Bond's decision against defences or because he simply had no money. On this last point, it is amazing to read that neither Simson himself, nor Percival, knew of the War Office's allocation of £60,000 for defences made to Dobbie in 1939, only one third of which had been spent.

Simson had no better luck from local commanders, and

in frustration reported the situation in late October 1940 to General Cave Browne (Director of Fortifications and Works, and thus the senior Engineer appointment in the War Office at the time). No reply was ever received to this letter, and it seems likely that Cave Browne never received it in the first place, since he had left his appointment the previous month. But the letters should have been forwarded to him, and he should have passed their contents on to his successor. Likewise, he should have ensured that Sir John Dill, then Chief of the Imperial General Staff, should write to Percival clarifying Simson's appointment. Simson's being armed merely with verbal instructions was clearly a great hindrance to him in putting plans forward and having them accepted.

On the specific issues, perhaps the defence against tanks is the most interesting for Malaya, and the water supply the most important for Singapore. Simson agrees with Brigadier Stewart's interpretation of the importance of the road system:

> In a modern army control is decisive . . . break control and an army will disintegrate . . . Jungle prevented visual control; within a battalion there was no wireless; maps and compasses were scarce. Control therefore depended on keeping open the single artery of the road. It became the absolutely dominant tactical feature. The only one to attack or defend. Battle was always for control and therefore always for the road . . .
>
> Under these conditions a static defence has no hopes of success. It will be walked round, infiltrated, the road in rear cut . . . there are only two alternatives – to attack or to delay by gradual withdrawal to avoid the encircling move.[4]

By a curious coincidence, Stewart's metaphor for one form of attack is almost exactly the same as that used by one Japanese commander. The Argylls called it 'filleting': enemy control of his battle is cut by an encirclement on to the road or ripped in two by a frontal attack straight down the road to great depth on the frontage of the road itself. Colonel (later Major-General) Iwakuro, in command of 5

Guards Regiment, considered himself the inventor of this tactic and called it 'The Fishbone Tactic'.

> In the tactic called by the name 'Fishbone Tactic', the tanks were on the road and pushed forward while giving flanking fire into the rubber plantations on either side. The artillery was to annihilate the enemy's fire which was being brought to bear on our tanks. The infantry advanced behind a curtain of fire made by the tanks' guns, cutting a wide swathe in the rubber on either side. Three arms co-operated, infantry, armour and artillery, and the tactic was most suitable for terrain like rubber plantations which were planted with great precision. The name 'Fishbone' was derived from the fact that the path of the tanks was like the backbone of a fish, and the radiating fire like its lateral bones.[5]

Iwakuro used the tactic to devastating effect on 22 January 1942, in the battle for Parit Sulong.

What did Simson propose to counter a tank attack? Effective demolitions, for one thing. Mine chambers prepared in bridges with ample notice, and engineers to live in dugouts close to them to ensure that the demolition was effectively carried out. Anti-tank blocks, pillboxes, modern demolition techniques – information on all these was available and Simson wanted to train engineers in them. He was told that his function was limited to the supply of engineer stores to the Commander Royal Engineers of each division. It was not part of his duty to train engineers in combined field training with other troops. The limitation of the Chief Engineer's role was particularly disastrous in the kind of campaign the British had ultimately to fight in Malaya – a campaign of imposing delay on an enemy until the army could halt behind fixed defences and strike back, all of which implied a heavy and detailed reliance on engineering works.

One specific example which was to have fatal effects was the Jitra Line. Percival sent Simson up to Jitra in November 1941. The anti-tank line was not Simson's responsibility, but that of the civilian Public Works Department. He found Murray Lyon's men keyed up and ready to go for Operation Matador. Not unnaturally, Murray

Lyon was not thrilled by the suggestion that his men should start digging trenches and build anti-tank and machine-gun positions to cover the main road and the anti-tank ditch.

At this date [writes Simson] (1 and 2 December), just a week before the war started, I saw no defences of any sort at Jitra, other than the anti-tank ditch still under construction . . . I saw no trenches, barbed wire, etc., and so far as I could ascertain, no defences had yet been reconnoitred, sited or even contemplated in future planning. I informed General Murray Lyon that I regarded all this as a vital necessity. But he pointed out that he was on 'two hours call' to move off in a race against time to occupy the Matador positions before the Japanese did. He was reluctant, on this account, to risk delay in unpacking tools and carrying out the work. I understood work did start in very bad weather shortly after I left, and after Matador was called off.

On my return to Singapore, I informed Command H.Q. that there were no defences for the road across the Jitra anti-tank ditch. It caused no anxiety.[6]

Neither, apparently, did the lack of instruction on anti-tank warfare. Simson discovered that War Office pamphlets on defence methods against tanks were still lying in unopened bundles in the General Staff cupboards, as late as November 1941. Neither the pamphlets, nor orders based on them, had been passed to the troops who would need them most.[7] Simson set to work to produce one consolidated forty-page pamphlet to condense the information. It was ready on 6 December, two days before the Japanese attack. The lessons were accurate enough: light and medium but not heavy tanks were to be expected, and their manoeuvre would be limited to roads and rail tracks and occasionally to rubber plantations; tanks on the move were hard to hit, and the purpose of the obstacles was to force them to stop so they could be destroyed – hence obstacles must be almost invisible until the tank was nearly on them; draining ditches should be deepened so the tank could not turn off, once blocked; obstacles should be installable within fifteen to thirty minutes; 3,500 concrete cylinders, with steel ropes attached to chain them together in groups of ten, were being made and these would make 350 anti-tank blocks; they should be kept under small arms fire.

By the time the pamphlet was written and approved by Percival, it was too late, even though Simson was authorized to deliver it personally to all formations down to brigade level. Simson acted on this, and saw every formation commander in the next few days – except Key at Kota Bharu and Painter at Kuantan. He asked them to specify where anti-tank material should be dumped. Not from a single formation did he ever receive an answer to this request. As a result, engineers dumped the material where they thought suitable.

That Simson's pamphlet was never read seems clear from Gordon Bennett's disparaging comments – which Simson quotes – on the concrete cylinders:

> Personally, I have little time for these obstacles for tanks, preferring to stop and destroy tanks with anti-tank weapons. An obstacle merely makes the tanks shy clear . . . I prefer to use anti-tank gunners to cover the obstacle.[8]

But as Simson pointed out, there was no question of an alternative here. Both obstacles and anti-tank guns (25-pounders if necessary) were part of the same tactic.

The Slim River defeat is a prime example of the results of a defective anti-tank defence system. There were other factors, of course: the field artillery should have been employed in an anti-tank role, and was not; the Japanese achieved surprise, though warnings of approaching tanks had been given; full use was not made of anti-tank weapons. But Simson had indicated the defensive possibilities of Slim River to Heath, the III Corps Commander, and the anti-tank cylinders might have prevented the Japanese tank thrust if properly used. As it was, they appear to have been used singly, not linked up, as they were supposed to be; and they were not covered by fire, so both necessary conditions were missing.

The troops had never been instructed in anti-tank

methods, other than the use of mines. Simson puts the blame for Slim River, from this point of view, squarely on the shoulders of Malaya Command: it should have seen the War Office pamphlet was printed and training carried out in accordance with it. And the engineers should have been used, months before, to construct anti-tank defence systems.

Simson has a great admiration for Heath's skill in conducting the retreat down the Peninsula, and compares it with Napoleon's retreat from Moscow (550 miles to the River Niemen in fifty days, a speed of over eleven miles a day) and Sir John Moore's to Corunna (267 miles in twenty days, or over twelve miles a day). With specific orders not to allow his forces to become surrounded or annihilated, Heath fought a retreat of 515 miles in fifty-three days – just less than 10 miles a day, against an enemy using tanks and aircraft when he had none, and saved thousands of his men to fight again on Singapore Island. Yet, Simson adds, if only the engineers from Malaya Command had been allowed to prepare anti-tank obstacles and effectively demolish the major bridges, much enemy pressure on III Corps would have been reduced, as would casualties. The excuses of shortage of labour, materials, and money were only part of the answer. The real refusal lay in Percival's decision that defences were bad for morale, for both troops and civilians, a decision which horrified Simson.[9] Percival and Simson bitterly argued the issue into the early hours of the morning of 27 December, after Simson had returned from Heath with a (verbal) request to Percival that a strong defence area in Johore should be prepared for his Corps to retreat into. Percival continued to reject this. Simson pleaded for at any rate a strong defence line on the north shore of Singapore Island. If Singapore were lost it would be hard and costly to retake. And British prestige would be destroyed in Asia. Percival stubbornly refused to agree to a defence system and, writes Simson, 'the argument became dangerous for both of us. Whether General Percival realized this I do not know; neither of us has ever mentioned that midnight meeting again . . .'[10] But Percival did in fact admit later, on one occasion, to Simson, that he had been wrong not to order defences.

What is amazing is that Percival did in fact change his mind two days later, and ordered the Public Works Department to provide work groups to build anti-tank blocks in depth on the Peninsula. Even more amazing is that he never told Simson he was doing this, since the army engineers clearly knew more about defence works than a purely civilian organization could be expected to know.

Lack of anti-tank defences let the Japanese through. Lack of water forced the surrender. For a supposed fortress, Singapore's water supply system was a joke. The main source was at the pumping station at Gunong Palai ten miles north of the Island, in Johore State. The water was carried by large-diameter pipe across the Causeway and then on for sixteen miles until it reached Singapore City. Not only was the City's main supply therefore vulnerable to an enemy occupation of Johore, where it could be cut off at once; the line itself was open to damage by sabotage (which did not occur) or bombing attacks (which did) because for most of its twenty-seven-mile course the pipe-line was exposed above the surface, and in fact sections of it were raised on pillars. The line was in fact broken nine times between the outbreak of war and 27 January, by which date the Japanese had overrun the water source.

In addition to the Johore source, the Island had its own rainwater catchment area, draining into three reservoirs. Their supply was intended to provide water for half a million people, but, rationed in an emergency, it could have maintained a million. This in turn required a safe system of checks against bursts and breakages. That was precisely the snag. There were no overall plans of the water distribution to Singapore City. Valves and stopcocks were few and far between, so that to save water in case of a burst whole areas had to be cut off. As Simson comments, 'It is difficult to believe that, whenever the various water supply systems and extensions had been planned, the civil authorities had approached the military for their opinions. One can hardly imagine any G.O.C agreeing to exposed piping, unmapped systems, and so few valves and stopcocks, for a "fortress" that might be involved in war one day.'[11]

The Japanese succeeded in capturing the last water source in the island by 13 February – McRitchie Reservoir. Oddly enough, they neither cut the pipe nor closed the valve (Simson thinks they must have been sure of victory by this time and did not want the problems of a water-deprived population on their hands). But wastage proved a worse enemy than the Japanese. In the twenty-four-hour period of 14-15 February, five-sixths of the water supply from the Woodleigh pumping station – 800 yards from the Japanese positions – was going to waste. Percival himself, aware of the absolutely crucial importance of his water supply, came to the Municipal Offices twice on 14 February to check the supply figures personally. He was not surprised, then, when Simson reported to the Conference in Fort Canning on 15 February that water would fail within twenty-four hours; and there can be no doubt that this and the appalling dangers it implied for the civil population were the major factors in his decision to surrender.

(ii) THE CIVILIAN CASE

SIR MILES SHENTON-THOMAS

Sir Miles Shenton-Thomas, Governor of the Straits Settlements from 1934, gave the impression of an affable, sociable person, able to mix with a great variety of people. In appearance short, stout and red-faced, in manner distinguished and urbane, he was, wrote the *Times* correspondent Ian Morrison, 'one of those solid, imperturbable, unimaginative Englishmen who would face up to anything.'[12] But Morrison's description was qualified. Shenton-Thomas was stolid and dogged, but unrealistic.

He was over-sanguine to the verge of complacency, and had risen to the position he held not through outstanding ability but as the result of long and conscientious service.[13]

Morrison shows that at the head of civil affairs in Singapore and Malaya, as at the head of military affairs, there were able, competent and hard-working men, when perhaps what was most required were aggressive-minded personalities of striking force and vigour, with a touch of flamboyant leadership. Shenton-Thomas, like Percival, lacked colour and decisiveness. Cecil Brown, Singapore correspondent for the Columbia Broadcasting System, was less concerned to euphemize his judgement of the Governor: '. . . an uninformed individual . . . a slave to Civil Service clichés, bromides and banalities. He lives in a dream world where reality seldom enters, and where the main effort is to restrict the entrance of anything disturbing.'[14] Shenton-Thomas bore the brunt of much criticism of the conduct of affairs in Malaya both during the campaign and after it. There was an attempt to have him removed and replaced by a Military Governor in January 1942. This idea seems to have originated with Duff Cooper who, as Minister Resident, wrote to Lord Moyne, then Secretary for the Colonies, that a breakdown on the civil side might paralyse the fighting services. There existed, he claimed, a widespread and profound lack of confidence in the administration, and suggested the appointment of Major-General Keith Simmons as military governor for the duration of the emergency. If this appeared too drastic, he proposed that at any rate the Colonial Secretary, S. W. Jones, should be removed and replaced by Hugh Fraser. He also urged that Jordan, the Secretary for Chinese Affairs, should go. The Chinese had made up their internal quarrels, were 'behaving splendidly', and there was no further *raison d'être* for Jordan's post.[15]

A copy of the signal was sent to Wavell, and Moyne telegraphed to Wavell the following day:

On several of these matters of suggested failure to discharge responsibilities my view is that Shenton-Thomas is *not* blameworthy and on the whole on information at my disposal I should not myself have thought that a change of Governor at the same time as Colonial Secretary is changed is desirable.[16]

But he told Wavell that he (Wavell) was the best judge and asked him to consult Layton and Brooke-Popham and recommend a change if he thought it necessary. The replacement of Jones by Fraser was agreed.

Churchill wired Wavell on 14 January, after seeing Duff Cooper's telegram, that he favoured the latter's proposals, which were very like his own. Wavell, however, after consulting with Brooke-Popham and Layton, refused to recommend a change of Governor, provided the Colonial Secretary was changed: 'With strong backing consider Thomas a good figurehead. . . . If I form a later opinion that even with Fraser's help Thomas does not fill the bill I will let you know.'[17]

Moyne accepted this, and wired to Churchill that it would be confusing to change both Governor and Colonial Secretary at the same time. But he added that he was instructing Shenton-Thomas to ensure that civil personnel were 'such as enjoy the confidence of the military.'[18]

The unfortunate impression left by Shenton-Thomas upon those who wished to galvanize the scene in Singapore has undoubtedly become fixed in the histories and personal accounts of the time. Yet Shenton-Thomas has a case, and it has largely gone unheard. In 1954, nine years after his liberation from imprisonment by the Japanese, he wrote an account of the conditions in Malaya and Singapore in 1940 and 1941 from the viewpoint of the civilian administration. *What Malaya Did* is a single-spaced typescript of over forty pages foolscap followed by a similar draft of comments – more than twice as long – on Woodburn Kirby's official history and it meets the points raised by the military critics and by those whose sojourn in the East was brief, perhaps too brief for their comments to be informed, like Duff Cooper or Wavell. It shows that the attempt to shift the responsibility for pre-war unpreparedness onto the shoulders of the Malayan civilian community and its leaders will not stand up. The report and the comments are too long to quote *in extenso* but some salient points emerge.

First, in maintaining what seemed to be a peacetime stance in the midst of the European war, Malaya was properly carrying out the function allotted to it by the British Government: the maximum possible production of tin and rubber and the conservation of foreign exchange. Malaya sold more to the USA than any unit of the British Empire except Canada. In 1937, for instance, the USA bought from Malaya to the value of 235 million Straits dollars (the dollar = 2s 4d). Just under 90,000 tons of tin and over half a million tons of rubber were produced annually. The currency this earned was not spent by Malaya in imports from the USA. In one year, the USA spent in Malaya more than twenty-five times as much as Malaya spent in the USA.

Europeans in key positions in Malayan commercial enterprises, which kept this very favourable trade position going, were nonetheless liable for service in the Volunteer Forces. The male European population was liable for service up to the age of fifty-five, and most had extra duties in addition to their normal civilian employment. The Malayan Security Branch of the civil police rounded up Japanese agents on the outbreak of war, and was quite *au fait* with espionage networks in pre-war days. There were about two and a half thousand Japanese nationals who had to be interned when war broke out, and although naval and military co-operation was supposed to be available for this, it was not forthcoming. The civil police did it alone.

The provision of works and labour – as can be seen from Simson's account – was a constant point of friction between civil and military. As an instance of what *was* done, Shenton-Thomas quotes the details from one state – Selangor.

Works carried out for the Army:
   i. Construction of hutted camps, workshops, stores, hospitals, headquarters offices, etc.

  ii. Establishment of dumps for materials for road and bridge repairs; setting up of control offices for telephone contact for speedy repair work.

  iii. Beach defences and road blocks [Percival queried this item in a marginal note on his copy].

  iv. Obstructions on open spaces to prevent aircraft landing.

  v. Cutting of two defence lines to provide open lines of fire.

  vi. A/A gun emplacements built.

  vii. Military buildings camouflaged.

  viii. Several miles of by-pass road made through jungle to prevent traffic congestion.

  ix. Manufacture and supply of tank traps.

Works carried out for the RAF:

  i. Civil aerodrome runway extended by 650 yards.

  ii. Four aerodromes prepared for demolition.

  iii. Water supply to two workshops in two towns.

  iv. Manufacture of bomb racks.

Works carried out for the Royal Navy:

  i. Water supply to naval aerodrome.

  ii. Water supply to one port improved, so that it could act as alternative if Singapore and Penang proved unusable.

'I have no reason to suppose,' Shenton-Thomas wrote after listing these Selangor works, 'that similar help was not given in all the States and Settlements. It would certainly have been given if sought.'[19]

Telecommunications were expanded and a postal and telegraph censorship organization was set up which derived much useful intelligence from traffic to Japan and French Indo-China. 'Singapore was one of the most important overseas censorship stations in the Imperial chain. . . . The work was responsible . . . and the hours were long with frequent unpaid overtime. It might be added that on Malayan standards of the cost of living the pay of 125 dollars (say £15) a month for European women was almost nominal and was about half the pay of a senior Asiatic clerk.'[20]

The Singapore Harbour Board armed 89 ocean-going

ships by the end of June 1940, and converted many local
ships into armed auxiliaries.

Food control. Ninety days before the arrival of relief
from Great Britain was the figure on which Malaya was
supposed to work, if war broke out. But six months was
regarded as a safer period. The Customs Department took
over food control in April 1939, and on the outbreak of
war in Europe prompt action kept food prices down and
ensured adequate stocks. Rice was the greatest problem,
since it was the most important article of food: 900,000
tons was consumed annually, two thirds of which came
from Siam, Burma and French Indo-China. 300,000 tons
had to be bought and kept sweet for six months. Unmilled
padi in the husk would keep longer, but it required additional storage space, so experiments were carried out –
two years before the war – in Perak State, on the preservation of milled rice by a coating of powdered lime. Six
new rice mills were constructed and warehouses built, and
in Kedah alone, by the end of 1940, over 100,000 tons
had been stored. The reserve requirements for 180 days
were more than met when the Japanese attacked.[21]

In terms of manpower figures, Shenton-Thomas
showed Malayan participation in the war effort as follows:

18,095		
10,552	(Volunteers)	
1,500	(Malay Regt and Johore Military Forces)	
Total 30,147		

'This figure takes no account of numbers enrolled in civil
defence units other than those in the large towns, of those
employed on food inspection and control, on publicity, on
vulnerable points, and so on.

Nor is it possible to estimate the cost, and indeed there
is no need. It will suffice to say that every penny was paid
by Malaya as her war effort, and she paid it willingly. No
money was ever refused.'[22]

It seems to me that Shenton-Thomas makes a good case
for Malaya fulfilling its proper role in the early days of
the war in Europe: the country was to be an earner of

money, to enable the United Kingdom to buy the sinews of war. When it came to providing for its own defence, anything Malaya could spare detracted from the main purpose; and, anyway, like most colonies and protectorates, Malaya justifiably looked to the mother country for her defence. Otherwise what was the strategic relationship for? Many of the achievements listed by Shenton-Thomas would not be immediately evident to servicemen looking for constructions and establishments of directly military value.

His case seems equally good when it comes to specific points raised by various military commanders in their despatches or in the official history. Wavell is quoted as saying that had 5,000 labourers been available, organized under vernacular-speaking British officers, much of the chaos in December 1941 and January 1942 might have been avoided.[23] Percival's predecessor, General Bond, had seen the need for organized military labour and had got two labour companies from India. In April 1940 Malaya Command received permission to recruit labour locally, but, according to the Official History, the Labour Controller in Singapore advised against this on the grounds that forming six labour companies would harm production of rubber and tin.[24] It would also be difficult to raise them since they would need to leave their homes and would refuse to do so. Percival realized that all he could raise would be one Chinese company. Even the hopes of this were dashed by the decision – *reached in the UK* – to pay 45 cents a day. The rate was not only unrealistic, it was nonsensical: it was in fact below the rate paid to the lowest type of unskilled female labour.

Shenton-Thomas gives much more detail than does the Official History on this point. Tamil labour was paid less than Chinese. In January, 1941, the wage was 60 cents a day for an adult male Tamil, 50 cents a day for an adult female Tamil. A Chinese contract tapper in the rubber industry received 80-85 cents a day. No Tamil male had been rated as low as the proposed War Office authorized rate since September 1939. In August 1938 the Singapore Municipality was paying 80 cents a day to nightsoil coolies.

'I should be very interested to know' Shenton-Thomas comments, 'on what advice the War Office fixed 45 cents and why Bond did not immediately protest. The civil government would surely have backed him.'[25] The upshot was that the only ready-formed labour units in Malaya at the outbreak of war against Japan were the same two Indian companies which had arrived in 1940.

What the Official History fails to add is that the Services were still offering their absurd rate after the campaign had begun, at a time when the local rate was 100 cents a day plus free food and quarters. 'The Services were therefore offering less than half the proper rate, with no food, no protection, no compensation for casualties.'[26] And so far from the civilian authorities being backward in solving the Services' problems – and Shenton-Thomas declares it was no part of Civil Government's duties to recruit labour for the Services or indeed for anyone – the Governor himself wired home for *carte blanche* to be given to the Services and authorized them, pending a reply, to draw on civil government funds for what they needed.

Percival's interpretation of the pre-war labour issue is also questioned. 'Pre-war plans to organize civil labour had never reached finality,' Percival wrote 'and efforts made to raise additional Army labour companies had . . . been frustrated through delay in obtaining official sanction.'[27] Shenton-Thomas wrote to his former Secretary for Chinese Affairs (Jordan), one of whose responsibilities had been to see that Chinese labour was not exploited in Malaya, and to negotiate settlements in disputes. If any scheme for Service labour in wartime had been put up to the Government, Shenton-Thomas claims, Jordan would have been the first to be consulted. As it was, Jordan denied that Malaya Command, the Navy or the RAF had put in such a request on any occasion.

Shenton-Thomas amplified the problem involved:

A properly worked out scheme would have cost quite a large sum, depending on the numbers required . . . There would have to be skilled supervision . . . There might have to be labour lines, some sort of uniform, provision for compensation in the case of wounds or death, and arrangements for food or transport. On the top of this would be the cost of wages in peace time. And whether there was to be a pool, or a separate and distinct establishment for each of the three Services, or even for the Army and RAF alone, the conditions of service would have to be jointly approved: otherwise the men would play off one Service against another. There is no suggestion that Bond put any of these problems to the War Office, or that he discussed them with Percival when he handed over, or that Pulford on arrival was apprised of the need. I can only guess that, having regard to the War Office attitude in regard to wages and to the impossibility of working out a scheme with Babington [here the reference is to the intense hostility between the Army and RAF commanders before Percival and Pulford took over], Bond decided to accept the rate of 45 cents and hope for the best. At the end of 1940 he was a very tired man.[28]

No blame attaches to the civil authorities, therefore, for failure to provide organized bodies of labour for service needs in the event of war and later during the campaign. The assistance of the civil authorities in forming labour units was never invoked.

The criticisms of the civil authorities' air raid precautions implicit in the official account of the first air raid on Singapore are also dealt with in detail.

Fighter Control Operations Room in Singapore, at 3.30 am on 8 December, reported unidentified aircraft approaching from the north-east. All Service establishments were warned and A/A defences brought to readiness. 'It was not possible for similar warning to be given to the civil defence authorities' writes the Official Historian 'as the headquarters of the Air Raid Precautions organization was not manned. The civil air defence scheme could not therefore be put into effect, in spite of the fact that more than thirty minutes elapsed from the time of the first radar reports before the enemy aircraft [seventeen in number] arrived over Singapore'.[29]

But the official historian aims at more than the ARP headquarters: the city was fully illuminated when the raid took place, there had been no attempt at any blackout and the street lamps were not extinguished until after the all-clear at 4.40 am. The raid had a profound effect on the civilian population, writes Woodburn Kirby, and took them completely by surprise, particularly those members of the European community who still believed war with Japan was unlikely.[30]

Shenton-Thomas's detailed refutation of this interpretation of events, by timetable, is most convincing. Brooke-Popham ordered a first degree of readiness on 6 December, 1941, at 3.30 pm. This did *not* provide for black-out nor for 'brown-out' (precautionary dimming of lights intended to be permanently in force from dusk to dawn). Institution of 'brown-out' entailed automatic shift manning of the ARP control room and posts.

Percival telephoned Shenton-Thomas at 1.15 am on 8 December to say that the Japanese were attacking Kota Bharu. The Governor promptly put into force the rounding up of Japanese nationals and confiscation of their power boats. At 4 am Pulford telephoned to say hostile aircraft were approaching and were within twenty-five miles of the city. All the lights were on. Shenton-Thomas just had time to phone the Harbour Board and ARP before the Japanese planes appeared. The raid took place at 4.15 am, so the Governor had precisely fifteen minutes' warning. Air Vice-Marshal Maltby says the RAF had thirty minutes' warning, ie they received a warning at about 3.45 am, and Shenton-Thomas naturally deduces that they must have spent fifteen minutes trying to contact ARP HQ – a long time in the circumstances. If the Official History time is right, and the RAF were warned at 3.30 am, then they took even longer to get in touch with the Governor.

Shenton-Thomas is amazed that the various commanders did not see the lights in the city and do something about it.

I put it to Maltby that it was not 'conceivable that on the night in question the C. in C. Far East, the C. in C. China Station, the G.O.C., the A.O.C., and myself should all have gone happily to bed with every light on the island blazing if any one of us had thought that a raid was even remotely possible. Of course it isn't: it just doesn't make sense.' He did not answer.[31]

Any one of those commanding officers had two and a half hours between the news of the landing and the warning of the raid, to request the Governor to have the city's lights put out. It is obvious, Thomas concludes, that they did not expect the raid, and this is not surprising 'seeing that we knew that no Japanese aircraft was nearer than French Indo-China some 600 miles away. I have heard that to make the raid the Japanese aircraft were fitted with supplementary petrol tanks.'[32]

No one mentioned either the lights or the ARP organization's supposed failure in the subsequent period, to Shenton-Thomas. Naturally, he thought, if the civil administration was to blame, he should have been questioned. The question was not in fact raised until five years later in the Service Despatches.

'Brown-out' as a precautionary measure was *not* ordered for the night of 7/8 December. Therefore the ARP was not manned nor were the municipal services altered in any way. They were in their beds as on any other night in peacetime.

Shenton-Thomas recalls his Colonial Secretary enquiring if the Service chiefs had made any suggestion that the city should be on the alert. Shenton-Thomas told him they had not. Nor was it possible to put on a crash black-out in Singapore, because much of the lighting was by gas which had to be extinguished by men going round with a pole to each lamp. The Services were supplied by electricity and so could put out their own systems easily.

The official historian even goes wrong on the lack of provision of night fighters to counter the Japanese. They were standing by, apparently, but in order to avoid confusing the defence, which was inadequately trained to distinguish aircraft, they were not allowed to take off, and defence was restricted to anti-aircraft batteries.[33] The reason given by Maltby to Shenton-Thomas *at the time* was totally different. When asked why night fighters were not sent up, Maltby is said to have replied that Buffalo fighters were day fighters only. The only night fighters in Malaya Command were with No. 27 Squadron whose war station was Sungei Patani, ie hundreds of miles to the north in Kedah.[34]

Lastly, on the impact on the population, Shenton-Thomas is surely right when he affirmed, against the official version, that Singapore was 'quite composed' after the raid, which had no adverse effect whatever on the civilian population. Everyone, of whatever colour and whatever calling, was naturally surprised, but not shaken: far from it.[35] Ian Morrison confirms this view. Singapore's first air raid, he wrote 'was not serious enough to cause panic but it served as a spur to galvanize all the civil defence organizations into wartime activity.'[36]

Perhaps at this point Cecil Brown's comment on Shenton-Thomas may be seen to have some point. No doubt the Governor was right in thinking that the Services had a responsibility for warning the civil authorities of the likelihood of air attack. On the other hand, if he had been really alive to the full possibilities of war, would he not have taken the precaution, once Percival had telephoned him about the Kota Bharu landings, to alert his own ARP people *without waiting for further Services intervention?*

He is also, and very naturally, keen to defend his own officials. It is clear from Simson's book, and from Duff Cooper's report to the War Cabinet, that two of those officials were found wanting by the military authorities. One was S. W. Jones, Shenton-Thomas's Colonial Secretary. The other was Jordan, the Secretary for Chinese Affairs. Wavell had been told that Jordan was 'difficult', and passed this on to Shenton-Thomas.[37] Later still Wavell heard from Duff Cooper 'a gloomy account of the efficiency of Civil Administration and of the lack of co-operation between the Civil and Military'.[38] Simson is more specific: when Wavell asked him the one most pressing item in each of Simson's military and civil spheres, the reply was,

defence works on the north shore of the Island and full
Chinese co-operation as labour and guerrillas.

> I stated that there were no defences at all on the north shore
> of the Island; and we seemed unable to get full Chinese co-
> operation, while two civil servants remained in the Chinese
> Secretariat. I was asked to name these men, and I stated
> that I understood both of them had been unpopular with
> the Chinese for many years. I added that this state of affairs
> had continued despite overtures to the Governor from Gen-
> eral Percival, Mr Duff Cooper and myself, to replace the
> officials in the public interest.[39]

Now Shenton-Thomas is quite right to suppose that
Jordan, one of these officials, could not conjure up labour
for the Services at less than half the ruling rates of pay. On
the other hand, as far as raising guerrillas was concerned,
there was a good deal of suspicion of the Chinese, and
Jordan's attitude to certain Chinese officials can hardly
have been helpful. Cecil Brown recounts the treatment accorded to George Yeh, head of the Chinese Information
Board in Singapore, and thus an accredited representative
of the Chinese National Government in Chungking:

> When I came here [Yeh said] I was treated with the
> greatest suspicion by a man named Jordan, who was in
> charge of Chinese affairs in the Colonial Secretary's office.
> Jordan cross-examined me like a common immigrant,
> although I came here as an official representative of the
> Chinese Government. He asked my name, age, father's
> name, where born and the usual rigmarole. He was very
> suspicious of my purpose in coming here. I explained that I
> was a liaison man, that I was to facilitate the work of cor-
> respondents and to do what I could to give publicity to the
> Chinese cause.
>
> I guess he thought I came to make speeches and stir up
> the Chinese. Jordan seemed to thaw out a bit when I told
> him I had studied at Cambridge. When I told him that I
> was a graduate of Amherst and did post-graduate work at
> Harvard it seemed to have no effect on him, but the fact
> that I had gone to Cambridge made me somewhat less of a
> Chinese in his eyes.
>
> I explained to Jordan that after all China and Britain

were allies in that we had a common front against Japan. I said that we were both fighting the Axis powers. To that Jordan said, 'I wish to remind you that Great Britain is not at war with Japan' [October 1941]. I am convinced that the British do not consider China an ally in any way.[40]

Whatever the justice or otherwise of the complaints made against Jordan, and the compulsory retirement of the Colonial Secretary, S. W. Jones, there is no doubt that Duff Cooper thought this the only way open to him to sweep away what he regarded as the sluggish apathy of the civilian administration. On 6 or 7 January, 1942, he spoke to Simson about the possibility of superseding Shenton-Thomas himself and setting up a strong and efficient Military Governor in charge of both civil and military spheres, with the country under martial law: 'it would be very distasteful to him to supersede the present Governor, who was the King's Representative,' Simson records him as saying, 'but he would not hesitate to do so, if the right man could be found.'[41] Duff Cooper left Singapore on 11 January, on Churchill's orders: there was, anyway, at that time, little he could do since his function to report had been overtaken by events. But there were repercussions from his recommendation that a Military Governor should take over. The change at the very top was obviously considered too drastic, but certain changes among the senior members of the administration were recommended. As a result of this recommendation, Jones was selected as the scapegoat. The manner of his dismissal, wrote the editor of the *Malaya Tribune* (E. D. Glover) 'was as unjust as it was undeserved, but he was too good a government servant to comment on the personal aspect of the matter.'[42]

Not everyone would agree on this point either with Glover or with Shenton-Thomas, who claims that the accusations of inefficient organization of civil defence levied against Jones were baseless and that neither he nor anyone else ever had the opportunity of defence because the charges against him were never disclosed. One such is the prickly C. A. Vlieland, who provides the second of the civilian cases.

C. A. VLIELAND

It may seem odd to make a case for someone who is never mentioned by name in any of the official war histories dealing with Malaya. But the role he played, the views he championed, and the opposition – and final defeat – which he encountered, are vital to an understanding of what happened in Malaya. Vlieland's case is not only a case for the civilian administration of Malaya and Singapore. It is an anti-Churchill case, and behind him, an anti-Whitehall case of great cogency. It also raises a number of side issues of considerable interest. Major-General S. Woodburn Kirby, the author of the official history, made some amends for his omission of all reference to C. A. Vlieland, when he wrote his own short account some years later (*Singapore: The Chain of Disaster*, Cassell, 1971). He points out that as Secretary for Defence in the immediate pre-war period Vlieland had great power, having direct access to the Governor and being able to initiate action on defence by the civil administration. But he uses this as grounds for accusation:

> Had Vlieland carried out his duties purely as Secretary for Defence and executive head of the civil administration for defence matters, Malaya, by 1941, might have been well organised to meet a Japanese invasion. Unfortunately, Vlieland, holding strong views on the necessity of defending the whole of Malaya, and incensed by Bond's apparent unwillingness to spread his meagre resources throughout the country, entered into matters which lay outside his sphere of responsibility. He allied himself with Babington, with whom he was on very friendly terms and whose views he accepted, and set out to try to impose those views on Thomas and Bond. He had, as will be seen, no difficulty in getting the Governor to accept them with the result that the War Committee was divided into two opposing camps and everything that Bond suggested was opposed. In these circumstances the Committee accomplished little of value.[48]

This is taking Bond's side, of course, as perhaps might be expected from a General who, like Bond, clearly thought Vlieland should have confined himself to civilian affairs.

He refers later to Vlieland's 'lip-service to the idea of holding all Malaya' (*ibid.* p.52) on the grounds that the civil defence system was confined solely to the Straits settlement. On the other hand, he does not explain why he omitted all consideration of Vlieland's views and career from the official history, nor does he give a fair account of Vlieland's remarkable prescience in anticipating the very details of the Japanese advance.

C. A. Vlieland was a Malayan civil servant who was appointed by the Governor, Sir Shenton Thomas, to be Secretary for Defence, Malaya, in December 1938. He held this post until his resignation in December 1940. Vlieland's case can be summed up as follows:

i Contrary to what is usually supposed, the civil authorities in Malaya had a good idea of what Japan was planning, and what the likely points of invasion and defence would be. They made recommendations in this sense, which were ignored by London and – most often – by the army authorities on the spot.

ii Backed by an ignorant Whitehall bureaucracy, the Army was intent on the defence of Singapore in isolation, and did not realize until it was too late that it could not be defended without the whole of the Peninsula being defended too. Vlieland drew up an Appreciation in July 1940 which is startlingly accurate in its assessment of what was to happen.

iii Whether Churchill alone was responsible for the low priority of the Far East, in relation to the Middle East, which determined the way the entire war developed, or whether he shared it with others, that low priority was wrong, in terms of the value of the Middle East and in terms of the value of holding on to Malaya.[44]

The British Government's actions were based on an 'incredibly fallacious' set of assumptions. They completely misunderstood the political philosophy of the Japanese, their intentions and designs, their efficiency and military power. They were ignorant of the elementary geographical and economic realities of Malaya which should have corrected their judgement. The core of the fallacy lay in the notion of 'fortress Singapore'. Not only was it not a fortress, it was of little strategic consequence, by itself, in the circumstances of 1941-2. The naval base was useless, and the attempt to protect it from a vast sea-borne attack was a waste of money, energy, and equipment. If the British had lost Singapore and still held the Malay peninsula, 'the whole grand Japanese design could still have been wrecked and the most valuable and strategically important parts of our Far Eastern dependencies saved from enemy occupation – to say nothing of a hundred thousand potentially useful fighting men.'[45] In addition, not only were the military commanders in Malaya starved of forces, they were prevented by Whitehall's obsessions from making the best use of what they had.

Vlieland's domestic complaints are about philosophy of government, and although he was clearly a very embittered man when he wrote his memorandum, his own bitterness does not affect the facts. Broadly speaking, even at the worst periods of the war, the principle of supremacy of the Civil Power was maintained in the United Kingdom. In Malaya, this was sapped from the start. Duff Cooper, of course, irritated by what he supposed to be Shenton-Thomas's inability to get things done for the forces, recommended a Military Governor who would control civil and military affairs. But long before this recommendation was made, Vlieland declares that the role of the Army in Malaya's Defence Committee was already working in this direction by 1940. Shenton-Thomas was, by title, 'Governor and Commander-in-Chief'.[46] He and his officials were therefore responsible for defence policy, and it was in pursuance of this that Vlieland began to plan the defence of Malaya. But when Lieutenant-General L. V. Bond arrived to take over as GOC Malaya Command in 1939, he told Vlieland that his orders were to defend Singapore and he was not permitted to interest himself in the defence of the Peninsula. This was a major contradiction to the policies recommended to the civil government, and Vlieland rightly points out that it implied that the War Office had arrogated to itself the right to dictate defence policy overseas without reference to governmental authority as far as Malaya was concerned. There was a sharp conflict of views here. The Air Officer Commanding, Air Vice-Marshal Babington, the Governor and Vlieland believed in 'the extended defence of Malaya'.[47]

Vlieland's assessment of the Japanese idea of Singapore is the correct one:

> Singapore was *not* a main strategic objective from the Japanese point of view. To them it represented, in the short view and for the purposes of their war of acquisition, no more than a desirable 'extra' which they could claim automatically at the end of their programme of giddy dances down the Malay peninsula; in the longer view, it bulked large as the future capital of their new overseas empire.[48]

He under-estimates the *moral* value to the Japanese of the capture of Singapore, but he is right strategically.

His views on what Malayan civilians thought about Japan is greatly at variance with General Piggott's (cf. p.5). During World War I, Malaya was very conscious of the threat from Japan, so that there was a division of views between those who regarded the training in the local volunteers as preparation for the Western Front and those who insisted they be trained to meet a Japanese invasion from the north. 'Neither school had any faith at all in the Anglo-Japanese alliance; the dispute was purely over priorities in the national interest.'[49]

During those days Vlieland remembers being given the job of mapping the position of all Japanese land holdings in Selangor, as a very junior assistant in the secretariat. He found the proximity of the holdings to road and rail junctions, bridges and other vulnerable points suggestive, and thinks they were significant of questions exercising higher authories. He made the acquaintance of the then GOC Malaya, Sir Theodore Fraser, who told him many years later, in 1938, 'we shall never be safe in Singapore until we hold Lower Siam.'[50] What Fraser had in mind was the fact – which Vlieland says both of them were fully aware of – that the British Government could have *bought* all it wanted of Lower Siam in 1925 'and bought it in great amity and for a trivial price'.[51]

So he views Japan's ambitions as going further back than 1940 or 1941, and rightly dismisses Percival's view that the Japanese entered the war as a result of German pressure upon her to attack Singapore.

> I cannot swallow the suggestion [he writes] that the Japanese expansionists and militarists were actuated by an altruistic desire to aid their western allies or that the latter were in any way responsible for the Japanese grand strategy . . . Is it conceivable that the German government would have favoured plans for a Far Eastern diversion which were to begin by deliberately precipitating the entry of the U.S.A. into the war?[52]

Nor does he think the fall of France and the acquisition of French bases at little cost in Indo-China radically altered the Japanese plans. 'The long-standing Japanese plan, as I envisaged it, always involved the use of Indo-China as a springboard and they must have been prepared to put in any necessary military effort to secure it.'[53]

But whatever the Japanese plans, British plans were vitiated, once war came, by the irrational priority accorded to the Middle East. The reasons given for this were i) Britain's traditional claim to dominate the Mediterranean, to keep open the route through Suez and ii) the vital need to secure sources of oil. To i), he answers that there was no point in keeping a route open if you lost the destination the route led to. To ii), he answers that after 1941 'we got most of our oil supplies from across the Atlantic from America and the Caribbean' and that 'we were *not* at any stage dependent on oil from the Middle East.'[54] The priority derived more from tradition, sentiment and the romantic imagination, particularly Churchill's. Vlieland points out that Sir John Dill, who preceded Lord Alanbrooke as Chief of the Imperial General Staff, placed Singapore second only to the United Kingdom on the list of priorities, and relegated the Middle East to the bottom.

This case was lost to those who believed Japan was unlikely to go to war, and if she did, her prime objective would be Singapore. These ideas led to an 'elaborate set of fictions':[55] i) that a Japanese offensive would be a vast sea-borne armada, rendered hazardous by a presumed US intervention in the Pacific; ii) 'the invention of the imaginary fortress of Singapore',[56] or as Vlieland puts it the 'Singraltar' legend. The so-called fortress had a hinterland, he points out. It had *none* of the characteristics, natural or artificial, which a layman associates with the term 'fortress', a fact which was fully concealed from Mr Churchill himself until late in January 1942. Not only from Churchill, either. As John Connell remarks in his *Wavell, Supreme Commander*, the future supreme commander in the Far East 'had at no time in his service been east of Calcutta. He did not know Burma, Malaya, Siam or the Dutch East Indies. He knew nothing of Japan or China.'[57] The ignorance was on a very simple level. There was an imaginary picture of swamp and jungle which did not correspond in the least to the highly developed and well-roaded parts of Malaya in which the campaign was actually fought. The third fiction was that the 'fortress' would hold out until a relieving fleet arrived. The period before relief was originally one month, then extended ultimately to six. 'Long before this stage was reached,' says Vlieland, 'two things had become quite clear. The first was that it was impossible to postulate any limit to the period before relief; the second was that the Singapore naval base had lost its very *raison d'être*.'[58]

About the 'jungle' fiction Vlieland is correct. The campaign against the Japanese invaders was fought over the developed countryside and on or near the excellent road system of the western coastal plains. Had tanks, field guns and aircraft been provided in sufficient numbers, the enemy could have been decimated in the large open areas of north-west Malaya which he had to cross.

Why was Malaya so important in Vlieland's eyes as to outweigh the Middle East? Its wealth made it unique. He gives a 'league table' of export/import values, in millions of US dollars, for 1938, which makes his point:

Country	Exports	Imports	Total Trade
UK	2746	4600	7346
France	881	1324	2205
Denmark	334	354	688
Switzerland	302	366	668
South Africa	161	503	664
MALAYA	327	315	642
Netherlands E. Ind.	380	255	635
Brazil	289	295	584
USSR	257	268	525
Norway	198	292	484
New Zealand	225	225	450
Egypt	147	185	332
Spain	98	152	250
Ceylon	104	86	190
Nigeria	70	56	126

43% of the world's natural rubber came from Malaya, 33% of its tin. The U.S. bought large quantities of both (half the rubber in the world and ⅜ths of the tin) which made Malaya a vastly important dollar earner.[59]

Malaya was accurately described in 1927 in relation to countries like India and Burma, as 'trim, neat Malaya, with a surplus revenue amongst bankrupts'.[60] Yet having jettisoned Malaya, Churchill was prepared to scrape the bottom of the barrel to save Burma. This is special pleading, of course, and the date is deceptive. It needs to be rectified with reference to Shenton-Thomas's comments on the Malayan economy, when he is discussing Malaya's financial potential in the inter-war years:

If it should be thought that in these pre-war years Malaya was a rich country, it might be well to show the export quotas of tin and rubber for the years 1934-1938. . . . Between 1926 and 1929 the price of tin fell from £284 a ton to £120 per ton. By 1935 the International Tin Committee had been able by creating buffer stocks to maintain a stable price of £200-£300 per ton. In 1931-33 the price of rubber dropped to 3d per lb, that is, to about one-fiftieth of its highest price in 1912. About half the crop was Asiatic owned, most of it being on small holdings which totalled more than 1,000,000 acres.

For several years before the war Malaya was therefore a poor country. Between 1927 and 1937 the revenue of the Federated Malay States fell by just on 25 million dollars, say more than a quarter; and the revenue of the Straits Settlements dropped by 17 million dollars, nearly one third. Obviously every item of expenditure had to be most carefully scrutinised.[61]

Within the Defence Committee itself until Vlieland took over the Army was overwhelmingly represented on all subcommittees (Food, Transport, Medical, ARP, Manpower) and exercised almost the sole initiative. A staff officer at Fort Canning acted as secretary, and the upshot was that the Navy, RAF and civilian representatives regarded their committee service as a time-wasting chore. But the Committe had no executive powers and no funds. It merely made recommendations on problems without the least notion of how they were to be carried out. What was needed was a central defence secretariat for the whole of Malaya, which would avoid going through the separate governmental structures of the various states, which were jealous of their own rights. It must also be able to spend money. Shenton-Thomas had already been under pressure from the RAF to change the system. Months before Vlieland was appointed, the then Air Officer Commanding, Air Marshal Tedder (later Marshal of the Royal Air Force Lord Tedder) had recommended a civilian appointment 'to provide a counterpoise to the excessive weight of the Army command in defence counsels.'[62] The GOC Malaya, Lieutenant-General Dobbie, whole-heartedly agreed, and accepted Vlieland's appointment gladly. The initial atmosphere was one of good will and mutual co-operation, with the Governor, the three Service chiefs and Vlieland acting in concert. All matters dealing with defence were removed from the purview of the general secretariats of Malaya and became the sole concern of the new office. Vlieland was theoretically subordinate to the Colonial Secretary and the Federal Secretary in the pecking order, but in his position as Secretary for Defence he dealt directly with the Governor and neither of the other two Secretaries interfered with defence matters unless their advice was asked. All correspondence dealing with the defence of Malaya and Singapore went through Vlieland's office.

The system ceased to function properly, in Vlieland's view, when General Bond arrived on 1 August 1939. He could not – or would not – accept Vlieland's constitutional position, and began to press for the return of the old committee system in which the Army ruled the roost. He clearly thought that Vlieland should not concern himself with purely military matters but should confine his activities to civil defence. Defence policy and military strategy were no concern of his or the Governor's. Now Vlieland was no ignoramus in military matters, quite the contrary, and he was also a firm believer in Clemenceau's dictum that war was too serious a matter to be left in the hands of soldiers. Certain matters entailed much more than personal animosity. Policy was involved: Bond told Vlieland specifically that his orders were to defend Singapore, and not the Peninsula.[63] The balance of opinion, in spite of these irritations, was still even until the Governor went on leave in April 1940. He was away for the astonishing period of eight months. During his absence two things occurred. Vlieland is convinced that he was brainwashed in London and made to accept a point of view about Malayan defences radically contrary to the one he had held. And new arrivals on the military scene in Malaya weighted the scales against Vlieland.

In April 1940, he had done a great deal: the stockpiles of food would soon reach the provisional target of six months' reserve supplies. Babington had done what he could with his slender resources to plan the air defence of the whole of Malaya. Only Bond was out of step, with his insistence on the defence of the Island. Vlieland is convinced that there never was any intention in Whitehall to provide either the air or army manpower to defend the Peninsula or to provide the modern weapons it required. He is convinced that the directive of the Chiefs of Staff, issued on 1 August 1940, was secretly countermanded by instructions to Bond and to the C-in-C, China Station,

Admiral Sir Geoffrey Layton, who was later to take over the naval chair in the War Committee in Singapore. Vlieland is sure that Jones, the Colonial Secretary, who acted as Governor in Shenton-Thomas's absence, and Brooke-Popham, when he arrived in October 1940 as C-in-C, Far East, were privy to the *real* intentions of the Government in London.

Vlieland was certainly shaken by Shenton-Thomas's volte-face when he returned. On his departure from Singapore, 'Remember, Vlieland,' he had said, 'I rely on you to hold the fort while I am away and not to let Bond get away with it. Jones knows very little about the defence side and you'll have to keep him straight.'[64]

Jones was 'profoundly unhelpful',[65] and once Brooke-Popham and Layton collaborated on the revised War Committee, Vlieland found himself suddenly out-numbered, since his ally, Babington, found himself unable to speak against Brooke-Popham, who was his superior officer. The committee, which had finally and officially replaced the old moribund Defence Committee on the outbreak of war in Europe, had no agenda, no minutes and no secretary. It did not record decisions, nor did it issue corporate orders. The members 'took any action they saw fit to take within their own competence in the light of the discussions.'[66]

General Bond began to take a number of decisions against Vlieland's wishes: he had piers and beach pavilions on Singapore Island demolished, called up the Volunteers, and gave out a number of orders which made it transparently clear that he assumed Singapore would be a battlefield while the Peninsula remained relatively untouched: hospitals in the States were told to make room for military casualties expected from Singapore, planters in southern Johore were ordered to fell trees on their estates to clear fields of fire *southwards* over the Island, barbed-wire entanglements were put up on Collyer Quay. 'Don't these madmen know,' Vlieland's Malay chauffeur asked him, 'that the Japs will come down on us from Siam?'[67]

Although Bond, in a memorandum to the War Office on

13 April 1940, had in fact stressed the need to widen the defence of Singapore beyond the area he had originally envisaged and spoke of necessary increases in the garrison to cover the defence of airfields at Alor Star, Sungei Patani and Kota Bharu, he and Babington still did not agree on the general deployment of resources. Bond thought of holding the whole of Malaya largely in order to guarantee air reinforcements (this was the importance of Alor Star). But he still believed in concentrating nearly the entire army force on the Island. Babington, whose view was that air action would be the controlling factor, wanted Bond to guarantee far more than the infantry battalion promised to defend Alor Star. Because they could not agree, the matter was referred to London. Vlieland wanted Jones, the Colonial Secretary, to espouse Babington's cause, and prepared a telegram for him to despatch to London. Jones agreed on a less committed version, but, Vlieland claims, even this was not finally sent, and Jones's telegram ultimately came down on neither side, but merely asked for strong reinforcements.

Two months later, Vlieland submitted his own Appreciation to Jones (printed in full in Appendix C), who asked him not to submit it, since it would only anger Bond, and he refused to read it himself in case he became compromised. The Appreciation quoted Percival's of 1937 in which the probability of the Japanese using Thailand was stressed, and the consequent need to defend northern Malaya. Vlieland thought the Japanese intelligence was so well organized that they must know they could sweep down from Thailand right to the back door of Singapore with ease. Direct assault on Singapore was quite improbable, subsidiary landings on the southern east coast possible, an invasion of Kelantan certain, with a view to crossing to the west coast to move down the western coastal plains. The balance of air power would move progressively against the defenders. Air power would be decisive. The economic life of Malaya must continue, and the mobilization of Volunteers should not be allowed to wreck the economy. The whole military effort should be directed to the north-western plains. Alor Star was the key to the whole defence. No large garrison should be kept in Singapore, nor any large reserves south of Kuala Lumpur:

> I maintain that, if the enemy succeeded in driving us out of the north-western plains, complete disaster would follow inevitably. Not only should we lose Malaya, including Singapore, but the Japanese would be well on the way to achieving their whole grand design.[68]

He made an uncanny prediction of the fate of the battle for Kampar:

> If we were forced back out of Kedah and northern Perak, I think the only area where a considerable stand could be made is in the vicinity of Kampar and I should expect a distinct battle there. But I do not think it would be a success for us. It seems to me too certain that we should be forced to withdraw by a threat to the left rear of our positions *via* the Telok Anson-Bidor road since, by that time, the enemy would be in a position to make landings on the west coast.[69]

Vlieland naturally felt that the Chiefs of Staff Appreciation of August 1940 was very much a confirmation of his own views.

They recommended that the *whole* of Malaya was to be defended, that the forces required were estimated at 336 first-line aircraft and six brigades with ancillaries, the target date to be the end of 1941, and additional land forces to act as reinforcements until the air reinforcement reached the level estimated. The last point was the exception. Vlieland found it profoundly disturbing. He decided to put to the test his own feeling that the Chiefs of Staff Appreciation – after the first euphoria – was going to be swept under the carpet. He sent Jones a file dealing with a regional evacuation scheme, and added a minute beginning with the words, 'Now that our whole defence is to be re-orientated to meet the overland threat from the north . . .' 'I am not at all sure,' Jones replied, 'that there is going to be any such re-orientation.'[70]

Vlieland felt powerless until Shenton-Thomas returned.

But a further shock was in store. He had already found that his successful plan to store 100,000 tons of rice in new granaries at Alor Star had been criticized by Admiral Layton, who arrived in September 1940. Vlieland ignored the criticism, only to find that Layton appealed to the Admiralty, who worked on the Colonial Office to such good effect that a brusque telegram was dispatched to Vlieland ordering him to comply with the wishes of the military without delay. The *padi* was despatched to Singapore where accommodation had to be found for it, and where it was virtually useless for lack of mills. Having interfered in the rice storage operation, the services omitted to bring the collection of rice to an end, so the Alor Star granaries filled up again. But the Navy-Army collusion against the Secretary for Defence and against his ally, Babington, who also believed that defence and retention of the Alor Star area was vital, had won the day as far as representations to the home Government were concerned.

Shenton-Thomas returned to Malaya on 5 December 1940. Vlieland had always been *persona grata* with him before. Now, for a whole week, he tried to see him, and was fobbed off through the Private Secretary. Shenton-Thomas did not summon him for an account of what had happened, and saw him for the first time on 13 December at what proved to be Vlieland's last meeting of the War Committee. He entered the council chamber and took up his usual seat at the Governor's right-hand. Shenton-Thomas did not greet him. He did not even look up. Instead, he turned to the C-in-C, Far East: 'I think you have something to bring up, Sir Robert?'[71] This was Brooke-Popham's cue to make a savage attack on Vlieland, who was convinced it was the result of careful briefing by Bond and Layton. Babington said nothing. Vlieland exonerates him by saying 'The A.O.C. could not of course rally to my support in defiance of his own titular superior'[72] but since Vlieland's views were Babington's own, it seems pretty pusillanimous. (It is clear from later correspondence between Brooke-Popham and Babington that they were extremely friendly. When Babington was back in London he lobbied the

Chief of Air Staff to have Brooke-Popham kept as C-in-C, Far East: 'I told the C.A.S. point-blank that I personally regarded your continued presence at Singapore as absolutely indispensable, [he wrote to Brooke-Popham] since your departure from the scene would mean the risk of the next C-in-C. being a War Office nominee, in which case we should be back where we were in the bad old days . . .'[73] No wonder Vlieland found him a broken reed.)

Brooke-Popham had already taken a dislike to Vlieland. Writing to Ismay on 5 December 1940, he complained of the lack of touch 'and indeed the latent hostility'[74] between the Central Government, the Services and the Civilian Community.

> The Heads of the Services get pretty wild at times with the Civil Government because of their procrastination, whilst the officers generally, who are paying a heavy Income Tax without complaint, feel that they have a grievance against the Civil Community who appear to be accumulating fortunes from War profits and scream out when any suggestion is made to impose an Income Tax on them . . . You have doubtless heard of Vlieland the Secretary for Defence? [he continued] I have seldom met anyone who is, with two or three exceptions, so universally distrusted, by Government officials, by the Services and as far as I can judge by the Civilian Community. He also seems to have established procrastination as a fine art. On the other hand he has got a brain, he has got all the details of the civilian side of Defence preparations at his finger-tips and he is trusted by the Governor, Sir Shenton-Thomas. My present policy is to try and work with him and make him useful. We have had one brush together at which the Officer Administering the Government [Jones] fully supported my view and I think was secretly rather glad of having the opportunity for letting Vlieland have a bit of his mind.[75]

Brooke-Popham was no doubt right about the hostility between Vlieland and Jones, and also about Vlieland's genuine abilities. But his decision to 'work with him' didn't last very long. Writing again to Ismay on 6 January 1941, 'progress has been made in some directions' he said.

At a Defence Council meeting, I let loose some winged words over a silly memorandum put in by Vlieland, the Admiral sitting next to me to pinch my elbow if I looked like losing my temper. The next definite thing I knew about it was that Vlieland had put in his resignation from the Colonial Service . . . This was the only satisfactory solution of the problem. As I've told you before I should have liked to have made use of Vlieland, but it would have taken too long to wean him from his habits. He had a brain but it was only second class and he failed to realise that though he had a certain facility for sarcastic phrase, he lacked the wit that converts irony into humorous criticism.[76]

Vlieland saw the attack as a complaint against his persistent refusal to toe the Army line and co-operate unilaterally in the strictest 'Singraltar' policy. He waited for the Governor to speak. Shenton-Thomas remained with bowed head. Vlieland began to answer the case: he was not answerable to military authority, he had not changed his ground, he had no reason to suppose the Governor had. He thought the idea of close defence of Singapore was absurd, and he referred to the Chiefs of Staff appreciation as the only authoritative directive he knew of. Unless the military changed their policy and concentrated on the defence of Kedah, disaster was certain.

On the way back to his office, Vlieland decided to resign. He saw the Governor's support had gone, and he could not be a party to a policy which he regarded as an inexcusable betrayal.* Back in London in April 1941, he

---

* Shenton-Thomas interprets this very differently, as might be expected. Discussing the Official History's view that there was friction between civilians and military, he denies that this was general and restricts it to the dispute between Bond and Babington in which Vlieland took the latter's side:

There was friction between Bond and Babington and the latter was strenuously supported by one of my officers. Therefore there was antipathy between him and Bond. But the officer in question [*i.e. Vlieland*] had no executive authority, and indeed at this distance of time I should say that his duty was confined to an expression of opinion in favour of or against either of the two schemes put up by Bond and Babington, for the consideration of the Acting Governor. It is clear . . . that they were put up. That would be the normal duty of a Senior Secretariat Officer.

lobbied influential individuals and at the Colonial Office
without success. He tried to get in touch with Duff
Cooper when the latter's mission to Singapore was first
announced. A stereotyped reply came when Duff Cooper
had already left England. Vlieland was convinced nothing
would be done, and the fate of Malaya and Singapore was
as he predicted. He acknowledges that Churchill was no
doubt right, taking a larger strategic view, in assuming that
the doom of Japan was sealed and Britain was saved – ultimately – once the results of Pearl Harbour were known. 'It
is easy to understand his joy and thankfulness,' he comments, 'at the knowledge that the United States were at
last in the war and that we no longer stood alone. It might
be considered ungenerous to cavil at a certain suggestion
of callousness over the forfeits he anticipated in the Far
East. He seems to have been little troubled by the twinges
of regret which are apt to afflict hunters, and anglers after
predatory fishes, for the fate of baits which have served
their purpose.'[77]

It is not difficult to feel here that Vlieland is jumping
beyond the evidence. The case he insinuates is very like
the historian Charles Beard's case against Roosevelt: that
he consciously weakened Pearl Harbour vigilance in order

But this does not amount to a 'divergence of views between the
Services and the civil authorities'. The divergence was between
my officer and Bond who at that time was not well served by
some members of his staff. I should like to say that on my return
the Acting Governor [*Jones*] told me of the matter and spoke in
the highest terms of Bond who, he said, had behaved extremely
well throughout.

... No directive which I received from the Colonial Office ever
conflicted with the military needs of defence. And I wish to say
that Brooke-Popham did solve what the History calls the lack of
co-ordination etc. He arrived in Malaya shortly before my return
from leave at the end of 1940. He spoke to me quickly about my
officer, and my officer went home. I imagine that he wrote to the
Air Ministry, because Babington went home soon. He says himself
in paragraph 15 [*the reference is to Brooke-Popham's dispatch*]
that Service relations with civilian officials were satisfactory, in
most cases. Here beyond doubt he had my officer in mind: I do
not remember friction with any other. (*Draft Comments on the
Official History*, unpublished TS, paras. 66-68)

to let the anticipated Japanese attack succeed, and so bring America into the war on the side of the Allies, which was his profoundest wish. That Churchill allowed Malaya to become so conspicuously weak that it offered itself as a tempting prize to the Japanese, and so ultimately induced their aggression and brought the Americans into the war, saving Great Britain's position in the West vis-à-vis the Germans, implies not just a Machiavellian circuitousness (of which Churchill was perfectly capable), but a guarantee that a number of links in the chain of events would automatically be produced – something that it would have been impossible for him to foresee. In addition, many of the weaknesses in the Malaya planning go back beyond the defeat of France and Britain on the Continent of Europe. Rather than the workings of a Machiavellian master-mind, the defeat in Malaya shows a much more familiar and more probable failure of imagination at the top, a Europe-centred and US-centred attitude on the part of Churchill and his advisers, which was perfectly understandable in the days of Dunkirk and the Battle of Britain. The pity of it is that those attitudes persisted well into 1941, and that a false idea of the nature of Singapore dictated the dispositions of forces.

Vlieland quotes Percival as saying that the object of the defence was the protection of the Naval Base, and later of the Air Bases also, at Singapore, and that the holding of any part of Malaya was merely a means to that end. The result of this was that Percival was bound to hold a large part of his forces on the Island and in Johore and could not defend Kedah adequately. 'In short,' Vlieland concludes, 'H.M.G. never intended that the job of defending Malaya be undertaken at all and, even if General Percival had been disposed towards an outrageous "Nelson touch", he simply had not the tools to do that job.'[78] Even so, there were difficulties that need not have arisen, and Vlieland blames the determination of Bond and Layton to get rid of him for Percival's later difficulties with civil labour and the complexities of Malayan government. If the Europeans had not been pulled out of the economy in the mobilization of the Volunteers, civil labour would have been effectively provided under its 'experienced and familiar *tuans*'[79] and Vlieland's 'pan-Malayan procedure'[80] in his Defence Secretariat would have ensured effective dealing with a number of semi-independent authorities.

Percival's being hamstrung by the War Office closely supervising his expenditures could have been got round by the local governments approving finance for defence measures under the guise of civil expenditure: 'The War Office need never have been consulted and could not have protested if they became aware that the government of a Malay State was undertaking construction of a new road . . . or clearing a patch of forest or draining and reclaiming a swampy area.'[81]

To those who might think such contriving fanciful, Vlieland quotes the example of a former Governor, Sir Laurence Guillemard, who circumvented the halt in work on the Naval Base, decreed by the Labour Government of the 1920s, by carrying out work on the Base under the guise of anti-malarial drainage measures.

Vlieland sums up his 'inquest' under three heads:

i The Malayan theatre of war was starved of defence resources, especially air forces, in order to avoid interference with the build-up of overwhelming military power for offensive operations in north Africa.

ii A subsidiary factor was a perverse plan of defence which assumed without justification that Singapore was the prime Japanese objective and that its defence was our sole concern. These ideas derived from assumptions about Japan's aims and about the Malayan theatre, which bore no relation to realities.

iii No failure of anyone in Malaya at the time, combatant or non-combatant, contributed to the disaster, 'which was the inevitable consequence of the policy of His Majesty's Government'.[82]

To objections that there were other calls on resources, such as aid to Russia and home defence, Vlieland retorts that 'H.M.G. did *in fact* find it possible to pour into the Middle East forces and munitions on a scale beside which the maximum requirements for the defence of Malaya seem almost insignificant.'[83] This is true. If one remembers the havoc wrought on the Japanese landing vessels off Kota Bharu by the pitifully few Hudsons flying from local airfields on 8 December, it seems likely that air forces provided on the scale requested, and *approved by the Chiefs of Staff*, might well have wrecked a sea-borne invasion, and altered the course of history.

Vlieland accepts that in a sense the diversion of strength to North Africa could be justified on Clausewitzian grounds, even if the oil and Suez arguments are inadequate. After Dunkirk, the British could do nothing in Europe, but the Italians could be met in Africa, and so could any Germans sent to help them. This was the obvious theatre, then, for the destruction of the enemy's *forces*, even though Britain had no treaty obligations there and no territorial possessions. But the effort was exaggerated. Three-quarters of a million men had piled up in the Middle East by November 1941. Of the sixteen field divisions in Middle East Command, six were involved directly in the battle with Rommel, two were mopping up in liberated territories, two were in Palestine and Syria, four were in Iraq and Persia. It is difficult to believe that an adequate supplement to Malaya's sketchy three and a half divisions could not have been found *without* dangerous consequences to the Middle East.

In terms of air strength, the RAF put over 800 planes into the battle of El Alamein against Rommel's 300. That victory, Vlieland suggests, would have been anticipated by General O'Connor if he had been allowed to continue his early series of victories, in which his force of one Indian infantry division and one weak armoured division destroyed ten Italian divisions, taking 130,000 prisoners, 400 tanks and 850 guns [Vlieland's figures].[84] As it was, Alamein was unnecessary in a purely military sense, though 'a victory of some sort somewhere was very badly needed to boost British morale and restore confidence in our war leaders.'[85] Even so, Vlieland affirms, 'the cost of preparing and staging that particular victory was shockingly high in terms of global strategy. Amongst other things, the cost of the preparation included disaster utter and complete in the Far East.'[86]

This is not armchair strategy. Vlieland is quite prepared to contemplate the deductions to be made from his case. Without an immense effort in North Africa, he concedes that the Mediterranean might have been lost. He would accept this, provided it could have been 'bottled up'[87] at both ends, with the British keeping out of North Africa altogether and maintaining purely defensive holding operations in the Middle East. This would have freed powerful air and naval forces for other theatres, have strengthened the Indian Ocean and Atlantic, let alone Singapore. Without the drain to the Mediterranean and North Africa, the build-up for victory in North-Western Europe might have been more rapidly achieved.

On the positive side, Vlieland proceeds on a series of deductions from the holding of Malaya. He doubts whether the Dutch East Indies would have been lost, since their conquest, if significant British forces had remained in Malaysian waters, would have involved long-range amphibious warfare 'promising very inferior rewards for much greater effort and risks.'[88] Baulked of their conquest of Malaya, the Japanese would have consolidated their hold on Indo-China and Siam, and possibly taken Burma. But if the occupation of Malaya had been prevented by Britain according due priority to the Far East, 'the whole grand design of the Japanese expansionists would have collapsed in ruins. Nothing they could then do could hurt us very much, while they waited for the nemesis they could not hope to escape when the full power of the United States was ready to deal with them.'[89] Their forces were not unlimited, and reinforcement from the home islands would not have been easy or safe. With Singapore retained, not as a 'fortress' which it never was, but as a supply base and channel for reinforcements which it could easily have been, the British could have moved to the offensive. 'Air forces could strike deep into Siam from the northern Malaya airfields and if we got as far as Victoria

Point with our counter-offensive, the air reinforcement route from the west would have been open.'[90] Vlieland insists on this point, because he wishes to emphasize that the strategy he envisaged does not do violence to the principle that the prime aim in war must be the destruction of the enemy's forces. 'The policy of His Majesty's Government' he concludes 'was defensive to the verge of defeatism. It further failed to take account of the fact that the advent of air power had invalidated, or at least modified, the old concept of proportionality between the extent of a given area and the force required to hold it. It has now to be recognized that it is impossible to hold less than a considerable area however large the force you manage to cram into it.'[91]

XI

The Factor of Race

'The issue of race . . . rested at the heart of power politics in the Far East.'*

The campaign for Malaya and Singapore was a struggle between two great powers for possession of empire. But it was fought out on territory on which lived three of the races of Asia. Malays, Chinese and Indians were all involved in the battle to some extent, but the attitudes of the great combatant powers towards them had more effect in the moral aftermath of the surrender. On the British side, the majority of the forces were Indian troops. It has been too easily assumed that they were very different from the Indians who put up a splendid fight in the North African desert, or who later were the main element in the defeat of the Japanese in Burma. Certainly many of them were only half-trained, and they were flung into situations – outgunned by armour and aircraft – which had in the past overcome far better-trained troops. But something odd happened to these Indian forces after the surrender. Thousands of them, from the first moments of their imprisonment, were subjected to pressures from the Japanese and certain of their own countrymen, to forswear their allegiance to the King-Emperor and to join an army raised by the Japanese to fight against their former comrades in arms. It is futile to pretend that only moral weaklings joined the Indian National Army, or that the motives of all those who did so were suspect. This is simply untrue. Some of the very best joined, and from motives not of self-seeking but from a deep sense of national pride, not unmingled with injustice and resentment at their previous treatment at the hands of the British. What went wrong?

* William Roger Louis, *British Strategy in the Far East*, Oxford, Clarendon Press, 1971

To answer this question, we have to see what role the factor of race played in Malaya. This has been touched upon by other writers on the subject, but my purpose is more direct. I want to single out racial prejudice as a conspicuous factor in the demoralization of the native population and many of the Indian troops. It should have been possible to interest the peoples of Malaya in their own defence, but this did not happen on a large scale at all. And on a number of occasions the native populations undoubtedly felt themselves discriminated against when the question arose of evacuation in face of the advancing enemy.

Let us take the Chinese first. In theory, they had been fighting the Japanese longest. In spite of Japan's conquest of her richest industrial areas and almost all of her coastline, Nationalist China under Chiang Kai-shek had steadfastly continued to resist the Japanese invader. Overseas Chinese contributed greatly to the support of the Nationalist Government, and there was a two-million strong community of them in Malaya, one-third local born, but most of them retaining Chinese citizenship. Why was it not possible to arm these against the Japanese? The suggestion had been made. Brigadier Simson proposed to Percival, in October 1941, the creation of guerrilla forces for operations behind the Japanese lines if and when they advanced into Malaya. He suggested that caches of arms, ammunition and explosives should be buried at suitable sites in the jungle. As Simson points out, the time and effort it took after the war to cope with Chinese terrorist organizations in Malaya was ample proof that the Chinese were suitable for guerrilla warfare.[1] But, as an engineer, Simson was in fact more interested in raising labour companies, each 500-strong, on the lines of the Chinese labour companies which the Allied armies had used in France in the First World War. The difficulties of recruitment caused by the laying-down of unrealistic rates of pay by a Whitehall unaware of local conditions made this an almost impossible task, when it should have been relatively easy, because there had been, as the Governor recalled, unemployment in Singapore.

But besides the Chinese labourers, there were other Chinese, Malaya-born, well-educated, who might have been used in responsible positions and were not. When Brooke-Popham visited Hong Kong early in 1941 he wrote to Sir Arthur Street at the Air Ministry (15 January 1941) that he had been 'very impressed by the Chinese'.[2] 'What they definitely resent, and, I think, with a good deal of justice [he rightly pointed out] is being regarded as an Eastern Race in the early stages of development who must be led and guided by Europeans. They are fully ready to acknowledge our genius for mechanics and make use of our abilities in that respect, but though they might ask for an engineer officer to take technical charge of, say, a repair depot, I do not see them asking for a British Commander and Staff to take charge of the war against Japan.' It would have helped if that recognition had been transferred to the situation in Malaya.

In *The Jungle is Neutral*, Spencer Chapman is very cutting about Malaya Command's lack of interest in guerrilla warfare, though 101 Special Training School had been set up in Malaya to organize it. He attributed the apathy to the fact that so far there had been no example from occupied Europe of a successful resistance movement and many at Headquarters, Far East Command, thought in terms of the First World War. 'The idea of stay-behind parties', he wrote, 'consisting of Europeans and Asiatics seemed an extravagant and impracticable notion . . .'[3]

When Percival read this in Spencer Chapman's book he claimed this was far from the truth, and that he himself was acknowledged to be one of the leading experts in guerrilla warfare, including stay-behind parties, during the Sinn Fein operations in Ireland in 1920/21 'and for some time went about with a price on my head.'[4] Whatever Percival's past, Spencer Chapman remembered chiefly how firmly the authorities in Malaya turned down his guerrilla plans in the months before war began. The highest authorities in Malaya, he claimed, had expressly forbidden plans for irregular warfare. In August 1941 a detailed plan was put up to organize stay-behind parties, to include Chinese, Malays and Indians, selected for reliability and knowledge of the country. They were to supply intelligence and, if over-run by the enemy, would operate against his communications. They were also to organize sabotage and anti-Japanese propaganda in occupied areas. The scheme was discussed on a high level and early in October 'turned down without any alternative suggestions being made.'[5]

The reasons given were half-realistic, half-fantasy. The scheme would be a drain on European man-power, for one thing. This was true, if we bear in mind the still overriding need to keep the Malayan economy working at full blast. White men could not move freely in occupied territory. This was true, as Spencer Chapman later discovered to his cost. Asiatics could not be employed, on the grounds that a scheme which admitted the possibility of enemy penetration would 'have a disastrous psychological effect on the Oriental mind.'[6]

More to the point was the objection to Communism. It was not safe to arm the Chinese since many of them belonged to the Malayan Communist Party, then an illegal organization. Finally, under further pressure, permission was given to create an Intelligence organization as envisaged by Spencer Chapman, but only in the states of Kedah and Kelantan. Permission was given to proceed with the fuller earlier scheme after the Japanese had bombed Singapore, by which time it was too late for an effective plan and an orderly procedure had to give way to hasty improvisation.

Percival objected to this account too. He told Chapman that in July 1941 he (Percival) had been sent for to Government House, where the Governor introduced him to an emissary from the Ministry of Economic Warfare, Killery, who was to be in charge of what Percival was led to believe was a very secret mission from the Foreign Office. It was, of course, the kind of thing that SOE had begun to set up all over occupied Europe. Percival was asked to give Killery facilities but not to enquire about the nature of his work. He agreed. Six weeks later, Percival was again invited to Government House where he was shown a plan devised by Killery in conjunction with certain police officers for stay-behind parties.

Percival admits it took him longer to study this plan than it should have done. It was obviously part of the military plan for defence, in his view, and therefore properly his preserve. He was put off by the implication that further withdrawals of European manpower would be needed, but the plan was not expressly forbidden, and he claims the counter-proposal came from him, viz. to restrict the plan to frontier areas. When more Europeans became available, as a result of the Japanese advance, Percival agreed to the full scheme.[7]

But it will be seen that Percival speaks in terms of European-controlled operations.

As regards the Chinese [he wrote to Chapman] there were many armed Chinese in the Volunteers and we had several Chinese administrative units. We had an Asiatic Recruiting Office in Singapore. On various occasions the Chinese had asked to be allowed to form their own combatant unit of Regulars. This was refused for two reasons. Firstly, we had no arms with which to arm them. Secondly, political considerations came in. The policy of H.M. Government up to the entry of Russia into the war was to support the Kuomintang regime and to keep a tight control on the Communists. If we had had arms and had agreed to the Kuomintang supporters having their own units, it would have been difficult to refuse the Communists. The long-term danger of Communism was fully realised at that time and there was an official reluctance to give them power – a reluctance which has, I think, been fully justified by recent events.[8] [The letter was written on 12 November 1949. He has a point.]

In the event, the only Chinese military organization which played any part in the defence of Malaya and Singapore was the tiny 'Dalforce' of locally enlisted Chinese under British officers, with an initial strength of 2,000. Detachments of this force were allotted to local commanders on the Island, in the last phases, to help patrol mangrove swamps as scouts against possible landings. A company of 'Dalforce' fought alongside 22 Australian Brigade on the west of the Island.

The Official History – dated 1957 – is cool and brief on this organization.[9] A more dramatic account of its activities is given by Ian Morrison, who refers to it as 'Dalley's Desperadoes'. Colonel Dalley was a middle-aged policeman of somewhat unconventional views, who proved to be a tough and skilful commander of a unit which, in the end, in spite of the cautious attitude 'higher up', used both Kuomintang and Communist Chinese, in separate units. Of course by the time they were ready to be put into the front line – 5 February was the day they left their training camps – the surrender was only ten days away. Morrison visited one of the forward companies in the mangrove swamp on the north-west of the Island, going through a battered and jittery Australian company to reach them. He found their three British officers worn out. The Chinese, without uniforms, but looking 'somehow like Chinese soldiers in old photographs of the Boxer rebellion', had exactly seven rounds of ammunition each for their shot-guns, and asked for more. They had stood up well to the bombardment, and were amazingly cheerful.[10]

Had the training of these men begun two years before, Morrison comments, had they been better trained and equipped, their mobility and ability to live off the country would have enabled them to play a vital role in the mainland fighting, of which they were deprived. As it was, their bitter hostility to the Japanese invader laid them open to terrible reprisals after the surrender.

Shenton-Thomas points out that the Chinese took an active part in civil defence and there were many Chinese in the Volunteers, particularly in the Colony (ie Straits Settlements) where they were British subjects if they had been born there. (Chinese born in the Malay States were *not* British subjects but British-protected subjects. The Malay States were not British territory.) China herself had always maintained that every Chinese in Malaya, wherever born, was a Chinese national.

He also pointed out that it had never been the policy of HM Government to 'turn the peoples of the Colonies and Protectorates into soldiers and, even if we had attempted to do so, the Chinese themselves would not have responded.'[11] The evidence is against him here.

The reconciliation between Kuomintang and Communists in Singapore on Christmas Day, 1941, which permitted the functioning of Dalforce, he comments on as follows:

> The important point about the meeting on Xmas Day, 1941, was that the *communists* were at last accepted by the other Chinese political parties, thus making it possible to form a united front. It may not be realized that communism had been active in Malaya for over 20 years and was a constant menace, kept under reasonable control by very efficient Police forces and by the use of the power of banishment. In actual numbers the Party was not very large, but its nuisance value was high, as indeed it is today [ie 1954]. The alliance secured by the meeting was therefore very helpful in the political sense, and saved the police a lot of trouble. More important was the fact that at the meeting a Chinese Mobilization Council was set up and its leader appointed. It did much useful work in watch and ward, and in providing labour.[12]

At the outbreak of war, there were roughly two million Malays in Malaya – about the same number as the Chinese. The Official History describes them, with patronizing paternalism, in terms which will surprise nobody. They are, it says, 'a gentle, dignified but somewhat easy-going race, content to lead a simple life and accept the edicts of their rulers with good grace.'[13] The description accords ill with the acknowledged bravery of the Malay Battalions in the defence of Singapore. When, for example, the Japanese 18 Division attacked along the Pasir Panjang Ridge west of the city, on 13 February, when it was vital to prevent the Alexandra area with its ammunition dumps falling into their hands, the 2 Malay Battalion stood its ground until it was almost annihilated.

Shenton-Thomas's evidence is that a high proportion of the volunteers in the State units was Malay. Malays also enrolled in the various civil defence units, which were almost entirely Malay in the northern States. Time and time again they guided retreating British troops to safety through jungle or rubber plantations. Accusations of fifth-column activities were frequently made against the Malay population after the surrender, but with little foundation in fact. The Inspector-General of Police, in his capacity as Civil Security Officer for all Malaya, put to all commanders the question, 'to what extent has fifth-column activity contributed to our military defeat?' and the general answer was 'not at all'.[14] This is not the same as saying there was *no* fifth-column activity. But if it had been on a massive scale, involving large segments of the population, then the effect on operations would have been considerable. The Japanese confirmed this. Lieutenant-Colonel (as he then was) Fujiwara, when interrogated in Kuala Lumpur in December 1946 about his unit, whose function was to carry out sabotage and pro-Japanese propaganda, admitted that fifth-column activity had been 'militarily of no use whatever before and during the actual fighting.'[15]

The fifth-column scare was overdone, and the rumours which were spread, often by well-intentioned people, no doubt slandered the Malays. 'I found not one single case of fifth-column activity' wrote Gordon Bennett on his return to Australia, and he did not receive a single report of unfriendliness on the part of the people of Malaya during the operations. Yet Colonel Harrison, the GSO 1 of 11 Indian Division, who wrote a vivid and detailed account of its operations, describes the final scenes in Singapore in these terms: 'Fifth-columnists, Japanese infiltrators, and panic-stricken members of our own troops vied with each other in causing alarm and despondency by their shooting matches within the city. And the poor wretched crowded, nerve-wracked [sic] civilians, the tally of their killed and wounded ever mounting, crowded in their hovels or padded aimlessly up and down the streets, hating the soldiers whose presence had brought them to this pitch of misery and longing for the end of it all.'[16] Shenton-Thomas described Harrison's picture as pure imagination. There were, he affirmed, some cases of indiscipline, but very few, and very mild. No Japanese entered the city proper until 15 February. Percival agreed with him. 'Colonel Harrison,' he wrote, 'is one of those writers who loves a little sensationalism, and therefore it is dangerous to quote him.'[17] The passage was quoted in an early draft of the Official History, and is given by Compton Mackenzie in his *Eastern Epic*.[18]

On the other hand, Percival refuses to accept Shenton-Thomas's view of the Malay population. There might be some difference of opinion on what 'fifth-column activity' implied, but there were plenty of people in Malaya, he thought, who helped the Japanese in different ways.

On balance, it seems that both the Chinese and Malays began to show military virtues which somewhat surprised the British Services, but for one reason or another these virtues were never fully exploited against the Japanese. Even after the tremendous fight the Malay Battalions put up on Singapore Island, Colonel Ashmore could write, some months later, 'the Malay, a nice fellow, is soft, idle and does not possess any martial qualities. He is vain, soft living and content to exist under any rule so long as his own way of life goes on. As a race I should say that they lack stamina and courage.'[19] But even Ashmore, who has that terrifying facility for dismissive racial generalizations which seems to afflict certain Englishmen, regrets the lack of use made of the Chinese: 'Had we taken the Chinese into our confidence early in 1941, and made it clear that we trusted them, I am convinced that there would have sprung up a great and valuable citizen force.'[20]

When we come to the Indian element in the Malayan community the picture is rather more disturbing. Most of them were Tamil labourers, who returned to the Madras area, from which they originated, after a three-year stint. They worked on the rubber estates or the railways. There were also Punjabis and Sikhs who joined the Malay Police, or acted as night-watchmen; and Indians of the professional classes. 'There was no racial discrimination in Malaya' says the Official History.[21] This was not what the Indian troops found when they arrived in Malaya to defend it. One of the leading officers of the anti-British Indian National Army, who had once held the King's Commission, Shah Nawaz Khan, wrote: 'Indian officers were not admitted as members of a large number of clubs in Malaya . . . there was an order by the Railway Authorities of Federated Malaya States that an Asiatic could not travel in the same compartment as a European, and the fact that they both held the same rank and belonged to the same unit did not seem to matter . . .'[22]

Nor will it do to attribute such views to those who were later to go over to the Japanese in mind and heart as well as in body. Those who remained loyal to their oath under circumstances demanding superhuman fortitude said much the same thing: 'The Indian officers were insulted at every opportunity,' says Lieutenant-Colonel Mahmood Khan Durrani, 'and often we wondered if this treatment was a natural return for all the enthusiasm with which we offered to defend the British Empire. The harsh and unjust dealings of the British officers awakened a sense of national pride and resentment at such injustice. . . . The biased treatment of Indians by British officers and the general discontent of Indian troops of all ranks was universal in Malaya.'[23]

The evacuation policy seemed to emphasize racial discrimination. In sublime unawareness, the Official History reports the Brigade Commander's decision to withdraw from Kota Bharu after the first landings:

> Key, after a personal reconnaissance, realized that the new line was not suited for prolonged defence and that his troops were too extended. Since all European women and children, the Sultan of Kelantan and his household, and many others had already left Kota Bharu, he had no further need to cover the town.[24]

But when a similar evacuation took place in Penang, there were ructions among the Indian community in Singapore.

Brigadier C. A. Lyon was in command at Penang, which was bombed by the Japanese on 11 December, without any opposition. There were no fighter aircraft in northern Malaya to oppose them, and the island was entirely without anti-aircraft defences. Aircraft were only stationed nearby when 453 Squadron arrived on the mainland opposite, at Butterworth, two days later in support of III Corps, and shot down five Japanese raiders. But the damage was serious. Half the town was ablaze, the police deserted their posts, and the labour force vanished. As the Japanese came southward through Kedah, it was obvious that Penang would soon be under attack from land forces too, and the two battalions which had been intended for its defence were no longer available after the defeat at Jitra. It was a valuable port, its stocks were enormous, and it was the terminal point of the ocean cables linking Malaya with Ceylon and India. It was nevertheless decided – sensibly enough – that Penang could not be held if the position on the mainland was lost. If that happened, the garrison and stores were to be withdrawn by sea.

The day before this decision was reached by the War Council in Singapore (14 December), the Resident Counsellor, Forbes, and the Fortress Commander decided that all European women and children should be evacuated with the sick and wounded. They were moved on the night of the 13th but, says the official historian, 'evacuation of Asian civilians was not considered feasible, since there was no possibility of providing transport for large numbers.'[25] Lyon, who talked at some length to the American journalist Cecil Brown after leaving Penang, declared 'We would have done no good by staying there. I know there is going to be a lot of criticism both about the native population and the military evacuation, but I did the only thing that could be done.'

'Did you get everyone off?' asked Brown. 'Well, it was a bit confused,' was the lame answer. 'All of our troops came away and six of the Asiatic volunteers. Five hundred of the Asiatic volunteers stayed with their rifles waiting for the Japs. They weren't going to resist. There was no native evacuation.'[26]

Not only was there no native evacuation. Many of the 'natives' stuck to their posts. When the practically deserted town was evacuated by the military, 850 members of Penang's ARP Corps were still on duty. After the bombing the administration of the town depended on them. They dealt with traffic control, food distribution, police work, and the Auxiliary Fire Service. The telephone operators worked all day and all night until the power station was blown up. Most of these operators were either Eurasian or Chinese. The members of the Medical Auxiliary Services also, both European and Asiatic, stuck to their jobs. The European sisters were compulsorily evacuated against their will on 16 December. That same day, Shenton-Thomas wired to Forbes, 'In any evacuation, preference should be given to those who are essential to the war effort without racial discrimination.'[27] But by then it was too late. The discriminatory evacuation had taken place. Shenton-Thomas was convinced this was the result of a purely military order, but he was wrong. The Resident Counsellor and Lyon consulted together before issuing the order.[28] To make matters worse, Duff Cooper gave a broadcast on 22 December in which he said the majority of the population of Penang had been evacuated. In fact, it was only the small European *minority*. His listeners were not slow to recognize his gaffe, as Duff Cooper himself did when the Governor pointed it out to him the following day.[29]

'Penang was a very discreditable affair and had a shocking effect on morale throughout Malaya,' Shenton-Thomas wrote years later.[30] Percival was, on the whole, unrepentant: 'In theory, Sir Shenton-Thomas is right' he commented on the Governor's no-discrimination policy, 'but in practice that is not so easy. In the case of Penang, there was not sufficient transport to move the whole lot, nor were they wanted in Singapore which was already becoming congested.'[31] On 22 December, Brooke-Popham, re-

alizing the rumours that had spread about the Penang
evacuation, held a general meeting for civic leaders and
representatives of the various communities in Singapore
to try to counteract them. His manner was far from calculated to inspire confidence. He appeared hesitant, unsure, and dealt in vague generalities. After he had sketched
the deteriorating military situation, a leader of the Indian
community jumped to his feet and shouted 'We are ready
to fight and die for the defence of Malaya, but we want to
be sure that you British also are ready to fight and die for
this country! We want to be assured that you are not going to abandon us the way the Asiatics of Penang were
abandoned. If there is going to be an evacuation of
Singapore, we want it to be on the basis of equality, not
just the English people.' When Brooke-Popham assured
him that the Asiatics would receive the same treatment as
the British, 'That's all I want to know,' was the answer.
'We will fight beside the British, but we don't want to be
discriminated against.'[32] After Penang, the fear of being
abandoned was understandably strong, particularly among
the Indian community. And among the Chinese too. 'The
sense of being the victims of a base desertion rankled in
the minds of all of us,' wrote one Chinese after the war.
'The memory of that unseemly stampeding from Penang
still had its sting, of launches cleared of Asiatic women at
the point of the bayonet, and of our chagrin and disgust
when, going to the railway station to meet relatives and
friends, we saw no Asiatics in that wilderness of Europeans,
whom the Governor was receiving as if they were
"conquering heroes come".'[33]

These episodes are merely indications of the racial
undertone of much of the campaign. The Japanese brought
it into the open once the British had surrendered, and the
fate of the Indian Army in Malaya changed hands.

For this is the real impact of the loss of Singapore: not
a strategic one, but a moral one. The British relationship
with those races of Asia they protected began to crumble,
as the Japanese moved down the Peninsula. The
Europeans moved out, the Asians were left in the path of

the invader. Appropriately enough, then, when Percival capitulated, his Indian troops were separated from their officers, and handed over to a renegade captain of the 1/14 Punjab Regiment, who had surrendered to the Japanese in the first week of fighting. Round him, the Japanese hoped to build an army of Indians which would fight against the British and speed the collapse of British power in India.

At the core of this attempt was the tireless Military Attaché in Bangkok, Colonel Tamura. In 1940 he had made contacts with a group of disaffected Sikhs in Bangkok, under Pritam Singh. An emissary from Imperial General Headquarters, Major Fujiwara Iwaiichi, took up the contact in 1941, and, with Pritam Singh's help, began to run Indians into northern Malaya on intelligence missions. Needless to say, he is nowhere referred to in the British Official History.[34] These Indians, and the few un-armed Japanese officers he brought with him, were organized into the Fujiwara Organization or 'F Kikan'. When war broke out, Fujiwara was in Bangkok, and sped at once to the Malayan border to join Yamashita's 25 Army. Throughout the campaign, his men followed the army, separating Indian prisoners from the rest, shepherding them into separate POW cages or allowing them considerable liberty in the rear areas, to show them that the Japanese were the enemy of Britain, not of India.

When the final surrender came, 45,000 Indian troops were herded into Farrar Park in Singapore. At 2 pm on 17 February 1942, a British lieutenant-colonel appeared on a balcony in front of them, accompanied by Mohan Singh and Fujiwara. 'From today,' he called out over a microphone, 'we are all prisoners of war. I now, on behalf of the British Government, hand you over to the Japanese Government, whose orders you will obey as you have been doing ours.'[35] The nominal rolls were handed over to Fujiwara, who then declared, 'On behalf of the Japanese Government, I now hand you over to the General Officer Commanding, Mohan Singh, who shall have power of life and death over you.' The British officer said nothing, but left the balcony. Fujiwara went on to make a long speech, which was translated into English, then into Hindustani:

> Japan is fighting for the liberation of the Asiatic nations which have been for so long trodden under the cruel heels of British Imperialism. Japan is the liberator and the friend of Asiatics. Japan wishes to inaugurate a New Order in East Asia. This new order will take the form of a Co-Prosperity Sphere of East Asia, which will consist of free and equal nations, co-operating with each other for the common good. The independence of India is essential for the independence of Asia and the peace of the world; and it is the duty of Indians to free themselves. Japan is willing to give all-out aid and assistance to Indians in East Asia to achieve their aspirations.[86]

Mohan Singh spoke in the same vein, and told the troops that the Japanese proposed founding an 'Azad Hind Fauj', an 'Indian National Army', from amongst Indian soldiers and civilians in the Far East. Some of the Indians yelled out 'Inqilab zindabad!' ('Long live the revolution!') when he had finished, but most were morose and silent. The idea of joining the Japanese to fight their own kith and kin did not appeal to them much. Among the officers in particular, there were many who knew Mohan Singh and wondered why on earth the Japanese had selected this very average officer to be commanding general of their new force. But in the weeks that followed, as hopelessness at their position set in – and often, in many cases, with the idea of joining the INA in order to be in a more favourable position to escape to India – of the 65,000 Indian troops who had been handed over to the Japanese, 25,000 agreed to join the Indian National Army.

Its future developments – the take-over by Subhas Chandra Bose in 1943, the Japanese defeat in Burma in which the INA shared, the trial of its officers in the Red Fort at Delhi after the war – are no part of this book. But that the men of the INA were, in the first place, the victims of racial prejudice which shook their loyalty to the British Crown is shown quite clearly by the letter which the Commander-in-Chief in India, Auchinleck, wrote at the time of the INA trials to formation commanders who had criticized his policy of leniency:

> It is quite wrong to adopt the attitude that because these men had taken service in a British-controlled Indian Army, therefore their loyalties must be the same as those of British soldiers . . . they had no real loyalty or patriotism towards Britain as Britain, not as we understand loyalty . . . The policy of segregation of Indian officers into separate units, the differential treatment in respect of pay and terms of service as compared with the British officer, and the preju-dice and lack of manners of some – by no means all – British officers and their wives, all went to produce a very deep and bitter feeling of racial discrimination in the minds of the Indian officers, who were naturally Nationalists, keen to see India standing on her own legs and not to be ruled from Whitehall for ever. It is no use shutting one's eyes to the fact that any Indian officer worth his salt is a Nationalist; though this does not mean that he is necessarily anti-British. If he is anti-British this is as often as not due to his faulty handling and treatment by his British officer comrades.[37]

That the Japanese were fully aware of the advantages to be reaped from British policies – or rather attitudes – of racial discrimination is obvious. It also goes a long way back in their modern history. The old Field-Marshal, Yamagata Aritomo, had spoken in August 1914 of Japan one day leading the coloured races of the world against their white overlords. That the dream survived is shown, indirectly, by the propaganda use the Japanese made of the British defeat at Singapore. Percival himself was later to realize the full force of the rising nationalism of Asia, and the role they played in his defeat. 'The more I look back at it,' he wrote in 1962, 'the more I feel that the spirit of nationalism, which was then in its infancy, had quite a considerable effect on the campaign. Early in 1941, Mr Nehru had toured Malaya and preached nationalism to the Indians. The Japanese came along with the cry "Asia for the Asiatics". Many of the Asiatics sat on the fence. I am convinced it had its effect.'[38]

I have in my possession a Japanese soldier's diary, picked up on the battlefield at Mawlu in Burma on 18 April 1944. It contains the usual items: war songs, Imperial proclamations, exhortations to a soldier's duty, maps of East Asia, introductions to the customs of various Asian peoples. But its illustrations show something else. One page has a line drawing of British POWs, head and shoulders; another the triumphant Yamashita facing Percival across the surrender table; overleaf is a pen drawing of the downcast 'defeated general Percival'; overleaf again a painting by the war artist Tsuruda Gorō, of British and Australian troops, naked to the waist, sweeping the streets of Singapore – the masters of the East performing the most menial tasks.

No purely military or strategic advantage can be compared to what those illustrations represented not only for the Japanese soldier who carried the diary, but also for the peoples of Asia. Clumsily, cruelly, hesitantly, he liberated them from the domination of Great Britain and her European allies. Even when Japan was defeated, she had made it impossible for the Allies to return to Asia on their own terms.

XII

Afterthoughts

It would be a mistake to think that the *bilan* in the battle for Malaya tells entirely against the British. Superficially, this may seem to be the right verdict: Britain lost her prestige in the East when she lost Singapore, and the loss of her Empire followed. Of course there were other contributory causes, including the lack of the will to retain an Empire in the first place; but these causes were interlinked. Yet, in spite of her victory, Japan lost something too.

One result, which can be traced along a very devious line of causality, was her ultimate defeat in Burma. The commander of 18 Division was Lieutenant-General Mutaguchi Renya. He had been involved in the Marco Polo Bridge incident in 1937 and regarded the conquest of Singapore as the second notch in his role in Japan's hegemony of East Asia. First China, then Malaya. What would be the third and last triumph? When his division was moved to Burma, and then when he was promoted to command XV Army in Burma, the answer was plain: the conquest of India.

This was no part of the plan put forward by Imperial General Headquarters. Burma was merely a buckler against the anticipated British attempt to re-take Japan's eastern possessions. It was not to be a springboard for further offensives. Then the success – relatively speaking – of the first Wingate expedition showed that a large force could cross the Chin Hills. What the British could do one way, the Japanese could do the other. Had not the triumph of Singapore shown the Japanese superiority over the British? Mutaguchi brushed aside the staff's objections based on lack of supplies. Malaya had shown this was no problem. The Japanese always managed to capture enough British supplies to keep going. Food, guns, ammunition had been there for the taking. Why should India be any different? Mutaguchi did not need the political pressure applied by Subhas Chandra Bose upon the Japanese authorities to invade India. The March on Delhi was the third Japanese victory in which he would play a major part.

He miscalculated. His troops fought with bitter bravery, but they did not succeed in capturing the British base at Imphal. 'Churchill rations' did not fall into their hands as easily as they had in Malaya. The two years between the fall of Singapore and the battle of Imphal had given time and opportunity to train an Indian Army that was more than a match for Mutaguchi, in determination, tactics and equipment. By the time his offensive was called off, with himself, most of his generals, and nearly every single member of his staff sacked, the March on Delhi had become what the Japanese called 'White Bone Road' where they left behind over 50,000 dead.

The over-confidence Mutaguchi had acquired in Malaya was undoubtedly a major factor in that defeat. But, like the British, the Japanese also suffered a moral defeat in their Asian campaigns. It is, of course, unfashionable to refer to atrocities more than thirty years after they occurred and there is a sound human instinct which recognizes faults on both sides and desires to forget. On the other hand, cruelty may be a method. On this score, perhaps it is in order to quote an ally of the Japanese, the INA brigade commander, Shah Nawaz Khan:

> The Japanese, in order to lower the morale and to shatter the nerves of British officers and men, had resorted to methods which were, by modern standards of civilization, quite brutal. They would tie captured prisoners to trees and then proceed to bayonet them one by one in the presence of their comrades. In some cases, they would ask the Indian prisoners to bayonet their British Officers. Those who refused to do so were themselves bayonetted by the Japanese. The Japanese soldiers were trained in such a manner that they took pleasure in this sort of work and treated it as a good pastime. While they were indulging in this sordid sport, the Japanese would release a few of the prisoners who were awaiting their turn to be bayonetted and send them back to

the British lines to tell these tales to their comrades and
thereby shatter the nerves of British officers and men.[1]

The campaign provided any number of such incidents.
Compton Mackenzie describes the massacre of prisoners
at Parit Sulong on 20 January 1942 when 110 Australian
and thirty-five Indian POWs were beheaded. For this
crime, Lieutenant-General Nishimura, GOC Imperial
Guards Division, was found guilty in June 1950 and
sentenced to death. His defence counsel claimed that the
survivors of the Guards divisional staff had 'manoeuvred
to put the whole of the responsibility of the massacre on
him.'[2] The commander of 5 Guards Regiment at Parit
Sulong was Colonel (later Major-General) Iwakuro Hideo.
When Iwakuro later wrote about the Parit Sulong battle,
no reference was made to the massacre:

> Our unit reached the bridge over the Sulong River and the
> Yoshida Battalion of 4th Imperial Guards made contact
> with it . . . I shall never forget the historic moment when
> this took place. The surviving Australian and Punjabis,
> about 300 men, were taken prisoner by our regiment. In the
> rubber plantation and in the village of Parit Sulong, at least
> 200 to 300 corpses lay scattered around, and on the surface
> of the River Sulong the bodies of dead Australians, with
> their brown boots, and dead Indians, with black boots,
> floated without number.[3]

Any reader of that text is bound to think the floating
bodies were battle casualties.

There were many other examples. The patients in the
Alexandra Hospital in Singapore were bayonetted when
the troops of 18 Division broke into it. Later, after the surrender, untold numbers of Chinese were massacred in an
attempt to cow the Singapore Chinese community into
submission. In all their campaigns, similar incidents
formed a pattern, as did their treatment of prisoners. The
episode which has received most publicity in this connection is, of course, that of the Burma-Siam Railway on
which worked prisoners taken in the Malayan campaign
and at Singapore. Not all the survivors from this terrifying
encounter with the malice of man and the horrors of the

virgin forest bear the Japanese continued ill-will. A good deal of magnanimity has been shown, and there is, of course, another side to the story, which has been written by David Nelson in *The Story of Changi*.[4] To Nelson is due the invaluable information derived after the war from the painstaking records he managed to keep of the prisoners in camp, their destination and ultimate fate, when known. He does not hesitate to lay the blame for deaths of prisoners not only on the Japanese but also on Allied ships and aircraft which sank transports carrying prisoners: '180 were lost when the ship *van Waerwyck* was torpedoed in Malacca Straits, and more than 1,000 were lost in each of the disasters involving the *Zyunyo Maru* off the coast of Sumatra and the *Ryuku Maru* in the vicinity of Bataan in the Philippines. These are only some of the losses, largely by the hand of our own people.'[5] Nelson ends his book with appreciation of the courtesy, tolerance and understanding of certain named Japanese officers and men and concludes:

> It is a pity the relieving troops felt obliged to destroy a memorial *torii* erected by the Nipponese Army on a hillock at Bukit Timah in memory of the fallen. Friend or foe, each was serving his country.[6]

Similar views have been expressed by Major Basil Peacock,[7] who worked on the Burma-Siam Railway, and by the novelist Laurens van der Post.[8]

What is missing, in the official records on the Japanese side, is some acknowledgement of the enormity of what is here being forgiven. A few pages in the account of the Imphal battles deals with the supply problems of the Japanese in Burma and the construction of the railway as an attempt to overcome them.[9] The decision to build the railway was taken by Imperial General Headquarters on 20 June 1942, the length to be 400 kilometres from Non Pladuk in Thailand to Thanbyuzayat in Burma, at a cost of seven million yen, employing a railway HQ, two railway regiments and a railway material stores, the labour to be found locally and from POWs. Orders to start were given to Southern Army Railway Unit in August 1942, and the date of completion was given as the end of 1943. Fearing a counter-attack to re-take Burma by the Allies after the end of the rainy season in 1943, this date was brought forward by four months. Cholera broke out in the labour camps in April 1943, starting at Niike near the frontier and spreading to the other camps. During the work, 10,000 Japanese troops, 55,000 Allied POWs, and 135,000 Asian labourers were involved. The labour force, through inadequate supplies and over-work, had little physical resistance with which to face cholera and the death rate rose quickly, reaching a peak in June 1943, when there were 6,000 sick of whom 4,000 died. Fear of cholera caused numerous desertions amongst the local labourers, and the work was held up. The GOC of the Railway Unit at the start, Major-General Shimoda, and a staff officer, Major Irie, were killed when their aircraft crashed during a survey of the line. Shimoda was succeeded by Major-General Takazaki from the No. 1 Railway Staff in Manchuria, who went sick with malaria in April, and was in turn succeeded by Major-General Ishida in June, by which time the prospects for completion looked very dismal indeed. The Army GHQ in Tokyo sent out Colonel Kato, chief of the Railway Bureau (No. 9 Bureau) to make an inspection on the spot, as a result of which the works period was extended by two months to November 1943. After July the cholera began to drop, supplies improved, and the work began to go smoothly again. In spite of innumerable difficulties the work was completed on 25 October 1943, when, under the protection of anti-aircraft guns, an opening ceremony was held in the presence of Major-General Ishida and his staff, a final memorial sleeper, in ebony, being laid by the two Railway Regiment commanders, Colonel Imai and Colonel Sasaki.

'The voices of all those present shouting, "Banzai!" echoed throughout the dense jungle'. As well they might. I have abridged this account,[10] but have reproduced faithfully the mood and contents of these pages. Admittedly, these Official Histories are intended as operational narratives. Somewhere, though, surely, an expression of regret might not be out of place?

This is what I mean by the moral defeat of Japan. During the Russo-Japanese War, her troops had a reputation not merely for courage but for decency. At some time in the four decades separating the two wars, that disappeared. The generals, of course, dismiss this, and say that Hiroshima and Nagasaki even up accounts. Possibly they do. But it is at least arguable that the use of the atomic bomb might *not have been able* to be considered, if, in the eyes of the Allies – peoples, not governments – the Japanese had not, at this moment in their history, put themselves beyond the pale. 'The kind of slaughter and violence that we have seen in this war,' said the old Field-Marshal, Hata Shunroku, in 1946, 'was in my experience very rare during the Russo-Japanese war. In modern war, the whole people are mobilized. Hence the majority of the troops correspond to the people as a whole. An army in which scandals and atrocities occur in great numbers, must surely reflect a decline in public morality?'[11] Is it not, on the other hand, disingenuous for a member of the military caste to try and shuffle off responsibility on to the Japanese as a whole? The novelist, Ōoka Shōhei, when discussing the return of Lieutenant Onoda from the Philippines, referred to Japan's no-surrender tradition and the contemptuous attitude towards prisoners, and pointed out that in the Russo-Japanese war a Japanese *general* had been taken prisoner and suffered no obloquy in consequence.[12] It follows that the Japanese Army, if not the people as a whole, underwent a moral decline, most probably as a result of the fighting in the China. The attitudes derived therefrom dictated their behaviour elsewhere in East Asia, beginning with the campaign in Malaya. This behaviour in turn created a stereotype of barbarous cruelty which it has taken the industrious post-war Japanese a long time to live down; if indeed, the process *is* complete. What they lost, to achieve their victory, may well have balanced what the British lost, to undergo their defeat.

APPENDIX I

Casualties

I BRITISH

a. British forces in the campaign numbered approximately 80,000 in the battle for the Peninsula, between 8 December 1941 and 31 January 1942. Casualties inflicted by the Japanese numbered 25,000, including 8,000 prisoners. Five brigades were annihilated.

b. British forces in the Singapore Island battle, including those which escaped from the mainland, amounted to over 100,000 men, most of whom were taken prisoner.

c. Equipment lost to the Japanese:
   i. Malaya

Aircraft	13
Armoured cars	50 approx.
Cars	3,600 „
Lorries	800 „
Artillery	330 pieces approx.
Heavy and light machine-guns	550 „ „

   ii. Singapore

Fortress artillery	54 pieces approx.
Mountain and field guns	300 approx.
Mortars	100 „
Armoured fighting vehicles	200 „
Cars	10,000 „
Lorries	1,000 „
Aircraft	10

Total British losses in manpower: 138,708, of which over 130,000 were prisoners. The British Official History breaks this figure down as follows:

Great Britain	38,496 men
Australia	18,490 „
India	67,340 „
Volunteers	14,382 „

2 JAPANESE*

Japanese troops taking part in the campaign numbered approximately 35,000 men.

a. Casualties in Malaya (8 December 1941 – 31 January 1942):

Unit	Killed	Wounded
TOTAL 25 ARMY	1,793	2,772
5 Division	695	1,292
Imperial Guards	900 killed & wounded approx.	
Takumi Force	1,000 ,, ,, ,, ,,	
Koba Force	100 ,, ,, ,, ,,	

b. Casualties in Singapore (two-fifths of these were sustained before landing):

Unit	Killed	Wounded
TOTAL 25 ARMY	1,713	3,378
5 Division	541	1,166
Imperial Guards	211	468
18 Division	938	1,708
Units attached to Army	23	36

Total killed:	3,506
Total wounded:	6,150
Total killed and wounded:	9,656

By formations:		
5 Division killed and wounded	3,694
18 Division ,, ,, ,,	3,646
Imperial Guards ,, ,,	1,579

3 THE CAMPAIGN

Campaign days:	55
Campaign distance:	1,100 kilometres (average per day 20 kms)
Engagements:	95 (average per day 2)
Movement by sea:	650 kilometres
Chief bridges repaired:	250 (average per day 5)

These can be briefly summed up: at a cost of 3,500 dead, and using three of its divisions, the Japanese Army conquered Malaya and Singapore in eight weeks, inflicting upon the British forces casualties in killed, wounded and prisoners, of nearly 140,000 men, and capturing immense booty.

* Discrepancies occur in these figures, the variations depending on which headquarters did the counting, and when.

APPENDIX II

Typescript, with manuscript alterations (indicated by square brackets), of a lecture delivered by Percival in January 1937 to officers taking part in a scheme or exercise on the Defence of Singapore. At this date Percival was a colonel, and GSOI to the GOC Malaya Command, Major-General W. G. S. (later General Sir William) Dobbie. The lecture is filed with the Percival Papers in the Imperial War Museum.

SECRET

MALAYA COMMAND

THE STRATEGICAL PROBLEMS
OF SINGAPORE

Lecture by
Col. A. E. Percival, D.S.O., O.B.E., M.C.

1. SCOPE OF LECTURE

You will remember that in my last lecture I discussed some aspects of Combined Operations from the point of view of the offensive. This morning I propose to discuss, first of all, the strategical position occupied by Singapore in the Far Eastern theatre and, later, to deal with some of the major factors which influence the problem of the defence of Singapore.

2. OBJECT OF THE SINGAPORE FORTRESS

Let us start by clearing our minds as to the object of this Singapore Fortress. Everybody, of course, knows Natural that we are here primarily to ensure the security of Strategical the Naval Base, but I think a good many people do Position of not realise that, even if there was no Naval Base here, Singapore yet a good many of us would very probably still be here to prevent other nations seizing this particular place and establishing a Naval Base here themselves. The fact is that Singapore is by nature endowed with such wonderful natural strategical advantages that,

272

in these days of international competition, somebody is bound to have it. You will find this is a point which a great many of the civilians here do not realise. One frequently hears them say "Oh, but we never wanted you to come here. We were much happier here before you came". This, in fact, is at the root of the constant struggle which has gone on in the past and still goes on here to get the Local Authorities to grant proper facilities for the installation of the defences.

I propose now to examine in rather greater detail these two reasons for our being here, i.e.

(a) Protection of the Naval Base,

(b) Denial of this strategical position to an enemy.

3. *THE NAVAL BASE*

Let us consider first of all the significance and importance of this Naval Base. What is a Naval Base? It has been described as *"a Naval Harbour from which a fully equipped fleet can strike"*. This definition describes many of its characteristics with an economy of words. Defences, docks, workshops, stores, equipment, fuel and a position from which operations can be conducted against an enemy are all implied in it. In short, *maintenance and operations* are its chief functions. The definition, however, is not completely adequate, for bases have an important defensive role also. They are havens where naval and merchant ships can take shelter, where transports and supply vessels can gather in safety before they are convoyed to their next destination – in fact barracks from which the Navy and police can protect our communications as well as harass those of the enemy. Defended ports have almost these attributes, but lack the facilities for docking and repairs which a base provides. As is well known, the great point about the Singapore Base when it is completed will be that it will be the only base East of Malta where our capital ships will be able to be put into dry dock and be repaired. In passing, I should like to make it clear that, apart altogether from enemy action, a ship loses speed and in consequence efficiency if it is not regularly docked and cleaned.

Why is it necessary to have a Naval Base at all in

What is a Naval Base?

Defended Ports

273

this Far Eastern theatre? I think to understand this problem properly it is necessary to go back a little to **Historical** past history. Before the emergence of Japan from her isolation towards the end of the last century there was, if we except Russia, no Naval Power in the Far East and, if we had gone to war with Russia, we should, I suppose, not have come all the way out here to fight a Naval action with her.

[During the opening years of this century we did from time to time maintain a Force of 6 Battleships in Chinese waters but these were withdrawn after the conclusion of our Treaty with JAPAN.]

Prior to Great Prior to the Great War we always had a two-Power **War** Naval standard, which meant that we could compete with the combined fleets of any two other Naval Powers and, of course, it also meant that, if we were at war with one Power only, it would only be necessary to concentrate for a Naval battle a portion of our total Naval strength. Of course, in those days we had an alliance with Japan but, even if we had been at war with her, we could, without the Singapore Naval Base, have concentrated sufficient capital ships in Far Eastern waters at any one time to ensure the necessary superiority. Docking and repair facilities at Hong Kong were sufficient to meet the needs of the Fleet of those times.

The Washington By the Washington Treaty after the War we ac- **Treaty** cepted a 5 : 5 : 3 standard in Capital Ships as between ourselves, the U.S.A. and Japan. The actual ratio agreed upon were 15 for the U.S.A. and ourselves and 10 for Japan. It was further agreed that, so long as the Treaty remained in force, neither of us would build any new battleships, the life of a battleship being fixed at 24 years. It is of special interest at the present time to note that this Treaty expired on the 31st December last and that work on our first new battleship commenced on the 1st January.

At first sight it may appear that the ratio of 5 : 5 : 3 was ample to enable us, provided we were not in- **Superiority at** volved elsewhere, to produce ample superiority at the **the Vital Point** vital point whenever we wanted to. But in fact this was not really the case. In the first place, it would, I suggest, only be in very exceptional circumstances that the British Public would agree to the whole of the Battle Fleet leaving Home waters and coming to the Far East. Certainly it could not happen as things are to-day. But let us suppose that in reasonably favourable conditions it was agreed to retain only one or two ships in Home waters. Again, it would seem that the margin would be ample. But here again another effect of the Washington Treaty comes in. If you are not allowed to build any new ships, it follows that all your ships are getting old at the same time, and an old ship, of course, requires much more repair than does a new ship. As a consequence, at any given time one or more of our battleships are in dock undergoing repair. You may say that the same applies to a potential aggressor. That is quite true, but an aggressor could so adjust his programme that he had the maximum number of ships available at a given time and he could select a time when we had the maximum number under repair. So the margin would be still further reduced.

I have dwelt on this aspect of the situation at some length to bring me to the point which I want to make now. It is this. Unless we have a base in the Far East **Reason for Naval** where our biggest ships can dock and be cleaned and **Base** repaired, we should be forced, unless we were prepared to accept reduced efficiency, to send them right back to Malta, and we should thus, from time to time, be forced to accept loss of the necessary numerical superiority. [Repairs of course will include both ordinary routine repairs and possibly after action repairs which may involve the expeditious repairs of numbers of vessels simultaneously.] Hence, when the Washington Treaty was signed, it became more necessary than ever to have a Naval Base in the Far East.

CONSTRUCTION OF NAVAL BASE

In 1923 the Imperial Conference drew attention to "*the deep interest of the Commonwealth of Australia, the Dominion of New Zealand and India, in the provision of a naval base at Singapore, as essential for ensuring the mobility necessary to provide for the security of the territories and trade of the Empire in*

Eastern waters". A floating dock was brought out from England and preliminary work was started in 1924. The progress of the work has been subject to many vicissitudes in accordance with the policy of the Government in power in England at the time. In 1929, under the Labour Government, work was suspended in accordance with their disarmament policy, except as regards the graving dock upon which they allowed work to continue on the plea that it might in any case be useful for ordinary maritime shipping.

About that time a considerable amount of pressure was brought by Australia and New Zealand for work on the base to be continued, as a result of which the Imperial Conference re-affirmed the policy of the ultimate establishment of a naval base at Singapore. Finally about 1933/4, when re-armament had become the order of the day, orders were issued for work on the base to be resumed at full speed.

4. THE STRATEGICAL POSITION OF SINGAPORE

We have seen that the primary object of the Naval Base is to enable the Battle Fleet to operate with the maximum efficiency in Far Eastern waters, so I think it may be as well to consider now why it is necessary for the Fleet to be able to operate in these waters. The key to this problem is contained in the resolution of the 1923 Imperial Conference which I have just quoted to you – "To provide for the security of the territories and trade of the Empire in Eastern waters". I think the interests to be secured can really be divided into three categories:

Why Fleet must be able to operate in Far Eastern Waters

(a) British lives, property and trade in China,
(b) The trade routes to and from Australia and New Zealand and the Southern Pacific Islands,
(c) The trade routes to and from India, Burma, Malaya and the adjoining territories.

China As regards China it has been estimated that the value of the British interests in that country aggregates something in the nature of 500 million pounds sterling. The loss of those interests, of course, besides the financial aspect, would be a very serious blow to British prestige. Those interests are centred mostly

276

in the Hong Kong – Canton area, the Yangtze Valley and the Tientsin Area.

When the decision to have a naval base in the Far East to protect the interests I have enumerated was taken there was, as you may remember, a considerable amount of discussion as to where it should be situated. The alternatives were Singapore, Hong Kong and Port Darwin. The latter, although it has many natural advantages and was naturally strongly advocated by a section of the Australian Press, was considered too far removed from the normal channels of communication between the Pacific and the Indian Ocean to be the ideal place for the principal British Naval Base in the Far East. A glance at the map will show that, without going South of Australia, there are only three gateways between the Pacific and the Indian Ocean. These are from South to North the Timor Sea, [and the passage leading to it from the East] the Sunda Strait between Java and Sumatra, and the Straits of Malacca between Sumatra and Malaya. Clearly the shortest route between East and West is the most important, and that of course is the Malacca Channel guarded by the Island of Singapore. Port Darwin is, of course, an important base and is to-day being fortified by the Australian Government, but as between Singapore and Port Darwin there can be no question as to which is the best position for the main British Base.

In 1824 Sir Stamford Raffles, writing to the Duchess of Somerset, said "You take my word for it. This is by far the most important station in the East, and, as far as naval superiority and commercial interests are concerned, of much higher value than whole continents." After giving his opinion as to the fortifications required he concluded "These defences, together with a Martello Tower on Deep Water Point will, in my judgement, render the Settlement capable of maintaining a good defence". It is of interest to note also that his vision went further than Singapore for he advocated the establishment of a similar settlement on Billiton Island astride the Straits of Sunda.

The next controversy, and a more bitter one, was

Situation of Base

Port Darwin

Sir S. Raffles View

277

Hong Kong between the relative merits of Singapore and Hong Kong. Again let us remember that we could only afford one really up-to-date naval base in the Far East. Many people contended that the proper place for it was Hong Kong, mainly on the grounds that Singapore was too far removed from our vital interests in China, so I think we might consider for a moment the relative claims of these two places and I will try to show to what extent the one is complementary to the other.

There were, I think, two main objections to the selection of Hong Kong as the site for our main Naval Base. The first was that it lay within the zone in which we had agreed, under the terms of the Limitations of Washington Treaty, not to develop our fixed de-Washington fences; and therefore if a base had been constructed Treaty there it would not have been possible to give it adequate protection. Secondly, it was considered by the H.K. experts that Hong Kong was too close to the Japanese Too Close Bases in Formosa and the Pescadores to make it a to Formosa suitable site for our main naval base. It does not and require much imagination to-day to see how very Pescadores correct this view was. Hong Kong is already within range of shore-based aircraft operating from Southern Formosa and it is fairly certain that in the next few years it will be within range of aircraft from almost anywhere in Formosa. The air defences of Hong Kong itself must necessarily be limited by the extent of British territory there and the geographical difficulties of finding suitable landing grounds. Thus, if our principal naval base had been constructed there, we should to-day have found ourselves in an almost intolerable position. There is therefore no question, I submit, as to which is the better site as between Singapore and Hong Kong.

Many critics then contended that, if Singapore was to be the main base, it was useless spending money on H.K. As the defence of Hong Kong. This argument, I suggest, Advanced lost sight of the fact that a Fleet based on Singapore Base to would be unable to operate in the East China Sea Singapore without an advanced base somewhere on the China Coast. Hong Kong is clearly the most suitable place for this advanced base and so, if we once surrendered it, the first step in any operations for the defence of our trade in China would necessarily be the recapture of Hong Kong. This would be a difficult and lengthy operation, necessitating as it probably would the establishment of shore-based aircraft on the South China Coast. In fact, the very difficulty of the operation might make the British Government sceptical of undertaking it.

From the point of view of the defence of Singapore the Fortress of Hong Kong in our hands is of great value, because light naval forces and air forces based on Hong Kong are in a position to act as distant reconnaissance forces for the Singapore Fortress and, in the event of an attack on Singapore, would be in a favourable position to harass the Lines of Communication of the attacker. — Defence Point of View

I hope I have said enough to show you that, from the point of view of our strategical position in the Far East, the retention of Hong Kong is of the utmost importance.

I said just now that one of the principal functions of the Singapore Fortress was to protect the trade routes to and from Australia and New Zealand, and the trade routes to and from India, Burma, Malaya and the adjoining territories. I think perhaps the best way to grasp the real significance of this will be to consider what the position would be if Singapore fell into the hands of an enemy. First of all, of course, the loss of Singapore would be a very serious, probably fatal blow, to our *prestige* among Eastern races. Then, it would give the enemy direct access to the Indian Ocean, around the shores of which lies three-quarters of the land territory of the British Commonwealth and more than three-quarters of its inhabitants. It has been estimated that through the Indian Ocean every year passes a *thousand million pounds* worth of trade. The distances of the following focal areas from Singapore show how vulnerable this trade would become to hostile forces based in the Singapore area: — Protection of Trade Routes

Calcutta and Colombo....................1500 miles
Madras.......................................1700 ,,
Port Darwin.................................1800 ,,

Rangoon......................................1130　　"
Nearest Point on the Perth –
Colombo Sea Route.......................1300　　"

Bearing this in mind, I would like to repeat the assertion with which I started this lecture i.e. that, if we were not here, somebody else would be. It shows, I suggest, a lack of appreciation of realities to imagine that this Island, with its marvellous strategical position, would ever remain for long unoccupied by any strong military nation which might aspire to supremacy in the East.

PART II

5. *THE DEFENCE OF SINGAPORE*

Having dealt with the strategical importance of Singapore and shown the necessity for the Naval Base here, I propose now to discuss shortly the strategical conception of the defence of this fortress. In the Exercises which are going to be held here next week, the The perspective of a great many of you will necessarily Forthcoming be very restricted. My object this morning, therefore, Exercise will be to give you a background which may help you to understand better what is going on and may thus, I hope, make the Exercise more interesting than it otherwise would be.

[THE SCHEME

DEFENDING SHIPS

NO SPECTACULAR FINISH

RESTRAINT ON TROOPS

I should like to take this opportunity of stressing that the object of this Exercise is to practise *(sic)* the personnel of the Fortress in operating the defence organization rather than to Test the Defences. Certain conditions must necessarily be unreal so that great care must be taken in deducing lessons.]

Object of Defence. It will be as well to clear our minds first of all as to what the OBJECT of the defence of a fortress like Singapore really is. We have seen that a Naval Base is necessary here to enable the British Fleet to interpose itself between British interests and the enemy's major naval forces and to enable our commerce protecting cruisers to operate in focal areas of British shipping. It is on the security of our sea communications that depend the strategical mobility of the armed forces of the Empire and the vital movements of the mercantile marine.

Consequently, the principal object of the defence of Singapore is to protect the Naval Base here against attack until the arrival of the British Main Fleet and to afford security to our forces subsequent to its arrival. [In the future the security of the Air Base may assume almost equal importance as Singapore is likely to become the base from which all offensive air operations in the Far East will be developed.] Thus any war in which we might be involved in the Far East would almost certainly be divided into two separate phases, i.e. the Phase prior to the arrival of the British Two Phases Main Fleet, during which we should be on the defensive, and the period subsequent to the arrival of that Fleet, during which we should hope to be able to assume the offensive. I think it is of the greatest importance to bear this in mind, because the object of the available forces during the first period will be to keep the fortresses intact so as to provide the necessary mobility for all Services when the main forces arrive.

Form of Attack. It is fairly certain that any attack which took place during the first phase to which I have referred above would be designed to deny to the British Main Fleet the use of the Naval Base, in which I include the oil depots and other facilities. Such attack might take the form either of a landing to capture the Fortress or at any rate to do the maxi- Phase I mum amount of damage to the naval facilities here, or else of an attack from the air, combined perhaps with naval action, similarly designed to do the maximum amount of damage to the naval facilities.

To deal with the latter first, this form of attack might be decided upon if a landing for one reason or another was not considered a practical proposition. Therefore, it would hardly be likely to be of a very sustained nature because it would have to be delivered from carriers and during the operations the carriers would necessarily be exposed to attack by ships, especially submarines, and by aircraft (provided of course that the range of the defending aircraft was greater than that of the attackers). As I pointed out in my last lecture, if there was any probability of a major fleet action in the near future the C-in-C might be loathe to allow his carriers to be used in this way. [He would have to weigh up the possible loss of one or more carriers against the possible advantage of depriving the enemy of the use of his Fleet Base.]

As regards the defence against this form of attack, A.A. Defence we have anti-aircraft land defences, but the value of these defences in a Fortress is necessarily limited by the difficulty of getting adequate warning of the approach of hostile aircraft and of pushing the defences far enough out to be able to engage them before they can deliver their attacks. We hope, however, that the cumulative effect of the anti-aircraft ground defence would be to gradually reduce the scale of attack by inflicting at any rate some casualties during each attack.

Possibly, however, the real form of defence against an attack of the nature I have described lies with the Air and Naval air and naval forces. For this purpose the defence Forces should have at its disposal sufficient air and naval forces, especially submarines, to make it too risky for the enemy to send his carriers within range of those forces.

I don't think I need say any more now about this form of attack, although I shall refer to it again later on when discussing the defence against attacks to capture the Fortress, because any such attack would almost certainly be accompanied by air operations.

Attack to Capture the Fortress. This, as I told you in my last lecture, might take the form of a 'Coup-de-main' attack or a deliberate attack, according to the amount of time which an enemy could reckon on having at his disposal and the degree of surprise which he could reasonably expect to attain. The plan Plan of defence to meet either form of attack is much the To Meet same, although as the 'coup-de-main' attack may be "Coup-de-main" expected to develop very much quicker than the de-Attack liberate form of attack the defence must be organized in such a way that it will be capable of dealing with the former. Later, if it becomes clear that the enemy intends to embark on a deliberate form of operation, the necessary adjustments can be made in the defence organization to deal with the new conditions.

Intelligence. The defence of a fortress begins in the enemy's country and takes the form of an intelligence organization to give warning of any military preparations which the enemy may be making. You will remember that I told you in my last lecture that many preparations have to be made before an expedition can be launched and so a good intelligence organization may get some inkling that something unusual is on foot. This would constitute the first warning to any fortress that might be threatened. In a modern military country, however, it must be expected that elaborate precautions will be taken to *prevent information leaking out* and so we must expect not to get very much warning from this source. I will refer to the other sources of information later as I discuss the various phases of the operation.

In Enemy's Country

The Voyage. We shall next hope to get some information of our enemy during the voyage from his port of departure to his advanced base or, in the case of a 'coup-de-main' attack, to the point from which he will launch his attack on the fortress. Our chances of getting news of him during this phase will depend on whether he is seen by naval or air patrols, or by some merchant vessel fitted with wireless or by some coast-watching post. The enemy will, of course, choose the less frequented portions of the ocean and will avoid, as far as he can, narrow waters. But a glance at the map will show that this is none too easy in the case of an enemy approaching Singapore from the East. In the first place he has either got to pass through the comparatively narrow channels between Formosa and the China Coast or between Formosa and the Philippines, or else he has got to pass South of the Philippines, which will bring him in among the Dutch Islands. He will, of course, try to pass the dangerous areas under cover of darkness but, even so, he will be rather lucky if he escapes detection. If he is detected, then the defence will prepare to strike him, as soon as opportunity offers, with such naval and air forces as can be made available.

Narrow Waters East of Singapore

Before I leave this Phase, I should like to put before you two possible developments in the future which, as I see it, may completely alter the situation

Two Future Developments

283

as regards the defence of Singapore during this phase of the operations.

The first is the probability of independence being Philippines restored to the PHILIPPINES by the U.S.A. within the next ten years. The intention is that by that time the Filipinos should be able to stand by themselves, but it seems to me very doubtful whether a group of islands with such great natural strategical advantages would ever remain in the hands of a militarily weak nation for very long. If they passed into the hands of the Japanese, then all the difficulty of making the voyage undetected would disappear with one stroke. That seems to me to be one of the greatest potential dangers in this part of the world in the future.

The second development is the rapidly increasing Range of Aircraft range of aircraft which would, I suggest, re-act to our advantage. For, when we are able to establish our aircraft in, say, British North Borneo with sufficient range to cover the waters within many hundred miles of that base, we shall have done much to make the problem of approaching unseen very much more difficult for the enemy.

The Fight for Air Superiority. In the exercise which we are going to do next week we have assumed Position at that the enemy has succeeded in preparing his ex-Beginning of pedition and in making the voyage undetected by us Exercise and that he has succeeded in reaching a position *300 miles* from Singapore before we get warning of his approach. We have also assumed that, during the period of political tension, certain air *squadrons from India and Iraq* had been ordered here and had arrived, and that the *Malay Regt.* had been brought down, but that the *Punjab Regt.* had only been ordered to move when the approach of the expedition had been discovered. And so it may be expected that the operations will open with a fight for air superiority. The attacking force is to have a carrier – the 'HERMES' – at her disposal. This carrier is to represent two carriers with a total of 126 Bombing Aircraft and each of her aircraft is to represent 15 aircraft in formation so if you see them flying over you will be able to get an idea of what the size of the attacking air force really is.

I think it is quite normal that an enemy attempting a 'coup-de-main' attack on this fortress should, as soon as he has reason to suppose that he has lost strategical surprise, attempt to establish temporary air superiority prior to his landing operations. Had he decided on a deliberate form of attack, he would probably have tried to establish *much more complete air superiority,* which would have involved establishing shore based aircraft either somewhere in Malaya or in some of the adjoining territory. It would be the task of the defence to prevent him so establishing shore-based aircraft – *a duty which would fall mainly on the naval and air forces available,* for the military forces in a fortress like this are insufficient to prevent an enemy establishing himself ashore anywhere except in the Fortress itself. If the defending aircraft are sufficiently strong and if they have the range of the attackers, it will be necessary for the attackers to establish temporary air superiority with carrier borne aircraft before they can put their shore-based aircraft ashore, because, as you will of course realize, these latter will have been brought to the theatre of operations crated in ships. From this you will realize how very difficult a really strong defending air force will make it for the attackers. *{Air Superiority}*

This fight for air superiority may go on for a considerable time, because we would hope that the mobility of our Air Forces would enable Singapore to receive air reinforcements, although we must of course always be prepared to find that there would be disturbances elsewhere in the Empire at such a time. *{Air Reinforcements}*

[ARMY A.A. DEFENCES
SEARCHLIGHTS]

The Reduction of the Fixed and Beach Defences. In the case of a deliberate operation, and possibly also to a minor extent in the case of a 'coup-de-main' attack, the enemy will then attempt to destroy or to neutralize the fixed and beach defences before attempting to land his troops. He may bombard these defences, either with high explosive or gas shell, both from ships and from the air. It will be the duty of the Army, in co-operation with the other Services, to repel these attacks.

For the benefit of those who do not belong to the Royal Regiment I should explain here that the Fixed Defences include the Counter-bombardment Batteries, which at present consist of the 15″ of the 'TERROR', of 9.2″ and will shortly be supplemented by heavier types of guns, and the Close Defence Batteries, consisting of 6″ guns. The role of the former is to destroy enemy ships which may be bombarding the Fortress and of the latter to protect the entrances to the main Fleet anchorage and to Keppel Harbour by engaging light surface craft which may be attempting to force an entrance. At each harbour entrance one of these batteries is told off as an examination battery, whose job it is to sink any vessel which may prove to be hostile while in the examination anchorage.

Fixed Defences

Examination Battery

Beach Defences

As regards the beach defences, they are unlikely, scattered as they are, to have much in the way of heavy stuff thrown at them, but the enemy might try to reduce their morale by machine-gun fire and gas-spray from the air. This form of attack they must be responsible for dealing with themselves.

The Final Approach. I come now to what will often be the *most critical part* of the operation, viz. the final approach from the advanced base, or from the position of assembly, to the positions selected for the ships to anchor and put the troops into boats. It is of the utmost importance that the defence should be able to *watch the enemy*, and attack him as opportunity offers, during this phase of the operation. The initial responsibility for this will rest with the *Royal Air Force*, by means of patrols and a striking force held in readiness to act on information supplied by the patrols, and on the *Royal Navy* by means of outer and in-shore patrols. Later, as information is supplied by these patrols, *the Army* may, if the enemy brings his ships close enough in, have an opportunity of engaging them with his Fixed Defences aided by search-lights to supply the necessary illumination.

A glance at the map will show how geographical factors facilitate our task of watching the enemy during this final approach for, leaving out the Malacca Straits, there are only three reasonably good ap-

proaches to Singapore and they are all through comparatively narrow channels, i.e.

SINGAPORE MAIN STRAIT

RHIO STRAIT

DURIAN STRAIT

The Approach to the Beaches. Finally there is the
approach to the beaches where the landing is to take
place. During this phase the in-shore patrols, if they
have not been sunk, will continue to watch the enemy, **Observation**
reporting direct to the Army Sector Headquarters,
and we may also try to watch him by means of Defence Electric Lights, Star Shell and aeroplane flares,
although any of these three agents might be required
for other work at the same time.

As soon as the enemy comes within effective range
of our beach defences, he will be engaged by each
weapon in turn according to its range and, we hope, **Engagement**
destroyed. If he succeeds in landing he will then be
engaged by the various reserves which are held for
that purpose.

NATURAL CONDITIONS
WEAK L. OF C. – ASSISTANCE OF NATURE
COMMAND.

I have tried to give you a picture of the defence of
a Fortress as I see it developing. I have only been able
to discuss selected forms of attack. There may, of
course, be others, such as attempts to reduce the for- **Other**
tress by starvation. But from what I have said I hope **Forms of**
you will have appreciated the really vital importance **Attack**
of close co-operation both between the Services and **Co-operation**
between the various branches of our own Service. For
unless a Commander of the Fortress is appointed –
which he may be in time of peril – the defence of a
fortress is a Combined Operation in exactly the same
way as the offensive operation about which I spoke
to you in my last lecture. In any case it will be a
Combined Operation during the planning stage and
the period of preparation in anticipation of attack.
So the old motto 'UNITED WE STAND – DIVI-
DED WE FALL' will apply to the defence just as
much as it does to the attack.

Jan. 1937.   A.E.P.

APPENDIX III

An appreciation of the defence of Malaya, written in July 1940 by C. A. Vlieland, then Secretary for Defence, Malaya. The appreciation is included as an appendix to Vlieland's memoir, which is preserved in the Liddell Hart Archive at King's College, London.

APPRECIATION BY THE SECRETARY FOR DEFENCE, MALAYA
July, 1940

INTRODUCTORY

If Malaya, including Singapore, is to be successfully defended, it is of vital importance to discard the idea that it is the defence of Singapore itself which is of prime importance.

2. The Naval Base has long lost its very *raison d'être*. It would be completely useless to either side in war if the other side occupied the peninsula. There is not the faintest chance of the arrival here during the war in Europe of a British fleet capable of dealing with the Japanese. Nor is there any justification whatever for believing that Japan regards Singapore as the prime objective. To the Japanese, it represents strategically for present purposes nothing more than a stepping stone in their southward drive. Looking further ahead, they would like it as a capital city for their projected Empire of the South Seas, as a valuable port and as a base for the defence of their Empire once achieved.

3. But such considerations are no justification for our attempting to hold the place as an isolated 'fortress' or indeed for according it any great priority in our defence plans. The whole idea of concentrating on close defence of Singapore is unreal and perverse. If we lost Singapore to direct assault the loss would not be fatal as long as we held the peninsula. If we lost control of the peninsula, even of the northern portion of it, we *should* lose Singapore, for what it is worth, too.

JAPANESE AIMS AND PLANS

4. There has never, I believe, been any question in the mind of any competent authority that the real threat from the Japanese is from the north. That was generally recognized as long ago as the 1914-18 war, although Japan was then nominally our ally. Gen. Sir Theodore Fraser, who was G.O.C., Malaya, here around 1925, repeatedly warned that Singapore would never be safe until we held Lower Siam. Gen. Dobbie wrote in May, 1939, that it was an attack from the north that he regarded as the greatest potential danger. Col. Percival, who was G.S.O. 1 in 1937, made an appreciation which stressed the probability of the Japanese making use of territory in southern Siam and the importance of defending northern Malaya.

5. With this I entirely agree and I would add considerations not brought into any purely military appreciations.

6. The permanent factors making for a break-out by Japan for the last thirty years have been over-population and the rice problem. With their small, mountainous home islands, terraced and intensively cultivated to the last available square foot, their already teeming population and a natural increase of the order of a million a year, the Japanese need for *lebensraum* is a real and compelling thing. Above all, they must have rice.

7. To anyone who knows something of the scramble for rice in the Far Eastern markets and has his ear to the ground in Bangkok it seems certain that Japan will not wait much longer to strike.

8. Rice is one of the most important keys to the whole situation. It spells control of Indo-China and Siam. Another key is the unparalleled wealth of Malaya, which Japan has long coveted. Another is to be found in the fact that she already has her foothold in Indo-China and can penetrate Siam at will, without fear of effective opposition. The obvious course for the Japanese to pursue is to proceed to military occupation of Indo-China and Siam and then sweep south over the whole length of the Malay peninsula, occupying it as they go. When they reach the southern tip of Johore, Singapore will fall into their hands like a ripe plum and will serve as a useful springboard for the final leap on the Dutch East Indies.

9. From the Japanese point of view, there would be no ob-

ject in a direct sea-borne attack on Singapore and little, if any, in invading the south of the peninsula before occupying the north. It would be quite irrational to proceed in that way when they mean to have Siam and the whole of Malaya.

10. I submit that there is little doubt that the Japanese programme reads

    (i) Indo-China – for its rice and as a base;

    (ii) Siam – for its rice;

    (iii) Malaya – for its multifarious wealth and for 'Face'.

    (iv) The Dutch East Indies – to complete the South Seas Empire.

11. This programme presents, from the Japanese point of view, the additional advantage that it calls for the minimum of naval forces and would leave the main sea-power of Japan available to meet any threat which might arise from American intervention.

12. I should add that Japanese intelligence is probably better than ours and, as all appearances go at present, it must be abundantly clear to them that a sweep all the way from the Siam-Malaya frontier down to the back door of Singapore will be so easy that they would be mad to plan their adventure in any other way.

13. One small point of the kind on which I personally place more reliance than I have ever felt able to do on official intelligence – an old Malay tracker friend of mine tells me that the Japanese have been very busy in the frontier forests lately, constructing or improving rough roads and tracks.

14. I would rate the chances of a direct assault on Singapore as negligible; the likelihood of anything more than subsidiary landings by small forces on the southern section of the east coast I consider slight; invasion in force of the Kelantan coast I regard as certain. But this last only with a view to transit *via* Siamese territory to the frontier west of the main range. Thence will start the main sweep down the western coastal plains which, if not decisively stopped early (I should say north of Bagan Serai at worst and preferably north of Alor Star) will, in my opinion, mean the loss of the whole of Malaya including Singapore.

15. Throughout the whole operation the Japanese will have land-based air forces at their disposal and, whatever air forces we have available in the Malayan theatre at the start, the balance of air power will move progressively against us as the enemy occupation proceeds – if it is allowed to proceed to

the south of Alor Star. Long before the enemy reached Johore his air power would be decisive.

THE PRINCIPLES OF A SUCCESSFUL DEFENCE

16. Without invading the tactical field which should be left to the professionals of the Services, I would lay down the following principles: -

(i) The aim must be to keep the whole of Malaya intact as far as may be found possible, to minimise disturbance of normal life and activity within the country and avoid anything in the nature of precautionary havoc.

(ii) The idea of mobilizing volunteers and transmogrifying them into conventional soldiers must be firmly discouraged. We cannot afford to pull out and remove from their normal occupations more than a thousand at most of the seven thousand European civilians who are the king-pins of the whole economy and will remain vital to the military effort.

(iii) Any of these civilians who are thus pulled out should be used on civil defence and on para-military duties as scouts, guides, interpreters, etc. and on no account as conventional soldiers. They should be carefully picked for their qualifications for such duties and should *not* as a rule be moved from their home districts.

(iv) The main military effort and maximum forces should be concentrated on the defence of the north-western plains and the aim should be to stop the main thrust as near the frontier as possible. *Alor Star is the key to the whole defence.*

(v) To achieve (iv) will necessitate stopping subsidiary thrusts *via* the Kroh-Baling- and the Kroh-Grik-Kuala Kangsar routes, penetration by which would force withdrawal from northern Kedah with disastrous effect.

(vi) It would be a grave error to waste any significant portion of the total forces available in the theatre by retaining a large garrison in Singapore or considerable reserves anywhere to the south of Kuala Lumpur.

(vii) The chance of direct invasion of the western plains *via* the Straits of Sumatra is very small. But account must be taken of probable landings on the west coast once the enemy has got a foothold in the north and can use small craft to travel southward along the coast.

(viii) It is quite likely that the enemy would try a subsidiary drive from a landing at Kuantan across to Kuala Lumpar to threaten the rear of our forces in the west and cut their communications with Singapore. This would, however, involve a long and difficult haul by a road peculiarly easy to block and/or render unusable over long stretches. It should be easy to counter without unduly weakening the vital defence of the north-west.

17. With regard to paragraphs 16(iv), (vi) and (viii), I would emphasize the considerations in paragraph 3 and also stress the fact that the defence would be operating on interior lines in a well roaded and highly motorized country. There should be no difficulty in moving considerable land forces to meet subsidiary incursions very rapidly.

18. I maintain that, if the enemy once succeeded in driving us out of the north-western plains, complete disaster would follow inevitably. Not only should we lose Malaya, including Singapore, but the Japanese would be well on the way to achieving their whole grand design.

19. That is my conclusion because there is no area south of the plains of Kedah, Province Wellesley and Krian which offers anything like the same advantages to the defence. I believe it is an accepted military maxim that close country favours the attacker and, if we fail to hold the invader in the finest large open area in the whole country, how can we hope to stop him further south? Especially as the balance of forces must move progressively against us. Kedah offers us the facilities for defence in great depth with extended fields of fire and optimum use of air power, especially in the virtual defiles by which the enemy would have to debouch on to the open plain. See also paragraph 15.

20. If we were forced back out of Kedah and northern Perak, I think the only area where a considerable stand could be made is in the vicinity of Kampar and I should expect a distinct battle there. But I do not think it would be a success for us. It seems to me too certain that we should be forced to withdraw by a threat to the left rear of our positions *via* the Telok Anson-Bidor road since, by that time, the enemy would be in a position to make landings on the west coast.

21. South of the Kampar area I do not think there would be any prospect of stopping the enemy's progress.

22. It has been suggested from time to time that we should go over the frontier into Siam to meet the enemy and I believe plans have been made for such a move. It would of course be

admirable if, as General Fraser suggested we held Lower Siam. But we don't and I see little point in plans to go in at the eleventh hour. H.M.G. would never agree to our doing so until the very last moment and I don't see how we could expect to do better on inevitably unprepared ground in Siam than on our own side of the frontier, where the open countryside is naturally favourable to the defence and we can do anything we think desirable in the way of preparing positions, satellite landing grounds, supplementary roads, 'hards', etc.

23. It seems to me that work of this kind should be put in hand without delay, but there is no sign of it as far as I am aware. What exactly should be done is of course a matter for the Service professionals, but it seems to me, as a civilian who is at least familiar with the terrain, that it would not be difficult to make northern Kedah into a modern equivalent of a 'fortress', which Singapore most emphatically is not.

APPENDIX IV

The 'Scorched Earth' policy

One of the reasons for the Japanese success was their ability to use the abundant stores and equipment left behind by the retreating British, or remaining undamaged in civilian hands. This naturally raises the question why a more effective 'scorched earth' policy was not enforced. The phrase had become popular since the summer of 1941, as a symbol of the Russian total will to resist the German invader, and many people, including Churchill himself, assumed the policy was transferable to the context of Malaya.

But the context was very different. General Woodburn Kirby points out (*Singapore, The Chain of Disaster*, p.159) that although the policy might have been correct from a purely military point of view, it was hardly feasible for a colonial power to apply it 'to the detriment of the indigenous Asian population'. To do so would have deprived them of many of the necessities of life.

In this, he echoes Percival's arguments in his Despatch, but there was another factor. It was taken for granted that the British, even if momentarily displaced by a Japanese onslaught, would soon be back, perhaps in a matter of months. Both Wavell and Duff Cooper had this sort of period in mind.* The principle was ultimately established that big facilities – power plants, water reservoirs – should be left alone, and property belonging to civilians likewise.

These plans were not evolved before war broke out, but in an exchange of signals between London and Singapore in mid-December 1941, as a result of which authority to destroy in-

---

* 'We had always the hope that even if Malaya fell we should be relieved before long. We had planned therefore to deny to the Japanese by removing or destroying essential parts while leaving bulk installations in a condition which enabled them quickly to be brought into action when relief arrived. Tin dredgers is a case in point. On December 33rd (1941), Duff Cooper asked the Foreign Office whether total destruction was enjoined in view of the possibility of our regaining Malaya within six months. It sounds fantastic now but so it was.' (Sir Miles Shenton-Thomas, comments on the draft War History, para. 128.)

stallations was left to the commander in the field unless very large installations were involved, such as the coal mines in Selangor, in which case the decision had to be referred back to government in Singapore (Woodburn Kirby, *op. cit.* p.189). On the other hand, destruction was to be on a 'do it yourself' basis: the owners were to destroy their own installations, with the help of army officers experienced in the use of explosives. Some owners were naturally reluctant to destroy expensive equipment, others actively resisted. Simson (*op. cit.*, p.97) points out that in many instances governmental sanction for the destruction of tin dredgers, stocks of rubber and processing plant were not given in time. Huge quantities of tin, as well as a harbour full of small boats, fell into Japanese hands when Penang was taken (Simson, p.98).

Seeing what had happened in Malaya as a result of lack of planning, Simson determined that things should be different on the Island. He recommended to Shenton-Thomas and Percival that a phased destruction policy should be prepared in advance. He got no decision. When he himself became a member of the War Council (23 January 1942), he raised the matter personally. Approval was given, but late, and it excluded water, electricity, gas and sewage installations. The Governor was to be responsible for destruction of rubber and tin stocks and radio stations, and Simson records that Shenton-Thomas refused to sanction the destruction of forty-odd Chinese engineering works for reasons of morale (Simson, p.98). There were forty-seven British-owned plants, and these were wrecked, although in some cases the owners opposed it. The Navy – helped by the oil companies – destroyed large stocks of petrol and oil. Soot from the fires fell on the city for two to three weeks afterwards. Also under pressure from Simson, the Governor ordered the destruction of all liquor stocks before the surrender to avoid a repetition of the atrocities perpetrated in China by Japanese troops inflamed with alcohol.

On 20 January 1942, there arrived a cable from the Chiefs of Staff instructing the Singapore authorities to apply a scorched earth policy rigorously to the Island. The implementation of this order was far from complete, among the services themselves. The Navy, for instance, withdrew its technical personnel from the Navy Base at the end of January, but they had done little to render it valueless to the Japanese before they left. The floating dock was sunk, the dry-dock gates were damaged, and auxiliary vessels were sunk. Otherwise, buildings, plant, machinery and oil tanks were left to the Japanese, and 11 Indian Division had to be ordered to complete the destruction (Woodburn Kirby, *op. cit.*, p.227).

This is hardly surprising when one reads the qualifications which hedge round the orders to destroy and deny, in Percival's letter of 1st February 1942, following up the Chiefs of Staff's directive. As much 'surplus' material as possible was to be disposed of immediately, provided that this could be done without damaging public morale (Percival, Despatch, p. 1,343). For the rest, plans for destruction should be drawn up at once, the responsibility lying with the military authority of the relevant area. Stocks of food, medicines, hospital equipment and water installations were not to be destroyed. 'If time permits', the orders were to be given by Percival himself, but he realized he would not always be able to be reached, and responsible authorities were to ensure that enough men under a reliable commander would be available, who would 'failing my orders, act on his own initiative.' The number of loopholes left is considerable.

It may seem surprising that it was necessary to await Simson's urging and pressure from the Chiefs of Staff to put such a policy on its feet. In fact, a denial scheme had already been devised early in 1941 (Percival, Despatch, paras. 233-4) but this was in no sense a scorched earth policy. Its purpose was to deny to an enemy the use of anything that would help the *movement* of an invading force: repair workshops, bridges, vehicles, boats.

When Duff Cooper, in mid-December 1941, transmitted London's orders to carry out a 'scorched earth' policy on the lines of Russia's, Percival pointed out that the Russians were retreating through their own people and could ask sacrifices of them which the British were not entitled to ask of a native population which looked to Britain for protection, by treaty:

> If we deprived these people of the necessities of life such as food, water, etc., or destroyed the symbols of modern civilization, such as the power supplies of their hospitals, they would claim that we were not treating them in accordance with our promises and they would become fertile ground for the seeds of the enemy's propaganda. (Percival, Despatch, para. 233)

Percival makes several valid points on morale. The use of fire and explosives to destroy installations was a sure indication to the enemy of a planned withdrawal; and the sight of smoke and the noise of explosives in the rear of a fighting army could hardly be expected to raise its spirits. As far as the civilian population was concerned, it was well known, Percival affirmed, that 'Asiatics tend to take the side of the more powerful and we feared that the sight of destruction being carried out well behind our lines would induce them to help the enemy rather than ourselves' (Despatch, para. 235).

These considerations of morale, always large in Percival's mind, caused him to query Wavell's instructions. Wavell sent a signal on 23 January 1942, stressing the ruthlessness with which he expected a scorched earth policy to be carried out:

> Policy is quite clear. As stated in special order I sent you Singapore will be defended to last. At same time preparations must be made to destroy material rather than allow it to fall into enemy hands. Of course this should be done as unobtrusively as possible. Best way to convince population of our intentions is to make them take part in defence especially by supplying necessary labour which must be done at once. Scorched earth policy of destroying what will assist enemy must continue, enemy will have no consideration for native population and will take what he requires from them if we leave it. This is no time for sentiment. Chinese population of Singapore know they need expect no consideration from Japanese [Connell, *Wavell*, p.120].

There is no doubt that on this point the views of Wavell and Churchill were at one, different though they might be on other topics. Churchill had sent a minute to General Ismay, for transmission to the Chiefs of Staff, in which he said he regarded it as indispensable that the Naval Base should be completely wrecked, to render docks and workshops unusable by an enemy for at least a year and a half. Likewise, all the fortress guns should be destroyed, leaving Singapore valueless to the enemy as a naval base. The work could be carried out, he averred, without causing public alarm, since it would be done in areas from which the public was rigorously excluded (2 February 1942, in Connell, *op. cit.*, p.140).

That destruction could be as absolute and as secret as the Prime Minister believed was implicitly denied by Percival in a signal sent the same day to the Chief of the Imperial General Staff – a copy was sent to Wavell in Java – reporting that plans for scorched earth policy had been worked out and that all was being done which could be done without causing alarm. But, he pointed out, Singapore and the surrounding islands were crammed with valuable war stores of all kinds, including oil, some of which might take not hours but days to destroy completely. If airborne and seaborne attacks were made simultaneously by the Japanese, the resultant confusion would mean that some demolitions could not be carried out. There was, too, a contradiction in his orders, as he saw them. He had been told a) to hold Singapore to the very last, and b) to carry out a total scorched earth policy.

> In existing conditions [he signalled] it is impossible to comply with both. In my view the holding of Singapore must be the primary object and I propose to continue in accordance with policy already approved [i.e. by the CIGS] ... I am still convinced that to put extensive scorched earth policy into effect immediately would so undermine the morale both of troops and public as to prejudice seriously our ability to hold Singapore [Connell, *op. cit.*, p.142].

It was another version of the reply which he and the Fortress Commander Major-General Keith Simmons had given Brigadier Simson when he asked permission to construct defences. Defences were bad for morale. Scorched earth demolitions were bad for morale. But at this stage, what was the alternative?

The destruction of civilian installations is only part of the story. 'Is nothing going to be said,' Shenton-Thomas asked plaintively (Comments on the draft War History, para. 151), 'about the denial of Service stores and plant?' More than stores and plant were involved. As Colonel Ashmore later pointed out (Ashmore, p.13), the loss of equipment to the Japanese was on a fantastic scale from the very first days of the campaign. On the basis of notes he kept from 8 December 1941 to 27 January 1942, he calculated that the losses in the first fifty days amounted to:

Rifles	30,000
Light machine-guns	1,500
Anti-tank rifles	70 per cent of unit scale in action
Thompson sub-machine-guns	30 per cent „ „ „ „ „
2-inch mortars	60 per cent „ „ „ „ „
2-pounders	25 per cent „ „ „ „ „
25-pounders	20 per cent „ „ „ „ „

'These losses should not have occurred,' he added, 'and the blame must lie firmly at the door of those responsible for training and physical fitness, with the climate and the terrain as subsidiary causes' (*ibid.*).

No wonder the Japanese were well-stocked with what they nicknamed 'Churchill rations'. After the storming of the Jitra Line, Colonel Tsuji pushed on to the hastily abandoned aerodrome of Alor Star. He was able to reach it fairly quickly, because the inadequate demolition of the road bridge over the river meant that Japanese vehicles were using it again within the hour:

> We pushed forward with the advance party, heading towards a large paved aerodrome which I had observed during my trip in the reconnaissance plane before the outbreak of hostilities, and unexpectedly found that it was scarcely damaged. Here was a gift of bombs piled high, and moreover in one of the buildings hot soup was arranged on a dining-room table. Among the surrounding rubber trees one thousand drums full of high-grade ninety-two octane petrol were piled up. About noon that day our planes successfully made their first landing at Alor Star . . . one squadron of fighter planes and one squadron of light bombers pushed forward and carried further our brief attack over the heads of the retreating enemy, using the enemy's abandoned gasolene and bombs. To our fighter groups who had risked their lives protecting our convoy of transport ships these were most acceptable gifts [Tsuji, *Singapore*, pp.128-9].

The same story was true in the other aerodromes in Northern Malaya:

> By high-speed assaults on Taiping and Sungei Patani the four large military aerodromes in Kedah Province were captured almost undamaged – we were able to repair them and put them into use in half a day. We called these 'the Churchill aerodromes'. They were provided with abundant equipment, ammunition, fuel and provisions . . .
> . . . Our hurriedly constructed air base in southern Indo-China could not be compared in equipment with these 'Churchill aerodromes'. Possession of twofold numerical air strength was one reason for our air superiority over the

Malaya theatre of operations, but the decisive factor was that we were able to take immediate advantage of the captured 'Churchill aerodromes' [Tsuji, *op. cit.*, p.130].

The final balance sheet of booty in the Japanese Official History reflects the scale of British losses of equipment (*Marē Shinkō Sakusen*, p.626):

Field/mountain artillery	300 pieces	approx.
Anti-aircraft guns	100 ,,	,,
Fortress guns	54 ,,	,,
1-pounder guns	108 ,,	,,
Mortars	180 ,,	,,
Heavy machine-guns	2,500 ,,	,,
Anti-tank rifles	63 ,,	,,
Sub-machine-guns	800 ,,	,,
Rifles	60,000 ,,	,,
Small arms ammunition	33,610,000 rounds	,,
Lorries and trucks	1,000 ,,	,,
Cars	10,000 ,,	,,
Armoured fighting vehicles	200 ,,	,,
Military wireless transmitter sets	600	
Aircraft	10	

In addition to the above, large stocks of ammunition, fuel, clothing and food were captured.

The above figures show what was taken on Singapore Island. To them must be added what was lost to the Japanese on the mainland (*Marē Sakusen*, Tokyo, 1966):

Aircraft	13	
Armoured fighting vehicles	50	approx.
Cars	3,600	,,
Guns	330	,,
Machine-guns	550	,,
Lorries	800	,,

REFERENCES

Introduction

1 *Kido Kōichi Nikki* (The Diary of Kido Kōichi), *Gekan* (Vol. II), Tokyo, Tokyo University Press, 1974, pp.945-6

2 Yoshihara Yanosuke (ed.), *Dai Shōri no Kiroku* (Records of the Great Victories) – *Dai Tōa Sensō Dai-ichi-nen* (The First Year of the Greater East Asia War), Tokyo, Bunshōdō Shoten, 1943, p.151. The Rescript was issued by Imperial General Headquarters at 11.40 am on 16 February 1942

3 D. Bergamini, *Japan's Imperial Conspiracy*, London, Heinemann, 1971, illuss. p.218 *et seq*. Bergamini wrongly gives the date of the surrender of Singapore as 19 February.

4 Yoshihara, *op. cit.*, p.159

5 Shiga Naoya, *Sōshun* (Early Spring), Tokyo, Oyama Shoten, 1942, pp.143-6

6 *Parliamentary Debates, House of Commons*, 5th Series, Vol. 377, 8 January – 18 February 1942, cols. 1671 – 1675. Unless otherwise stated, references to House of Commons debates are from this volume or Vol. 378, and will be referred to as *377 HC Deb.* or *378 HC Deb.*

7 *Punch*, Vol. ccii, 25 February 1942, p.158

8 *377 HC Deb.*, 1677

9 *Punch*, Vol. ccii, p.156

10 *377 HC Deb.*, 1681; *Punch*, Vol. ccii, p.158

11 *ibid.*, p.158

12 *377 HC Deb.*, 1683

13 *ibid.*, 1687

14 *378 HC Deb.*, 24 February – 26 March 1942, col. 44

15 *ibid.*, 45; *Punch*, Vol. ccii, p.179

16 *378 HC Deb.*, 61

17 *ibid.*, 69

18 *ibid.*, 98

19 *ibid.*, 271

20 *ibid.*, 273

References

21 *ibid.*, 306

22 *ibid.*, 230-7

23 *ibid.*, 156

24 *ibid.*, 158

25 *ibid.*

26 *ibid.*, 130

27 *ibid.*, 128

28 *ibid.*, 113

29 *Parliamentary Debates, House of Lords*, 25 March 1942

30 Lieutenant-General A. E. Percival, *The War in Malaya*, London, Eyre and Spottiswoode, 1949, p.295 : '. . . it was under German influence that [Japan] eventually decided to change her plans and to drive southwards instead of attacking Russia. That decision was not made until after the Tripartite Pact was signed in September 1940. It was made as a result of German pressure to attack Singapore.'

31 H. R. Trevor-Roper (ed.), *Hitler's War Directives*, London, Sidgwick and Jackson, 1964, p.58

32 *ibid.*, p.59

33 *ibid.*

34 William L. Shirer, *The Rise and Fall of the Third Reich*, London, Pan Books, 1964, p.1054

35 *ibid.*, p.1056

36 *ibid.*

37 *ibid.*, p.1060

38 *ibid.*

39 *ibid.*

40 Ōshima was named Military Attaché on 5 March 1934 and promoted to Envoy Extraordinary and Ambassador Plenipotentiary on 8 October 1938, a post he held until 27 December 1939 and resumed on 29 December 1940. He then held it until 1945. Cf. R. J. C. Butow, *Tojo and the Coming of War*, Stanford (Calif.), Stanford University Press, 1961, p.136, n. 9

41 Butow, *op. cit.*, p.136

42 Albert Seaton, *The Russo-German War 1941-45*, London, Arthur Barker, 1971, p.168

43 Generaloberst Franz Halder, *Kriegstagebuch*, Vol. III, Stuttgart, W. Kohlhammer Verlag, 1964, pp.152-3

44 *ibid.*, entry for 10 September 1941

45 Walter Warlimont, *Inside Hitler's Headquarters*, London, Weidenfeld and Nicolson, 1964, p.145

46 Shirer, *op. cit.*, p.1064
47 *ibid.*, p.1068
48 *ibid.*, p.1067
49 *Dai Hon'ei Rikugunbu* (Imperial General Headquarters: Army), *(3) (Shōwa jūshichi-nen shigatsu made)* (3) (To April 1942), Tokyo, Asagumo Shimbunsha for the War History Room, Defence Agency, Tokyo, 1970, p.447
50 *ibid.*
51 *ibid.*, p.448
52 *ibid.*, pp.556-7
53 *ibid.*, p.557
54 *Akten zur deutschen auswärtigen Politik 1918-1945*, Series E: 1941-1945, Vol. II, Göttingen, Vandenhoek and Ruprecht, 1972, p.312
55 *Dai Hon'ei Rikugunbu (3)*, *op. cit.*, p.529
56 Field-Marshal Sir William Slim (later Viscount Slim), *Defeat into Victory*, London, Cassell, 1956, pp.181, 187, 189
57 S. E. Morison, *History of United States Naval Operations in World War II*, Vol. III, *The Rising Sun in the Pacific, 1931 – April 1942*, Boston, Little, Brown and Co., 1950, p.386
58 Ōtani Keijirō, *Kempei*, Tokyo, Shinjinbutsu Ōraisha, 1973, pp.187-205, and *Sensō Hanzai* (War Crimes), Tokyo, Shinjinbutsu Ōraisha, 1975, pp.177-88
59 Quoted in G. Morgenstern, *Pearl Harbour: The Story of the Secret War*, p.117

Chapter I

1 F. S. G. Piggott, *Broken Thread*, Aldershot, Gale and Polden, 1950, p.196
2 Sir Stamford Raffles as quoted by Percival in his lecture
3 On the Beatty-Trenchard controversy cf. Wing-Commander H. C. Allen, *The Legacy of Lord Trenchard*, London, Cassell, 1972, p.56 *et seq.*; Andrew Boyle, *Trenchard*, London, Collins, 1962, pp.500-503, 552-9
4 *The Memoirs of General the Lord Ismay*, London, Heinemann, 1960, pp.236-7
5 cf. Winston (later Sir Winston) Churchill, *The Second World War*, Vol. 2, *The Gathering Storm*, London, Cassell, 1948, p.326
6 Piggott, *op. cit.*, p.260
7 *Dai Hon'ei Rikugunbu* (Imperial General Headquarters:

Army), *(I) (Shōwa jūgo-nen gogatsu made)* (I) (To May 1940), Tokyo, 1967, p.416

8   Seventeen-page typescript, Item 69.1 in Percival Papers, Imperial War Museum, London (see Appendix II)

9   *ibid.*

10 *ibid.*

11 Quoted by Percival in typescript notes 'The Defence of Singapore' (Percival Papers), and in his Despatch 'Operations of Malaya Command, from 8th December 1941 to 15th February 1942', London, HMSO, 1948 (hereafter referred to as Despatch)

12 C. A. Vlieland, seventy-seven-page typescript, 'Disaster in the Far East, 1941-2', in the Liddell Hart Centre for Military Archives, King's College, University of London (hereafter referred to as Vlieland)

13 William Roger Louis, *British Strategy in the Far East*, Oxford, Clarendon Press, 1971, p.212

14 Vlieland, p.11

15 Captain S. W. Roskill, 'The British Point of View', in *The Second World War in the Pacific – Plans and Reality*, London, National Maritime Museum, Maritime Monographs and Reports, No. 9, 1974, p.12

16 COS No. 39 to Brooke-Popham, Brooke-Popham Papers (hereafter referred to as BP) (Liddell Hart Centre), v/4/6, paras. 3-22

17 Major-General S. W. Woodburn Kirby, *The War Against Japan*, Vol. I, London, 1957, p.54

18 *ibid.*, p.60

19 Squadron-Leader G. H. Wiles to Brooke-Popham, 15 July 1948, BP v/9/30

20 Minute to Chiefs of Staff, 13 January 1941, in Woodburn Kirby, *op. cit.*, I, p.55

21 Brooke-Popham to Ismay, 6 January 1941, BP v/1/4

22 Cecil Brown, *Suez to Singapore*, New York, Halcyon House, 1943, p.149

23 Brooke-Popham to Ismay, 6 January 1941, *op. cit.*

Chapter II

1   Nobutaka Ike (ed. and tr.), *Japan's Decision for War: Records of the 1941 Policy Conferences*, Stanford (Calif.), Stanford University Press, 1967, p.12

2   Joseph C. Grew, *Ten Years in Japan*, London, Hammond, 1944, pp.367-70

3   Ike, *op. cit.*, p.152
4   *ibid.*, p.153

Chapter III
1   W. N. Medlicott, *The Economic Blockade*, Vol. II, London, HMSO, 1959, p.64
2   *ibid.*, p.74
3   Sir Llewellyn Woodward, *British Foreign Policy in the Second World War*, Vol. II, London, HMSO, 1971, p.122
4   H. J. Van Mook, *The Netherlands Indies and Japan*, London, Allen and Unwin, 1944, p.39
5   Medlicott, *op. cit.*, II, p.80
6   Ike, *op. cit.*, p.8
7   *ibid.*, p.10
8   *ibid.*, p.11
9   *ibid.*, p.13
10 Van Mook, *op. cit.*, p.105
11 For a Japanese account of the negotiations see Chapter 5 of Matsumoto Shunichi and Andō Yoshirō, *Nihon Gaikōshi* (A History of Japanese Diplomacy), Vol. 22, *Nanshin Mondai* (The Southward Advance), Tokyo, Kajima Kenkyūjo Shuppansha, 1973
12 Van Mook, *op. cit.*, p.103
13 Medlicott, *op. cit.*, II, p.100
14 *ibid.*, p.106
15 *ibid.*, p.107
16 *ibid.*, p.117
17 Ike, *op. cit.*, p.109
18 *ibid.*
19 *ibid.*, p.220
20 *ibid.*, p.222
21 *ibid.*, p.223
22 *ibid.*, p.224
23 *ibid.*
24 *Foreign Relations of the United States 1941*, Vol. IV, *The Far East*, Washington, US Government Printing Office, 1956, p.833 (hereafter referred to as *For. Rel. US 1941*)
25 *ibid.*, p.834
26 Medlicott, *op. cit.*, p.123
27 *ibid.*

Chapter IV

1 Brooke-Popham to Ismay, 3 February 1941, BP v/1/5
2 *ibid.*
3 Admiral Jean Decoux, *A la Barre de l'Indochine*, Paris, Plon, 1949, p.141
4 *ibid.*, p.127
5 *ibid.*, p.145
6 Memo by Sumner Welles, 25 November 1940, *Foreign Relations of the United States 1940*, Vol. IV, *The Far East*, Washington, US Government Printing Office, 1955, p.221 (hereafter referred to as *For. Rel. US 1940*)
7 Memo by Hamilton, 18 November 1940, *ibid.*, pp.214-6
8 Johnson to Secretary of State, 23 November 1940, *ibid.*, pp.218-9
9 Grant to Secretary of State, 26 November 1940, *ibid.*, p.222
10 Murphy to Secretary of State, 17 December 1940, *ibid.*, p.242
11 Matthews to Secretary of State, 30 December 1940, *ibid.*, p.250
12 Memo by Sumner Welles, 23 December 1940, *ibid.*, p.246
13 Ike, *op. cit.*, p.50
14 Woodward, *op. cit.*, II, pp.144-5
15 Ike, *op. cit.*, p.119
16 *ibid.*, p.120
17 *ibid.*
18 *ibid.*, p.235
19 *ibid.*, pp.242-3
20 *ibid.*, p.281
21 *ibid.*, p.243, n. 39
22 *Sugiyama Memo*, Tokyo, Hara Shobō, 2 vols., 1967, Vol. I, pp.169-73
23 Roberta Wohlstetter, *Pearl Harbour Warning and Decision*, Stanford (Calif.), Stanford University Press, 1962, p.48
24 *ibid.*, pp.329-30
25 Asada Shunnosuke, 'Wanitto no higeki' (The tragedy of Wan Nit), *Minnami*, No. 4, 1954, Tokyo (privately printed), pp.2-3
26 'Notes by the Commander-in-Chief Far East on conversation with Colonel Sura Narong', 15 July 1941, BP v/4/15

27 Brown, *op. cit.*, pp.132-3
28 *ibid.*, pp.133-5
29 *ibid.*, p.141
30 *ibid.*, p.186
31 *ibid.*, pp.147-8
32 *ibid.*, p.130
33 Lieutenant-Colonel B. H. Ashmore, 'Some personal observations of the Malaya Campaign 1940-1942' (twenty-six-page memorandum with Percival's penned queries in margin), p.12. Percival Papers
34 Percival, *The War in Malaya*, pp.91-2
35 Sir Andrew Gilchrist, *Bangkok Top Secret*, London, Hutchinson, 1970, p.12

Chapter V
1 Percival, Despatch, para. 21
2 *ibid.*, para. 29
3 Playfair to War Office, 20 August 1941, BP v/4/26
4 Roger Parkinson, *Blood, Toil, Tears and Sweat. The War History from Dunkirk to Alamein, based on the War Cabinet papers of 1940 to 1942*, London, Hart-Davis, MacGibbon, 1973, p.150
5 Chiefs of Staff to Brooke-Popham, 25 November 1941, BP v/4/39
6 Brooke-Popham to Chiefs of Staff, 28 November 1941, BP v/4/40
7 Parkinson, *op cit.*, p.320
8 *ibid.*
9 *ibid.*
10 *ibid.*, p.321
11 Woodward, *op. cit.*, II, p.172
12 *ibid.*, p.171
13 *ibid.*
14 *ibid.*
15 *ibid.*, p.172
16 *ibid.*
17 *ibid.*
18 War Office to Brooke-Popham, 5 December 1941, BP v/4/41
19 Note by Brooke-Popham, BP v/4/42
20 Quoted by Brooke-Popham in MS comment on draft of Woodburn Kirby, I. BP v/9/34

References

Chapter VI

1 Sudō Hajime, *Marē-oki Kaisen* (Sea Battles off Malaya), Tokyo, Shirogane Shobō, 1974, p.31
2 *ibid.*, p.32
3 *ibid.*, p.33
4 *ibid.*, p.34
5 *ibid.*, p.37
6 *ibid.*, p.38
7 Percival, *The War in Malaya*, p.110
8 *ibid.*
9 Brooke-Popham to War Office via Admiralty, No. 868, 7 December 1941, BP v/5/29. Cf. Brooke-Popham, Despatch 'Operations in the Far East, from 17th October 1940 to 27th December 1941', London, HMSO, 1948, para. 51 (hereafter referred to as Despatch)
10 Woodburn Kirby, *The War Against Japan*, I, p.181
11 Brooke Popham, Despatch, para. 98
12 Mahmood Khan Durrani, *The Sixth Column*, London, Cassell, 1955, pp.4-5
13 Tsuji Masanobu (tr. Margaret E. Lake), *Singapore, The Japanese Version*, London, Constable, 1962, pp.8-9
14 *ibid.*, pp.45-52
15 Louis Allen, 'Japan's Spy Network', *History of the Second World War*, Vol. 8, No. 3, p.3,211. London, Purnell, n.d. (1968)

Chapter VII

1 *Hi-tō: Marē hōmen kaigun shinkō sakusen* (Naval Operations in Philippine and Malayan Waters), Tokyo, Asagumo Shimbunsha for the War History Room, Defence Agency, Tokyo, 1969, pp.79-88
2 The best account of the landing details fom the Japanese side is by the landing force commander, Major-General Takumi Hiroshi, *Kota Baru Tekizen Jōriku* (The Opposed Landing at Kota Bharu), Tokyo, Press Tokyo K. K., 1968, pp.39-45
3 Woodburn Kirby, *The War Against Japan*, I, p.189
4 Tsuji, *op. cit.*, p.83

Chapter VIII

1 Percival to Professor J. R. M. Butler, comments on *Grand Strategy*, p.2. Percival Papers

References

2 Woodburn Kirby, *The War Against Japan*, I, p.185
3 Percival to Professor J. R. M. Butler, 7 January 1962. Percival Papers
4 Tsuji, *op. cit.*, p.117
5 Percival, Despatch, para. 280
6 Percival, *The War in Malaya*, p.197
7 Winston (later Sir Winston) Churchill, *The Second World War*, Vol. IV, *The Hinge of Fate*, London, Cassell, 1951, p.40: 'This command of the western shores of Malaya by the Japanese without the possession of a single ship of war must be reckoned as one of the most astonishing British lapses in naval history.'
8 Tsuji, *op. cit.*, p.156
9 Parkinson, *op. cit.*, pp.308-9
10 Captain S. W. Roskill, *The War at Sea 1939-1945*, Vol. I, *The Defensive*, London, HMSO, 1954, p.558
11 Churchill, *The Second World War*, Vol. III, *The Grand Alliance*, London, Cassell, 1950, p.547
12 Quoted in Brooke-Popham to War Office, 12 December 1941, BP v/5/42
13 Grenfell, *op. cit.*, p.114
14 In Brooke-Popham to War Office, 12 December 1941, BP v/5/42
15 Roskill, *op. cit.*, I, p.561
16 Quoted in Air Vice-Marshal Maltby to Brooke-Popham, 30 April 1946, BP v/8/12
17 *ibid.*
18 Roskill, *op. cit.*, I, p.566
19 Evidence of Ōno Shinichirō, in *Konnichi no wadai* (Topics of Today), Tokyo, July 1956
20 Compton Mackenzie, *Eastern Epic*, Vol. I, *Defence*, London, Chatto and Windus, 1951, p.242
21 Roskill, *op. cit.*, p.565
22 *ibid.*
23 Grenfell, *op. cit.*, p.118, n. 1
24 Brooke-Popham, Despatch, para. 108
25 Grenfell, *op. cit.*, pp.111, 117
26 Captain Geoffrey Bennett, *The Loss of the Prince of Wales and Repulse*, London, Ian Allan, 1973, p.57
27 Grenfell, *op. cit.*, pp.113-14
28 Marshal of the RAF Sir John Slessor, *The Central Blue*, London, Cassell, 1956, p.277
29 Roskill, *op. cit.*, I, p.568

30 Marcel Giuglaris, *Le Japon perd la guerre du Pacifique*, Paris, Fayard, 1958, pp.76-7

31 Mackenzie, *Eastern Epic*, I, p.322

32 J. H. H. Coombes, *Banpong Express. Malaya and After*, Darlington, Wm. Dresser and Sons, 1948, p.32

33 Frank Legg, *The Gordon Bennett Story*, Sydney, Angus and Robertson, 1965, p.209

34 Percival, *The War in Malaya*, p.218. The erroneous figure was repeated by Churchill (*op. cit.*, IV, p.37) and by Sir John Smyth, VC, *Percival and the Tragedy of Singapore*, London, Macdonald, 1971, p.222

35 Mackenzie, *Eastern Epic*, I, p.375

36 This is the figure given by Woodburn Kirby (*The War Against Japan*, I, p.362) and Smyth (*op. cit.*, p.227). It does not, of course, square with the Japanese post-surrender figure of over 100,000 prisoners.

37 Percival, Despatch, para. 456

38 *ibid.*

39 *ibid.*, para. 459

40 Percival, *The War in Malaya*, p.261

41 Ashmore, *op. cit.*, p.18

42 Smyth, *op. cit.*, p.218

43 John Connell, *Wavell, Supreme Commander 1941-1943*, London, Collins, 1969, p.112

44 *ibid.*, p.151

45 General Sir Archibald Wavell, 'Despatch by the Supreme Commander of the ABDA area to the Combined Chiefs of Staff on the Operations in the South-West Pacific 15th January 1942 to 25th February 1942', London, HMSO, 1948, p.12, para. 24 (hereafter referred to as Despatch)

46 Major-General S. Woodburn Kirby, *Singapore, The Chain of Disaster*, London, Cassell, 1971, p.221

47 *ibid.*, p.221, n. 1

48 Percival, Despatch, para. 460

49 *ibid.*

50 Brigadier Ivan Simson, *Singapore, Too Little, Too Late*, London, Leo Cooper, 1970, p.81

51 Moyne to Wavell, 13 January 1942, in Connell, *op. cit.*, p.97

52 Connell, *op. cit.*, pp.98-9

53 Churchill, *op. cit.*, IV, p.43

54 Simson, *op. cit.*, p.69

55 Connell, *op. cit.*, p.106; Percival, Despatch, para. 436
56 Woodburn Kirby, *Singapore, The Chain of Disaster*, p.221. Cf. Smyth, *op. cit.*, p.196; Wavell, Despatch, para. 24; Woodburn Kirby, *The War Against Japan*, I, p.404
57 Churchill, *op. cit.*, IV, pp.46-7
58 Tsuji, *op. cit.*, p.232
59 *ibid.*, p.237
60 Connell, *op. cit.*, p.151
61 Churchill, *op. cit.*, IV, p.87
62 Smyth, *op. cit.*, p.228
63 Tsuji, *op. cit.*, p.244
64 Kunitake Teruhito, 'Watakushi wa ano hi, mōshō Yamashita ni eikan wo sasageta' (That day I offered the crown of victory to General Yamashita), *Maru*, No. 324, Tokyo, August 1973, p.80
65 Ashmore, *op. cit.*, pp.18-19
66 Sir Miles Shenton Thomas, two-part draft on Malaya campaign, Part 2, 'Comments on the Draft History of the War Against Japan', para. 158. Percival Papers
67 Percival, 'Notes on Fort Canning Conferences', Conference of 13 February 1942, para. 3. Percival Papers 43
68 *ibid.*
69 Percival, MS notes 'Ammunition Situation' and 'Water Situation'. Percival Papers, Box 6, 64
70 Percival, 'Notes on Fort Canning Conferences', Conference of 15 February 1942, para. 5. Percival Papers
71 *ibid.*
72 *ibid.*
73 Major Cyril H. D. Wild, typescript 'Note on the Capitulation of Singapore', para. 3
74 *ibid.*, para. 4
75 *ibid.*, para. 14
76 Sugita Ichiji, 'Shingapōru kōraku-ji Yamashita chūjō no mondō' (Questions and answers of Lieutenant-General Yamashita at the Fall of Singapore), *Kokoro no hikari*, February 1965, no. 30, pp. 8-16, Tokyo, Naigai Jōsei Kenkyūkai; Defence Agency, Tokyo (ed.); *Marē Shinkō Sakusen* (The Campaign in Malaya), Tokyo, Asagumo Shimbunsha, 1966, pp.621-2; Louis Allen, 'The Surrender of Singapore: the Official Japanese Version', *Durham University Journal*, New Series, Vol. xxix, No. 1, December 1967, pp.1-6; Louis Allen, edition of Major

C. H. D. Wild's 'Note on the Capitulation of Singapore', *Intisari*, Singapore, Vol. III, No. 3, pp.109-16

77 Louis Allen, 'The Surrender of Singapore', pp.2-3
78 *ibid.*
79 *ibid.*
80 Oki Shūji, *Ningen Yamashita Tomoyuki* (Yamashita the Man), Tokyo, Nihon Shūhosha, 1959 (6th edn. 1961), p.235
81 Wild, 'Note on the Capitulation of Singapore', para. 19
82 Lieutenant-Colonel Harrison, draft typescript *History of 11th Indian Division in Malaya*, Chapter XXV, 'Envoi'. Percival Papers.

Chapter IX

1 *Marē Shinkō Sakusen*, pp.627-8
2 Cf. Chapter VIII, reference 34
3 *Marē Shinkō Sakusen*, pp.627-8
4 Ashmore, *op. cit.*, p.19a
5 'Further comments by Lieutenant-General A. E. Percival on Professor J. R. M. Butler's *Grand Strategy III*'. Percival Papers
6 Percival, Despatch, para. 611
7 Percival, *The War in Malaya*, p.296
8 *ibid.*, p.301
9 *ibid.*, p.302
10 Most Secret cipher telegram from CGS Australia to War Office, 2 April 1942. Twelve-page typescript, BP v/9/10/3
11 *ibid.*, I, Part 1, (b), 1
12 *ibid.*, II, Part 3
13 *ibid.*, IV, Part 12, 4
14 'Comments by Air-Chief-Marshal Brooke-Popham on Summary of General Gordon Bennett's Report on Malaya Campaign', p.1, BP v/9/10/2
15 *ibid.*, p.2
16 cf. pp.249-51
17 Brooke-Popham, 'Comments . . . on . . . General Gordon Bennett's Report . . .', *op. cit.*, p.2
18 *ibid.*, p.5
19 Most Secret cipher telegram from CGS Australia . . ., *op. cit.*, IV, Part 13, 4
20 Brooke-Popham, 'Comments . . . on . . . General Gordon Bennett's Report . . .', *op. cit.*, p.5

21 Percival, Despatch, para. 51
22 Confidential note marked 'given personally to AOC for issue to all units', 24 December 1941, BP v/5/49
23 Brooke-Popham to Ismay, 26 March 1941, BP v/1/8
24 *ibid.*
25 *ibid.*
26 Ashmore, *op. cit.*, pp.19a-20
27 Percival, Despatch, para. 80
28 Major-General I. S. O. Playfair, eighteen-page type-script 'Some Personal Reflections on the Malayan Campaign', April 1943, p.8, paras. 16, 17, in BP v/9/28
29 *ibid.*, p.11, para. 26
30 Slim, *op. cit.*, p.19
31 Connell, *op. cit.*, p.114
32 *ibid.*, p.162
33 Major-General Sir John Kennedy, *The Business of War*, London, Hutchinson, 1957, p.198
34 Percival, 'Comments ... on ... Butler's *Grand Strategy III*', *op. cit.*, p.7

Chapter X

1 Simson, *op. cit.*, p.81
2 *ibid.*, p.35
3 *ibid.*, p.37
4 *ibid.*, pp.42-3
5 On the 'fish-bone tactic' (*gyokotsu senpō*) see Major-General Iwakuro Takeo, *Seiki no shingun. Shingapōru sōkōgeki* (An Historic March. The Advance on Singapore), Tokyo, Shio Shobō, 1956, p.127
6 Simson, *op. cit.*, pp.47-8
7 *ibid.*, p.54
8 Lieutenant-General H. Gordon Bennett, *Why Singapore Fell*, Sydney, Angus and Robertson, 1944, pp.77-8; Simson, *op. cit.*, p.57
9 Simson, *op. cit.*, p.69
10 *ibid.*, p.70
11 *ibid.*, p.113
12 Ian Morrison, *op. cit.*, p.156
13 *ibid.*, p.157
14 Brown, *op. cit.*, p.210
15 Connell, *op. cit.*, p.97
16 *ibid.*, pp.97-8
17 *ibid.*, p.98

18 *ibid.*, p.99
19 Shenton Thomas, *op. cit.*, Part 1, 'What Malaya Did', para. 30
20 *ibid.*, para. 31
21 *ibid.*, paras. 34-5
22 *ibid.*, para. 42
23 Woodburn Kirby, *The War Against Japan*, I, p.162
24 *ibid.*, p.161
25 Shenton Thomas, *op. cit.*, Part 2, para. 87
26 *ibid.*
27 Percival, Despatch, para. 674
28 Shenton Thomas, *op. cit.*, Part 2, para. 87
29 Woodburn Kirby, *The War Against Japan*, I, p.153. This is Percival's view. Cf. his MS comment on Shenton Thomas's draft, dated November 1954: 'I think the whole point of this first air raid, which I agree came as a surprise because the R.A.F. did not think that the Jap. bombers had the range, was that the A.R.P. headquarters was not manned. This was a Civil Govt. responsibility. The responsibility for giving warning and ordering a "black-out" lay with the R.A.F.

Incidentally, we blacked out our Operation Room that night but it resulted in such an appalling waste of time that we never did it again.

Sir Shenton is quite wrong in trying to put the blame for what happened on the Military. It was a Civil responsibility.'
30 Woodburn Kirby, *The War Against Japan*, I, p.183
31 Shenton Thomas, *op. cit.*, Part 2, para. 95 (g)
32 *ibid.*, para. 95 (h)
33 Woodburn Kirby, *The War Against Japan*, I, p.183
34 Shenton Thomas, *op. cit.*, Part 2, para. 96 (i)
35 *ibid.*, para. 96 (ii)
36 Ian Morrison, *op. cit.*, p.49
37 Shenton Thomas, *op. cit.*, Part 2, para. 137
38 Wavell, Despatch, para. 9
39 Simson, *op. cit.*, p.89
40 Brown, *op. cit.*, p.229
41 Simson, *op. cit.*, p.88
42 E. M. Glover, *In 70 Days*, London, Muller, 1946
43 Woodburn Kirby, *Singapore, The Chain of Disaster*, p.42
44 All quotations in this section are from Vlieland's TS

draft (see Chapter I, reference 12), unless otherwise indicated
45 Vlieland, *op. cit.*, p.2
46 p.4
47 p.24
48 p.8
49 p.9
50 *ibid.*
51 p.10
52 p.11
53 *ibid.*
54 pp.12-13
55 p.14
56 *ibid.*
57 Connell, *op. cit.*, p.37
58 Vlieland, *op. cit.*, p.15
59 p.17
60 *ibid.*
61 Shenton Thomas, *op. cit.*, Part 1, paras. 52-3
62 Vlieland, *op. cit.*, p.22
63 p.24
64 p.26
65 *ibid.*
66 p.27
67 p.28
68 Vlieland, 'Appreciation by the Secretary for Defence, Malaya, July 1940', Liddell Hart Centre (hereafter referred to as 'Appreciation')
69 *ibid.*
70 Vlieland, *op. cit.*, p.32
71 p.40
72 *ibid.*
73 Babington to Brooke-Popham, 15 September 1941, BP v/11/2
74 Brooke-Popham to Ismay, 5 December 1940, BP v/1/3
75 *ibid.*
76 Brooke-Popham to Ismay, 6 January 1941, BP v/1/4
77 Vlieland, *op. cit.*, p.47
78 pp.53-4
79 p.54
80 *ibid.*
81 p.55
82 p.56

83   p.57
84   p.63
85   *ibid.*
86   *ibid.*
87   p.64
88   p.67
89   *ibid.*
90   p.70
91   *ibid.*

Chapter XI

1   Simson, *op. cit.*, pp.50-1
2   Brooke-Popham to Sir Arthur Street, 15 January 1941, BP v/2/3
3   F. Spencer Chapman, *The Jungle is Neutral*, London, Chatto and Windus, 1949; Reprint Society edn. (London 1950), p.22
4   Percival to Spencer Chapman, 12 November 1949. Percival Papers
5   Spencer Chapman, *op. cit.*, p.25
6   *ibid.*
7   Percival to Spencer Chapman, 12 November 1949, pp.1-2. Percival Papers
8   *ibid.*, p.2
9   Woodburn Kirby, *The War Against Japan*, I, pp.364, 371
10 Ian Morrison, *op. cit.*, pp.171-3
11 Shenton Thomas, *op. cit.*, Part 2, para. 76
12 *ibid.*
13 Woodburn Kirby, *The War Against Japan*, I, p.155
14 Shenton Thomas, *op. cit.*, Part 2, para. 159
15 *ibid.*
16 Harrison, *op. cit.*, quoted in Mackenzie, *Eastern Epic*, I, pp.399-400
17 Percival, comments on Sir Shenton Thomas's draft, p.5. Percival Papers
18 Mackenzie, *Eastern Epic*, I, pp.399-400
19 Ashmore, *op. cit.*, p.10
20 *ibid.*
21 Woodburn Kirby, *The War Against Japan*, I, p.156
22 Major-General Shah Nawaz Khan, *INA and its Netaji*, Delhi, Rajkamal Publications, 1946, pp.4-5

23 Mahmood Khan Durrani, *The Sixth Column*, London, Cassell, 1955, pp.2-3

24 Woodburn Kirby, *The War Against Japan*, I, p.190

25 *ibid.*, p.218

26 Brown, *op. cit.*, p.352

27 Shenton Thomas, *op. cit.*, Part 2, p.102

28 Percival, comments on Shenton Thomas draft

29 Shenton Thomas, *op. cit.*, Part 2, p.103

30 *ibid.*, p.104

31 Percival, comments on Shenton Thomas draft, p.4

32 Brown, *op. cit.*, pp.359-60

33 N. I. Low and H. M. Cheng, *This Singapore (Our City of Dreadful Nights)*, Singapore, Ngai Seong Press, n.d., p.10

34 Details in *Taikoku kankei Tamura bukan Memo* (referred to as *Tamura Memo*), MS by Colonel Tamura Hiroshi in War History Room, Defence Agency, Tokyo; and in Major Fujiwara Iwaichi, *F Kikan* (F Organization), Tokyo, Hara Shobō, 1966, Chapter I *passim*.

35 Shah Nawaz Khan, *op. cit.*, pp.18-19

36 *ibid.*

37 John Connell, *Auchinleck*, London, Cassell, 1959, pp.984-9

38 Percival to Professor J. R. M. Butler, January 1962, p.8. Percival Papers

Chapter XII

1 Shah Nawaz Khan, *op. cit.*, pp.11-12

2 Mackenzie, *Eastern Epic, op. cit.*, I, p.347

3 Iwakuro Takeo, *op. cit.*, p.128

4 David Nelson, *The Story of Changi, Singapore*, West Perth (Aus.), Changi Publication Co., 1974

5 *ibid.*, p.194

6 *ibid.*, p.195

7 Cf. Basil Peacock, 'Prisoner on the Kwai', *History of the Second World War*, Vol. 5, No. 10, pp.2068-72, London, Purnell, n.d. (1968)

8 Laurens van der Post, *The Night of the New Moon*, London, Hogarth Press, 1971

9 Cf. also the publications of the War History Room, Defence Agency: *Biruma Kōryaku Sakusen* (The Invasion of Burma), Tokyo, Asagumo Shimbunsha, 1967,

pp.485-8; *Dai Hon'ei Rikugunbu,* Vol. 4, pp.316-21;
Vol. 5, pp.445-8; Vol. 6, pp.90-1

10 War History Room, Defence Agency, *Impāru Sakusen –
Biruma no bōei* (The Imphal Operation – the Defence
of Burma), Tokyo, Asagumo Shimbunsha, 1968,
pp.130-42

11 'Kokumin ni wabu' (An apology for the people), interview with Field-Marshal Hata Shunroku in *Nihon Shūhō,*
December 1945. Quoted in Yasuda Takeshi and
Fukushima Jūrō (eds.), *Seigen. Shōwa nijūnen hachigatsu
jūgonichi. Haisenka no Nihonjin* (Witness. 15 August
1945. The Japanese in defeat), Tokyo, Shinjinbutsu
Ōraisha, 1973, pp.138-40

12 Ōoka Shōhei, Yamamoto Shichihei, Fujiwara Akira and
Hata Ikuhiko, 'Kōgun daraku no rekishi wo saguru'
(Investigating the history of the corruption of the
Imperial Army), *Shūkan Asahi,* 25 March 1974, pp.50-4

BIBLIOGRAPHY

I. PRIMARY SOURCES

A. *Japanese.*

1. Manuscript.

i. Tamura, Hiroshi, Colonel, *Taikoku kankei Tamura bukan Memo* (referred to briefly as *Tamura Memo,* memoranda of Colonel Tamura, Japanese military attaché in Bangkok). War History Room, Defence Agency, Tokyo.

ii. Nakamura Aketo, Lieutenant-General, *Chūtai Shinen Kaisōroku* (Memories of four years stationed in Thailand). War History Room, Defence Agency, Tokyo.

iii. Fujiwara Iwaichi, Major (later Lieutenant-General), *The Fujiwara Essays* (MS in author's possession).

2. Privately printed articles.

i. Asada Shunnosuke, 'Wanitto no higeki' ('The tragedy of Wan Nit'), *Minnami,* New Year 1954 to October 1954, Parts 1-4.

ii. Sugita Ichiji, Colonel,
'Yamashita Taishō to Shingapōru Kōraku' ('General Yamashita and the Fall of Singapore')
Kokoro no hikari, No. 30, Tokyo, Feb. 1965.
(Both the above in the War History Room, Defence Agency, Tokyo)

B. *British.*

1. Manuscript (or typescript).

i. Wild, C. H. D., Major (later Lieutenant-Colonel),
'Notes on the Malaya Campaign', 7 pp. pencil, incomplete.

ii. Wild, C. H. D., Major (later Lieutenant-Colonel),
'Note on the Capitulation of Singapore'. TS.

iii. Wild, C. H. D., Major (later Lieutenant-Colonel),
'Narrative of "F" Force in Thailand, April-December 1943' (The above in the possession of The Very Rev. J. H. S. Wild, D.D.)

iv. Manuscript material from the Liddell Hart Centre for Military Archives, King's College, University of London.

Bibliography

a. *Brooke-Popham Papers*

Brooke-Popham – Ismay Correspondence.

Brooke-Popham – Street Correspondence.

Copies of telegrams sent and received by Brooke-Popham as Commander-in-Chief, Far East.

Notes by C-in-C Far East on Conversations with Colonel Sura Narong.

Appreciation of the Situation in Malaya 18th December 1941.

First Sighting Report of Japanese invasion force and related signals.

Confidential Note on Evacuation of RAF Aerodromes.

Notes on the War in the Far East.

Notes on *Prince of Wales* and *Repulse*.

Statement of Fighting Units in Malaya at Outbreak of War.

Aeroplanes in the Far East at start of war.

Correspondence from Sir Josiah Crosby, British Minister in Bangkok.

Notes for Talk 2.30 pm 22 December 1941.

Correspondence with Air-Vice-Marshal F. C. Maltby.

Correspondence with Lt.-Gen. A. E. Percival.

Comment by Air Chief Marshal Sir R. Brooke-Popham on Major-General [sic] Percival's despatch 'Operations of Malaya Command'.

Narrative of Operations of Force Z.

Narrative of Aircraft Attacks on Force Z 10th December 1941.

Proposed Admiralty Amendments to reports on the loss of H.M. Ships PRINCE OF WALES AND REPULSE.

Summary of Major-General Bennett's report on Malaya Campaign, from CGS Australia to War Office.

Comments by Air-Chief-Marshal Brooke-Popham of [sic] General Gordon Bennett's Report on Malayan Campaign.

Major-General I.S.O. Playfair, C.B., D.S.O., M.C., *Some personal Reflections on the Malayan Campaign.* 18 pp. TS.

b. *The Vlieland Papers*

1. Copy of *Daily Telegraph article*, 13 Feb. 1967, 'Singapore: the Legend and the Facts'.

2. Memoir of C. A. Vlieland on experiences as Secre-

tary for Defence, Malaya from December 1938 to
February 1941, pp 1-70.
3. Vlieland's Appreciation, as Secretary for Defence,
Malaya.
v. Manuscript material from the Percival Papers in the
Imperial War Museum.

a. Shenton Thomas, Sir Miles,	Copy of two part draft on Malaya campaign. Part 1, 'What Malaya Did' (paras. 1-42) Part 2, Comments on the draft history of the War Against Japan, paras. 1-172.
b. Percival, Lt-Gen. A.E.,	Comments on Sir Shenton Thomas' Comments.
c. Percival, Colonel A.E.,	Lecture on Strategic Problems of Singapore (1937).
d. Percival, Lt-Gen. A.E.,	'Ammunition Situation', 'Water Situation'. Papers inserted into buttoned wallet of red leather (Percival's Hong Kong and Shanghai Bank-book folder).
e. Percival, Lt-Gen. A.E.,	Notebook containing record of proceedings of Fort Canning Conferences 13-15 February 1942.
f. Percival, Lt-Gen. A.E.,	Percival's correspondence with F. Spencer Chapman.
g. Percival, Lt.-Gen. A.E.,	Percival's correspondence with Major-General S. Woodburn Kirby.
h. Percival, Lt-Gen. A.E.,	MS Review of Campaign, written in Changi 16 May 1942, pp.31.
i. Percival, Lt-Gen. A.E.,	Percival's correspondence with Professor J. R. M. Butler.

j. Ashmore, Lt-Colonel, B.H., of the Royal Scots, 'Some
personal observations of Malaya Campaign 1940-42'.
26 pp. with Percival's penned queries in margin.

k. Lt-Col. Harrison's *The 11th Indian Division in Malaya* (draft TS in several folders).

II. SECONDARY SOURCES

1. *Despatches*

Air-Chief-Marshal Sir Robert Brooke-Popham, Commander-in-Chief in the Far East, *Operations in the Far East, from 17th October 1940 to 27th December 1941*. HMSO, London, 1948.

Vice-Admiral Sir Geoffrey Layton, *Despatch on Loss of HM Ships Prince of Wales and Repulse*, HMSO, London 1948.

Air-Vice-Marshal Sir Paul Maltby, *Air operations during the campaign in Malaya and the Netherlands East Indies from 8th December 1941 to 12th March 1942*. HMSO, London, 1948.

Lieutenant-General A. E. Percival, *Operations of Malaya Command, from 8th December 1941 to 15th February, 1942*. HMSO, London, 1948.

General Sir Archibald Wavell, *Despatch by the Supreme Commander of the ABDA area to the Combined Chiefs of Staff on the Operations in the South-West Pacific 15th January 1942 to 25th February 1942*. HMSO, London, 1948.

2. *Official Histories*
i. *British*

Gwyer, J. M. A., (Part I) and Butler, J. R. M., (Part II), *History of the Second World War. Grand Strategy III*, HMSO, London, 1964.

Roskill, Captain S. W., *The War at Sea*, 1939-1945, Vol. I, *The Defensive*, HMSO, London, 1954.

Woodburn Kirby, Major-General S., *The War Against Japan*, Vol. I, HMSO, London, 1957.

ii. *Indian*

Mackenzie, Compton, *Eastern Epic, Vol. 1, Defence*, (all published) Chatto and Windus, London, 1951.

ed. Prasad, Bisheshwar, *The Official History of the Indian Armed Forces in the Second World War (1939-1945). Campaigns in South-East Asia 1941-2*. Orient Longmans.

iii. *Australian*

Wigmore, Lionel, *Australia in the War of 1939-45 (Army): The Japanese Thrust*. Griffin Press, Adelaide, 1957.

Bibliography

iv. *Japanese*

Marē Shinkō Sakusen (The Campaign in Malaya), publ.
by Asagumo Shimbunsha for the War History Room,
Defence Agency, Tokyo, 1966.

Hi-tō: Marē hōmen kaigun shinkō sakusen (Naval opera-
tions in the Philippines and Malaya areas), publ. by
Asagumo Shimbunsha for the War History Room, Defence
Agency, Tokyo, 1969.

Marē Sakusen (The Campaign in Malaya), compiled by a
group of Military History Instructors at the Defence
Agency Academy, Rikusenshi Kenkyū Fukyūkai, Tokyo,
1966 (3rd ed., 1969)

Yoshihara Yanosuke, *Dai Shōri no Kiroku* (A record of
the great victories), Bunshōdō Shoten, Tokyo, 1943.

3. *Narratives by commanders or participants.*

i. *British*

Chapman, F. Spencer, *The Jungle is Neutral*, Chatto &
Windus, London, 1949.

Coombes, J. H. H., *Banpong Express. Malaya and After*,
Darlington, privately printed for the author, 1949.

Percival, Lieutenant-General A. E., *The War in Malaya*,
Eyre and Spottiswoode, London, 1949.

Roberts, Denis Russell, *Spotlight on Singapore*, Anthony
Gibbs and Phillips, London, 1965.

Simson, Brigadier Ivan, *Singapore – Too Little, Too Late*,
Leo Cooper, London, 1970.

Stewart, Brigadier I. MacA., *History of the Second Argyll
and Sutherland Highlanders (The Thin Red Line)
Malayan Campaign 1941-2.* Nelson, London, 1947.

ii. *Indian*

Durrani, Lieutenant-Colonel M. K., *The Sixth Column*,
Cassell, London, 1955.

Shah Nawaz Khan, Major-General, *INA and its Netaji*,
Rajkamal Publications, Delhi, 1946.

iii. *Australian*

Bennet, Lieutenant-General H. Gordon, *Why Singapore
Fell*, Angus and Robertson, Sydney, 1944.

Braddon, Russell, *The Naked Island*, Werner Laurie,
London, 1952.

iv. *Japanese*

Fujiwara Iwaichi, Major (later Lieutenant-General), *F
Kikan* (F Organization), Hara Shobō, Tokyo, 1966.

Hinoki Yohei, 'Marē sora ni Katō Hayabusa sentai no

gokui wo mita' ('I saw the mysteries of Katō Hayabusa squadron in the skies over Malaya'), *Maru*, No. 335, Tokyo, July, 1974, pp.86-91.

Itō Masanori *et al.*, *Jitsuroku Taiheiyō Sensō* (The Pacific War as it really was), Vol. 1, Chūō Kōronsha, Tokyo, 1960.

Iwakuro Takeo, Major-General, *Seiki no shingun. Shingapōru sōkōgeki* (A historic march. The advance on Singapore), Shio Shobō, Tokyo, 1956.

Kashiwagi Hiroshi, 'Marē oki ni POW no densetsu ga tattareta hi' ('The day the story of the Prince of Wales ended off the coast of Malaya'), Maru, No. 324, Tokyo, July 1973, pp.80-85.

Kunitake Teruhito, 'Watakushi wa ano hi, mōshō Yamashita ni eikan wo sasageta' ('That day I offered the crown of victory to General Yamashita'), *Maru*, No. 324, Tokyo, August 1973, pp.80-85.

Moritaka Shigeo, ed., *Hiroku Dai Tōa Senshi* (History of the Great East Asia War), Malaya volume, Fuji Shoen, Tokyo, 1953; reprinted together with Burma volume as one vol., 1971.

Shimada Kōsaku, *Samurai senshataichō* (In command of the *samurai* tanks), Kōnisha, Tokyo, 1969.

Sudō Hajime, *Marē-oki kaisen* (Sea battles in Malayan waters), Shirogane Shobō, Tokyo, 1974.

Takumi Hiroshi, Major-General, *Kota Baru Tekizen Jōriku* (Opposed landing at Kota Bharu), Press Tokyo K. K., Tokyo, 1968.

Tsuji Masanobu, Colonel, *Singapore. The Japanese Version*, trans. Margaret Lake, Constable, London, 1962.

4. *Contemporary Journalists' Accounts*

Brown, Cecil, (Columbia Broadcasting System), *Suez to Singapore*, Halcyon House, New York, 1943.

Gallagher, O. D., *(Daily Express)*, *Retreat in the East*, Harrap, London, 1942.

Glover, E. M., *(Malaya Tribune)*, *In Seventy Days*, Muller, London, 1946.

Morrison, Ian, *(The Times)*, *Malayan Postscript*, Faber, London, 1942.

5. *Later accounts*
i. *British*

Allen, Wing-Commander H. R., D.F.C., *The Legacy of Lord Trenchard*, Cassell, London, 1972.

Allen, Louis, 'The Surrender of Singapore: the Official

Japanese Version', Durham University Journal, New Series, Vol. xxix, No. 1. Dec. 1967, pp.1-6

Barber, Noel, *Sinister Twilight, the Fall and Rise again of Singapore*, Collins, London, 1968.

Bennett, Captain Geoffrey, *The Loss of the Prince of Wales and Repulse*, Ian Allan, London, 1973.

Bond, Brian, ed., *Chief of Staff. The Diaries of Lieutenant-General Sir Henry Pownall*, 2 vols, Leo Cooper, London, 1972 and 1975.

Boyle, Andrew, *Trenchard*, Collins, London, 1962.

Bryant, Sir Arthur, *The Turn of the Tide*, Collins, London, 1957.

Caffrey, Kate, *Out in the Midday Sun*, Deutsch, London, 1974.

Connell, John, *Wavell, Supreme Commander 1941-43*, Collins, London, 1969.

Cooper, Duff, *Old Men Forget*, Hart Davis, London, 1953.

Grenfell, Captain Russell, *Main Fleet to Singapore*, Faber, London, 1951.

Hough, Richard, *The Hunting of Force Z*, London, Collins, 1963.

Ismay, Lord, *Memoirs of General the Lord Ismay*, London, Heinemann, 1960.

Kennedy, Major-General Sir John, *The Business of War*, Hutchinson, London, 1957.

Leasor, James, *Singapore. The Battle that Changed the World*, London, Hodder and Stoughton, 1968.

Mackenzie, Sir Compton, *All Over the Place. Fifty Thousand Miles by Sea, Air, Road and Rail*, Chatto and Windus, London, 1948.

Moore, Donald, ed., *Where Monsoons Meet. The Story of Malaya in the form of an anthology*, Harrap, London, 1956.

Owen, Frank, *The Fall of Singapore*, Michael Joseph, London, 1960.

Moon, Penderel, ed., *Wavell. The Viceroy's Journal*, OUP, London, 1973.

Peacock, Basil, 'Prisoner on the Kwai', *History of The Second World War*, Purnell, London, Vol. 5, No. 10, pp.2068-2072.

Smyth, Sir John, V.C., *Percival and the Tragedy of Singapore*, Macdonald, London, 1971.

Sleeman, Colin and Silkin, S. C., *The Double Tenth Trial*, Hodge, Edinburgh, 1951.

Bibliography

Thompson, P. W., Lt-Col., Doud, H., Lt-Col., Scofield, J., Lt., *et al.*, *How the Jap Army Fights*, Penguin Books, London, 1943.

Wild, Major C. H. D., 'Expedition to Singrep', *Blackwood's Magazine*, No. 1572, Oct. 1946, pp.217-223.

Winstedt, Sir Richard, *Malaya and its History*, Hutchinson's University Library, London, 1948.

Woodburn Kirby, Major-General S., *Singapore, the Chain of Disaster*, Cassell, London, 1971.

ii. *Indian*

Ghosh, Kalyan K., *The Indian National Army*, Meenakshi Prakashan, Meerut, 1969.

iii. *Australian*

Firkins, Peter, *The Australians in Nine Wars* (Ch. 25, 'The Worst Disaster'), Robert Hale, London, 1972.

Legg, Frank, *The Gordon Bennett Story*, Angus and Robertson, London and Sydney, 1965.

iv. *Japanese*

Etchi Harumi, *Kyōran no Shingapōru* (Singapore madness), Hara Shobō, Tokyo, 1967.

Hatakeyama Seikō, *Taisen zenya no chōhōsen* (Espionage warfare on the eve of the great war), Rikugun Nakano Gakkō Shirizu, Sankei Shimbunsha, Tokyo, 1967.

Hatakeyama Seikō, *Hiroku Rikugun Nakano Gakkō*, (Secrets of the Japanese Army Intelligence School), Zoku (Continuation), Sankei Shimbunsha, Tokyo, 1971.

Hattori, Takushirō, *Dai Tōa Sensō Zenshi* (A complete history of the Great East Asia War), Hara Shobō, Tokyo, One vol. edn., 1968.

Imai Seiichi *et al.*, *Taiheiyō Sensōshi* (A History of the Pacific War) Vol. I, 1940-1942, Aoki Shoten, Tokyo, 1972 (3rd ed. 1974)

Imai Takeo, Major-General, *Shōwa no bōryaku* (Stratagems of the Showa Era), Hara Shobō, Tokyo, 1967.

Oki Shūji, *Ningen Yamashita Tomoyuki* (The Man Yamashita), Nihon Shūhōsha, Tokyo, 1959 (6th ed. 1961).

Saitō Yoshiki, *Mōshin! Marē: Shingapōru* (Advance! Malaya and Singapore), Ein Books, Tokyo, 1972.

Shinohara Mamoru, *Shōnan My Story-Japanese Occupation of Singapore*, Asia Pacific Press, Singapore, 1975.

v. *French*

de Belot, Contre-Amiral R., *La Guerre aéronavale du Pacifique*, Payot, Paris, 1957.

La Bruyère, René, *La Guerre du Pacifique*, Payot, Paris, 1945.

Decoux, Amiral Jean, *A la Barre de l'Indochine*, Plon, Paris, 1949.

Giuglaris, Marcel, *Le Japon perd la guerre du Pacifique*, Fayard, Paris, 1958.

vi. *Chinese*

Chin Kee Onn, *Malaya Upside Down*, Jitts & Co., Singapore, 1946.

Low, N. I., and Cheng, H. M., *This Singapore (Our City of Dreadful Nights)*, Ngai Seong Press, Singapore, n.d.

vii. *American*

Coffey, Thomas M., *Imperial Tragedy*, Pinnacle Books, New York, 1970.

Lebra, Joyce, *Jungle Alliance*, Asia Pacific Press, Singapore, 1971.

Louis, Wm. Roger, *British Strategy in the Far East 1919-1939*, Clarendon Press, Oxford, 1971.

Toland, John, *But not in shame*, Panther Books, London, 1964.

6. *Diplomatic background*

Allen, Louis, *Japan, the Years of Triumph*, Macdonald, London, 1970.

Butow, R. J. C. *Tojo and the Coming of War*, Stanford University Press, 1961.

Churchill, Sir Winston, *The Second World War*; Vol. III, *The Grand Alliance*; Vol. IV, *The Hinge of Fate*, Cassell, London, 1950 and 1951.

Crosby, Sir Josiah, *Siam: The Crossroads*, Hollis and Carter, London, 1945.

Foreign Relations of the United States, 1940, IV, *The Far East*, U.S. Government Printing Office, Washington, 1955.

Foreign Relations of the United States, 1941, IV, *The Far East*, U.S. Government Printing Office, Washington, 1956.

Gilchrist, Sir Andrew, *Bangkok Top Secret*, Hutchinson, London, 1970.

Ike, Nobutaka, ed. and transl., *Japan's Decision for War: Records of the 1941 Policy Conferences*, Stanford University Press, 1967.

Kase, Toshikazu, *Nihon Gaikōshi* (History of Japanese Diplomacy), Vol. 23, Nichi-Bei Kōshō (Japanese-American Negotiations), Kajima Kenkyūjo Shuppankai, Tokyo, 1970 (2nd ed., 1972).

Kennedy, Captain Malcolm D., *The Estrangement of Britain and Japan, 1917-35*, Manchester University Press, 1969.

Matsumoto Shunichi and Ando Yoshirō, *Nihon Gaikoshi* (A History of Japanese Diplomacy), Vol. 22, *Nanshin Mondai* (The Question of the Southward Advance), Kajima Kenkyujo Shuppankai, Tokyo, 1973.

Medlicott, W. N., *The Economic Blockade*, Vol. II, HMSO, London, 1959.

Nish, Ian H., *Alliance in Decline. A Study in Anglo-Japanese Relations, 1908-23.* University of London, Athlone Press, 1972.

Parkinson, Roger, *Blood, Toil, Tears and Sweat. The War History from Dunkirk to Alamein, based on the War Cabinet papers of 1940 to 1942*, Hart Davis, MacGibbon, London, 1973.

Van Mook, Dr H. J., *The Netherlands Indies and Japan. Their Relations 1940-41*, Allen and Unwin, London, 1944.

Woodward, Sir Llewellyn, *British Foreign Policy in the Second World War*, Vol. II, HMSO, London, 1971 (Chapters xxii, xxiii, xxiv).

INDEX

ABCD powers, 82
Acheson, Dean, 71
Aircraft: recommended Malaya establishment, 49-51; actual establishment, 51-3; obsolescence of most types, 52; lack of night fighters criticized, 222-3; losses during campaign, 270, 300; Vlieland's views on air defence, 243-4; Percival's views on air defence (1937 lecture), 282, 284-5. See also Royal Air Force

types: Avro Lancaster, bomber, 39n.; Brewster Buffalo, fighter, 52, 223; Bristol Blenheim, bomber, 33, sights and reports invasion fleet, 109; Consolidated Catalina, rescue/reconnaissance flying-boat, sent to shadow invasion fleet, 106, shot down, 107; Fairey Swordfish, torpedo bomber, 52; Hawker Hurricane, fighter, 33, 132, 155, diverted to Russia, 50, comparison with Zero, 52, patrols over Singapore, 171; Lockheed Hudson, bomber, 109n., sights invasion fleet, 105-6, attacks by, on invasion force, 118, 244; Mitsubishi Zero, Japanese fighter, comparison with Hurricane, 52, sea-reconnaissance variant (getabaki), 107; Vickers Wildebeeste, bomber, 52, attacks by, on invasion force, 118

Air raids, 220-3; casualties, 21; precautions, 220-2; absence of night fighters, 222-3
Akagi, cruiser, 33
Alanbrooke, Field-Marshal Viscount, 230

Alor Star, 47, 108, 114, 115, 123, 129, 134, 236-8, 299; airfield evacuated, 128
American-British-Dutch-Australian Command (ABDA), 131, 201
Anambas Islands, 29
Andaman Islands, captured by Japanese, 32
Anderson, Lt-Col C. G. W., 157
Ando, Col, and Ando Force, 147, 149
Anglo-Japanese Alliance, 42, 135, 229; ending of, 37, 38, 42
Arabia, 29-31
Argyll and Sutherland Highlanders, 53, 131, 135, 206
Arisue, Maj, 42, 113
Ark Royal, carrier, 138
Asada, Shunnosuke, 86-7
Ashmore, Lt-Col S.H., 90, 163, 165, 175, 188, 197-8, 255, 298
Atlantic Charter, 81
Attlee, Clement (Earl Attlee), 15, 82
Auchinleck, F-M Sir Claude (later Lord), 262
Australia, 31, 43, 184; and Operation Matador, 96
Australian troops, 185, 188, 190-1, 193, 201, 252; in Johore, 151-2, 154-9; reinforcements in Singapore, 158; on Singapore Island, 161-4, 170, 171, 177; British comments on, 196-8; prisoners massacred by Japanese, 266. See also British and Commonwealth army units
Awaji-San Maru, transport, 117-19
Ayato-San Maru, transport, 118
Ayer Hitam, 156, 157; road and railway to Singapore, 158

Babington, AV-M J.T., AOC

329

Far East, 49, 52, 55, 220, 226, 229, 234-6, 238, 240n.

Bakri, 152, 156, 157

Bangkok, 75, 77-9, 85, 86, 103, 104 107, 260

Bangkok Times, 79

Banzai, Lt-Gen, 26-7

Barham, battleship, 136, 137

Barstow, Maj-Gen A.E., 53, 117, 159; killed, 159

Batavia, 63, 66, 77

Battambang Province, 76, 103

Batu Pahat, 156-8; abandoned, 158

Beard, Charles, 241

Beatty, Admiral of the Fleet Earl, 39n., 40

Beaverbrook, Lord, 16

Bellenger, F. J., 15

Bennett, Capt Geoffrey, 145

Bennett, Maj-(Lt-) Gen Gordon, 53, 163, 209, 254; suggested role for Australians, 151-2; and battle for Johore, 151-2, 154-7; 'West Force', 154-8; and battle for Singapore, 170, 171; and surrender, 175, 177, 178 and n.; analysis of campaign, 191-3; blames Indian Army, 191, 193, 196; on inadequate air support, 191; criticism of British tactics and training, 192; on Singapore defences, 192-3; on civil population, 193; and Shenton-Thomas, 195

Bernam, River, 133-4

Betong, 114, 129

Bidor, 47, 237

Blenheim bombers, 33, 109

Bond, Lt-Gen Sir Lionel, GOC, Malaya Command, 45, 49, 55, 205, 218-20, 226, 228, 234-5, 238, 240n., 242; assessment of situation (1940), 49, 235-6; and defence of Singapore, 235

Bose, Subhas Chandra, 261, 265

Brewster Buffalo fighters, 52, 223

British and Commonwealth Army units: III Corps, 55, 106, 122, 129, 151, 152, 154, 157, 159, 161, 168, 169, 179, 191, 193, 209, 210; 8 Australian Division, 53, 162, 164, 170, 176; 9 Indian Division, 53, 55, 117, 154, 159, 161, 164 11 Indian Division, 55, 93, 94, 106, 110, 113, 122, 123, 127-30, 146, 150, 151, 154, 155, 158, 161, 163, 164, 171, 179, 183, 184, 296; 18 Division, 132, 152, 155, 161, 164, 165, 168, 177, 179, 183, 192, 201; 6 Brigade, 123, 124 126, 130; 6/15 Brigade, 131-3, 158, 170; 8 Brigade, 117, 118, 131, 154, 155, 159, 161, 193; 12 Brigade, 130-2, 135, 147, 151, 154, 155, 162, 170; 15 Brigade, 123, 124, 126, 130; 22 Australian Brigade, 152, 154, 159, 162, 170, 252; 22 Indian Brigade, 117, 154, 159; 27 Australian Brigade, 152, 162, 170; 28 Brigade, 124, 126, 130-3, 147, 151, 154; 29 Australian Brigade, 171; 44 Indian Brigade, 154, 158, 160, 170, 201; 45 Indian Brigade, 154, 156, 157, 159, 201; 46 Indian Brigade, 154; 53 Brigade, 155-8, 161; 2/4 Australian MG Battalion, 161; 2/19 Australian Battalion, 152; 2/29 Australian Battalion, 156; 157; 2/30 Australian Battalion, 155-6; 3 Indian Cavalry, 133, 135; Malay battalions, 161, 253-5. *See also* under names of individual regiments

British forces, 185; changes in command, 186; reasons for losing Malaya, 186-7; Yamashita's views, 187-8

British Eastern Fleet, 32, 101, 110, 185

British North Borneo, 44, 95, 202

British Strategy in the Far East (Louis), 247n.

Brooke-Popham, ACM Sir Robert C-in-C, Far East, 51-5, 109-118, 121-2, 142, 145,

214, 221, 235, 249, 258-9; and Thailand, 75, 76, 85, 87-90; and Operation Matador, 93, 95-7, 99-100, 106, 110, 112-13; relieved of command, 130; comments on Gordon Bennett's report, 193-6; on Indian troops, 193; takes part of blame for lack of defences, 194-5; on Shenton-Thomas, 195; and inadequate demolitions by RAF, 195-6; on Australian troops, 196-7; and Vlieland, 238-40

Brown, Cecil, US correspondent, 54, 88-90, 213, 223-5, 257

Bukit Timah, 168, 170, 171, 178, 179, 183, 267; captured, 172, 177, 187

Burma, 18, 34, 43, 55, 62, 74, 84, 92, 103, 119, 154, 184, 189, 217, 231, 232, 261, 263-8

Burma Road, 57, 88

Burma-Siam railway, building of, 266-8; cholera, 268; death rate, 268

Butler, Prof J. R. M. (Sir James), 52, 122, 188, 201

Butler, Nevile, 78, 80

Butler, R. A. (Lord Butler of Saffron Walden), 79, 80

Butterworth, RAF at, 257

Cambodia, 74, 76, 77, 103

Canada, and Operation Matador, 96

Cape Cambodia, 103, 104, 106

Carpendale, Brig W., 126

Casualty figures, 270-1; British, 270; Japanese, 271

Catalina flying-boats, 106, 107

Catroux, Gen, 57, 60

Cave Browne, Gen, 206

Ceylon, 28, 29; Japanese raids on, 31-4

Challen, Brig B., 158

Changi, 161-4, 169, 267

Changlun, 124, 126-7

Chapman, F. Spencer, 194, 249-51

Chiang Kai-Shek, 35, 57, 58, 61, 69, 248

Chiefs of Staff, 51, 92, 110, 234;
appreciation of Far East situation (August 1940), 49-50, 237, 240; limitation of aircraft for Far East, 50-1, 118; against unilateral action in Thailand, 81-2; and Operation Matador, 95, 96, 98; and 'scorched earth' policy, 295-7

Chiengmai, 77, 85

China and the Chinese, 44, 50, 54, 58, 61, 62, 71, 72, 247-53, 259; British lives and property in, 43; 'China Incident', 56-8, 62, 66-7, 70, 264; US supply of wheat, 68-9; British failure to use Chinese, 185-6, 248-53, 255; guerrillas, 193, 224, 248, 250; Chinese in Singapore, 193, 213; Chinese labour, 218-19, 224, 248; Nationalist Government (Kuomintang), 248, 251-3; Communists, 251-3; Dalforce, 251-3

Chinese Information Board, Singapore, 224

Chinese Mobilization Council, 253

Chinese Volunteer Force, 35

Chokai, Japanese flagship, 101, 109

Chungking, Chinese Nationalist Government in, 224

Churchill, (Sir) Winston, 14-16, 31, 55, 81, 95, 134, 136, 167, 168, 171, 186, 214, 225-7, 230-2, 242; and US entry into war, 16, 36, 241; on defence of Singapore (1939), 41-2; and aircraft for Far East (Jan 1941), 51; and Operation Matador, 96-9; and Force Z, 137-9; and 'scorched earth' policy, 294, 297

Clemenceau, Georges, 234

Climate of Malaya, 199

Colombo, 32; attacked by Japanese, 33

Columbian Broadcasting System, 54, 88, 213

Committee of Imperial Defence, appreciation of defence of Singapore (1937), 45

Index

Communism, 250-3
Connell, John, 164, 200, 231, 297
Coral Sea, Battle of, 34
Cornwall, cruiser, 33
Craigie, Sir Robert, 82-3
Cranborne, Lord (Marquess of Salisbury), 22
Cripps, Sir Stafford, 16
Crosby, Sir Josiah, British Minister in Thailand, 75-80, 91, 112
Curtin, John, 96

Dalley, Col, and Dalforce, 251-3
Darvall, Gp-Capt, 52
Decoux, Adm Jean, 57, 77-8, 80
Defence Committee (London), 139; and Thailand, 81-2, 89; decision to send *Repulse* to Far East, 136
Defence Committee (Malaya), 228, 233, 235; dominance of Army, 233
De Gaulle, Gen Charles, 79
De Ruyter, Dutch flagship, 32
Dill, F-M Sir John, 49, 206, 230
Dobbie, Lt-Gen (Sir) William, GOC Malaya Command, 43, 45-6, 49, 233, 272; on danger of attack from north, 46 and n., 92; building of pillboxes, 205; allocation of money for defence, 205
Doorman, Adm, 32
Dorsetshire, cruiser, 33
Duff Cooper, Alfred (Viscount Norwich), Resident Minister of State in Singapore, 55, 166, 167, 202, 203, 213, 214, 223-5, 228, 241, 258, 294, and n., 296
Duncan, Brig H. C., 154; killed, 157
Dunkirk, evacuation from, 56, 186, 242, 244
Dutch East Indies, *see* Netherlands East Indies

Eagle, carrier, 137

East Surrey Regiment, 2nd Bn, 124, 130, 133
Eastern Epic (Mackenzie), 144, 255
Eastforce, 158, 159
Eden, (Sir) Anthony (Earl of Avon), 66, 82, 137
El Alamein, battle of, 244
Electra, destroyer, 137
Empress of Britain, transport, sunk, 161
Endau, 103, 155, 158, 160
Express, destroyer, 137

Federated Malay States, 55
Fifth-column activity, question of, 255
Forbes, Resident Counsellor in Penang, 257, 258
Force Z, 137-46; in Ceylon, 138; in Singapore, 139; sails north, 139; absence of fighter protection, 141-2, 144; observed by Japanese submarines, 141, 142; changes of course for Kuantan, 141; *Repulse* and *Prince of Wales* sunk, 143
Fort Canning, 175, 177, 179, 212, 233
France, collapse of (1940), 48-9, 56, 60, 61, 74, 185, 230, 242
Frankland, Noble, 39n
Fraser, Hugh, 176, 178, 213, 214
Fraser, Gen Sir Theodore, 46, 229
Fujiwara, Maj (Lt-Col) Iwaiichi, and Fujiwara Organization, 254, 260, 261
Fushimi, Prince, 64-5

Gallacher, William, 16
Gammans, Capt Lionel, 21-2
Garreau, Roger, 78, 79
Garrett, Brig R. A., 126
Gemas, 151, 155-6, 197
Georgetown, 130
Germany: bombing of, 21; and Japan, 23-8, 230; invasion of Russia, 23, 24, 50, 82; unaware of Japanese plans, 25;

attitude to USA, 25-6; declares war on USA, 27-8; oil supplies, 64-5
Gilchrist, Andrew, 91
Glover, E. D., 225
Gneisenau, German battleship, 15, 21
Gong Kedah airfield, 119
Graham, Capt, 133
Grant, US Minister in Thailand, 79
Grenfell, Capt Russell, 145
Grew, Joseph, 58, 59
Grigg, Sir James, 16
Guerrilla warfare, 193, 224, 248-50; 101 Special Training School, 249
Guillemard, Sir Laurence, 243
Gunong Palai pumping station, 211
Gurkha battalions, 124, 128, 133; 2/1 Gurkha Rifles, 124, 149, 150
Gurun, defence of, 128-30; Japanese break through, 129; 6 Brigade's defences destroyed, 130; further withdrawal, 130

Haad'yai, 93, 94
Halder, Gen Franz, 27
Halifax, Viscount (Earl of), British Ambassador in Washington, 63, 67, 97-9
Hall, Noel, 71
Hamilton, Maxwell, 78-9
Hara, Yoshimichi, 65, 83, 84
Harada, Maj, 113
Harrison, Col, 163, 184, 254-5
Hart, Adm, 110
Hashimoto, Japanese escort commander, 118
Hata, F-M Shunroku, 269
Hawaii, 31, 33, 38, 117; US fleet at, 103, 137-9
Heath, Lt-Gen Sir Lewis, Commander of III Corps, 55, 106, 113, 121, 122, 128-31, 152, 157, 158, 163, 168, 180, 209, 210; and surrender, 175-9, 182
Hermes, carrier, 33

Hill, Prof A. V., 20-1
Hirohito, Emperor of Japan, 13-15, 57, 84-5, 99; Rescript to troops on fall of Singapore, 13-14
Hiroshima, atomic bomb on, 269
Hitler, Adolf, 25-8, 30; invasion of Russia, 23, 24; and co-operation with Japan, 23; and war with USA, 28; discussions with Mussolini, 30-1
Holland, German occupation of, 56, 61
Hong Kong, 28, 38, 50, 54, 55, 104, 135, 249
Hore-Belisha, Leslie (Lord), 19-20
Hornbeck, Stanley, 68, 71
Hoshino, President of Japanese Planning Board, 64
House of Commons, and discussion of Singapore, 15-22
House of Lords, and discussion of Singapore, 22
Hudson aircraft, 105, 106, 109n., 118, 244
Hull, Cordell, US Secretary of State, 66-8, 72-3; 'Four Principles', 58
Hull-Nomura talks, 25, 66, 73, 95
Hurricane fighters, 33, 52, 132, 155; diverted to Russia 50; patrols over Singapore, 171

Ike, Nobutaka, 84
Ikeya, Col, 181
Imai, Col, 268
Imphal, 265, 267
India: Japan and, 29-31, 184; Japanese submarine attacks off coast, 32
Indian Army and Indian troops, 185, 188, 190, 193, 194, 198, 201, 247, 248, 250, 256; blamed by Gordon Bennett, 191, 193, 196. *See also* British and Commonwealth Army units
Indian labour companies, 218, 219

Indian Mountain Artillery, 117;
22 Regiment, 124
Indian National Army, 247, 256,
261-2, 265
Indians in Malaya, 255-9; evacuation policy and Indian reactions, 256-9
Indo-China, French, 41, 47, 49,
61, 62, 64, 74, 80, 84, 97, 99,
103, 142, 185, 217, 222,
230, 245, 299; war with Thailand, 75-7, 88; Japanese occupation of, 25, 27, 48, 49,
57-8, 60, 67, 68, 72, 80-2;
Japanese reinforcements in,
98; Japanese aircraft based on,
141, 145
Indomitable, carrier, 138
Ipoh, 130, 168; captured by
Japanese, 131
Irie, Maj, 268
Iron and steel, Japanese needs,
61-2
Ironside, F-M Lord, 49
Ishida, Maj-Gen, 268
Ismay, Gen Lord, 40, 41, 45,
53, 75, 76, 196, 239, 297
Iwakuro, Col (Maj-Gen) Hideo,
206-7, 266

Jakarta, *see* Batavia
Japan: and Germany, 23-8, 230;
and Soviet Russia, 23, 24, 27;
naval bases required, 28-9;
aims in South-East Asia, 29,
47, 48, 59, 71; and India,
29-31; and Manchuria, 41;
leaves League of Nations, 41;
'China Incident', 56-8, 62, 66-
7, 70, 264; Imperial Conferences, 56, 57, 59, 60, 64, 83;
heirarchy, 57; Liaison Conferences, 57, 68-71, 81, 83;
occupation of Indo-China,
57-8, 67, 68, 72, 80-2; US
embargoes, 58, 66, 68-9, 71;
confrontation with USA, 58-
9; prepared to risk war, 59-
60; and Dutch East Indies,
63-6; Hull-Nomura talks, 25,
66, 73, 95; mediation and

influence in Thailand, 75, 77;
discussions on Thailand, 82-5;
espionage in Singapore, 88,
115; importance of Thailand
in Japanese plans, 92; signal
for war, 101; intelligence
activities in Malaya, 113-15,
185; actions after fall of
Singapore, 31-6. *See also*
Japanese forces
Japanese Air Forces, 141-3;
superiority of, 143
Japanese Army units: 15 Army,
264; 25 Army, 101, 103, 107,
116, 119, 170, 174, 180, 260;
5 Division, 34, 107, 119, 127,
128, 134, 154, 155, 169, 171,
172, 174, 187; 18 Division,
101, 119, 155, 169, 171, 172,
174, 187, 253, 264, 266; 55
Division, 101, 119, 56 Division, 103, Imperial Guards
Division, 103, 154-7, 164, 169,
171-2, 184, 187, 266; 21 Infantry Brigade, 174; 5 Guards
Regiment, 206-7, 266; 11 Infantry Regiment, 134; 42
Infantry Regiment, 147; 56
Infantry Regiment, 101; 143
Infantry Regiment, 101, 119
Japanese forces in campaign for
Malaya and Singapore:
Malaya Force, 101, 105;
Takumi Force, 101, 107, 113,
118, 119; Uno Force, 101, 108;
secret voyage south, 104; observed by Australian aircraft,
105-6; first air combat of war,
107; Malaya Force splits up,
107; composition of forces,
107-8; landings at Kota
Bharu, 116-19; its capture,
119; landings in Thailand,
119-20; in Northern Malaya,
121-35, 146; fighting for Jitra,
123-9; Gurun, 129-30; capture of Taiping and Ipoh, 131;
Kampar position, 131-5; control of west coast, 134; in
Central Malaya, 146-51; Slim
River battle, 146-52; battle
for Johore, 151-60; Kuala

Lumpur entered, 155; battle for Singapore Island, 160-74; crossing to Singapore, 169-70 qualities and advantages, 185, 188; local superiority at point of assault, 166, 185; mastery of air, 185, 189, 190; sea superiority, 189, 190

massacres by Japanese, 265-7; treatment of prisoners, 265-7; Burma-Siam railway, 266-8

Japan's Decision for War (Ike), 84

Jat battalion, 2/9, 124, 126

Java, 19, 64, 66, 184, 199; captured by Japanese, 28, 31-3. *See also* Netherlands East Indies

Java Sea, Battle of, 32

Jayanama, Nai Direck, 74, 91

Jellicoe, Admiral of the Fleet Earl, 38

Jemaluang, 152, 158

Jitra, defence of, 123-9, 146, 166, 207-8, 257; loss of guns and transport at Mannggoi, 126; penetration of Jat positions, 126; Japanese night attack, 127; surrender of 3,000 Indian troops, 127; withdrawal to Gurun, 128-9

Johore, 41, 55, 94, 166-9, 194, 195, 197, 203 and n., 204, 210, 235, 242; importance of its defence, 45; battle for Johore, 151-61, 164; line of defence, 151; Muar area, 151, 152, 154, 156-7, 170; forward position at Gemas, 151, 155-6, 197; Australians brought into battle, 151, 152; Japanese enter Kuala Lumpur, 155; ambushes by Australians, 155-6, 158-9, 197; resistance by 45 Brigade, 157; withdrawal to Southern Johore, 157-8; loss of Batu Pahat, 158; way to south blocked, 158; remnants evacuated by gunboat, 158; Eastforce arrives at

bridgehead, 159; difficulties of Westforce, 159; surrender of 22 Indian Brigade, 159; crossing of Causeway, 160; Causeway blown up, 160, 175; water supply for Singapore, 211

Johore Bahru, 159, 168, 204

Johore Causeway, 160, 174, 175, 187, 211

Johore Military Forces, 217

Johore River, 162, 163

Johore Straits, 39, 161, 162, 164, 171

Johore, Sultan of, 37, 203, and 204n.

Jones, S. W., Colonial Secretary, 176, 213, 214, 223, 225, 235-7, 239, 241n.

Jordan, Secretary for Chinese Affairs, 213, 219, 223-5

Jungle is Neutral, The (Chapman), 249

Jurong Line, 170, 171, 187

Kallang airfield, 162, 170

Kampar, 47, 131-5, 146, 147, 201, 237; bridge over Kampar River blown, 132; Japanese attack main position, 133; threat to flank, 133-4; seaborne landing on River Bernam, 134; resistance in Changkat Jong, 135; British withdrawal, 135

Kashii, cruiser, 108

Kato, Col, 268

Katsuno, Japanese consul in Singora, 119-20

Kawamura, Maj-Gen, punitive expedition in Singapore, 34-5

Kaya, Japanese Finance Minister, 70-1

Kedah, 47, 48, 55, 74, 94, 101, 129, 193, 194, 217, 223, 237, 240, 242, 250, 257, 299

Kedah River 128, 129

Keitel, F-M Wilhelm, 23

Kelantan, 47, 55, 74, 101, 193, 194, 236, 250

Kelantan, Sultan of, 256

Kempei (Japanese secret police), 35

Key, Brig (Maj-Gen) B. W.,
117-19, 155, 158, 184, 193,
209, 256
Khmers, 76
Kido, Marquis, 13
Killery (of Ministry of Economic Warfare), 194, 250-1
King George V class battleships,
137
King-Hall, Cdr Sir Stephen, 20
Kirby, Maj-Gen S. Woodburn,
165, 214, 221; on Vlieland,
226-7; and 'scorched earth'
policy, 294-6
Kluang, 154, 155, 157, 158,
201
Kobayashi, Japanese Minister
of Commerce, 63, 66
Koh Chang, naval battle at (Jan
1941), 77
Koiso, Gen, 63
Kondo, Adm, 116
Konoye, Prince, 58, 59
Kota Bharu, 101, 105, 107-9,
114, 122, 159, 193, 209, 221,
236; Japanese landings, 116-
19, 223; British air attacks,
117-18, 244; airfield evacuated
118-9; capture of town, 119;
evacuation, 256
Kra Isthmus, 76, 82, 93, 96-
101, 103, 112; significance of,
92; Japanese landing, 119
Kranji River, 170, 171, 187
Kroh, 47, 121, 129, 130, Kroh-
Patani road, 93, 121, 122
Krohcol, 121, 123, 128
Kuala Lumpur, 55, 106, 131,
132, 146, 152, 195, 237, 254;
entered by Japanese, 155
Kuantan, 47, 118, 132, 142, 143,
209; false report of Japanese
landing, 141, 144-5
Kunitake, Maj, 174
Kuomintang (Chinese National-
ist Government), 248, 251-3
Kurita, Rear-Adm, 32, 104
Kurusu, Japanese envoy to
USA, 14, 73, 95

Lancaster bombers, 39n.

Laos, 74-6
Layton, Vice-Adm Sir Geoffrey,
C-in-C, China Station, 55,
75, 89-90, 106, 109, 167, 214,
234-5, 238, 242
'Ledge, The', 93, 121
Leicestershire Regiment, 1st Bn,
124, 133
Lépissier, French Minister in
Bangkok, 77
*Loss of the Prince of Wales
and Repulse, The* (Bennett),
145n.
Louis, William Roger, 247n.
Lumut, Japanese assembly at,
133-4
Lyon, Brig C. A., 257-8

MacArthur, Gen Douglas, 167
McCollum, Cdr A. H., 85
Machang airfield, 119
Mackenzie, Sir Compton, 143-4,
187, 255, 266
Mahmood Khan Durrani, Lt-
Col, 256
Main Fleet to Singapore (Gren-
fell), 145
Malacca, 55, 155; abandonment
of, 151
Malacca Straits, 43, 132, 162,
163, 267
Malay people and troops, 161,
193, 217, 247, 250, 253-5;
British failure to use, 185,
250, 255; and Volunteer
Forces, 215, 217, 251, 253,
254; in civil defence units,
254
Malay Police, Punjabis and
Sikhs in, 256
Malaya, 43, 62-4, 74, 77, 80, 82,
84, 85, 87, 95, 120, 184; its
defences, 41-2, 45, 50, 236;
Japanese intelligence in, 42,
113-15; and Operation Matador, 92, 93
battle for Northern Malaya,
121-35, 146; Japanese control of west coast, 134; defence of Central Malaya,
146-51; battle for Johore,

151-60; demoralizing policy of withdrawals, 185
economic function, 215; trade with USA, 215; civil police, 215; and Japanese espionage, 215; effort in early days of war, 217-18; trade figures, 231-2
Malaya Tribune, 225
Malayan Communist Party, 250
Maltby, AV-M, 142, 221-3
Manchuria, 35, 37, 41, 58, 61, 66, 67
Margesson, Capt H. D. R. (Viscount Margesson), 16
Martin, J. H., 18
Matsui, Maj-Gen, 101
Matsunaga, Rear-Adm, 143
Matsuoka, Japanese Foreign Minister, 56, 58, 66, 81, 82
Matzky, Director of German Military Intelligence, 27
Maxton, James, 17
Mekong River, 74, 75, 80
Mersing, 103, 151, 157-9, 163
Middle East, British priority to, 227, 230, 243-5
Midway, Battle of, 34
Ministry of Economic Warfare, 62, 73, 194 and n., 250
Mohan Singh, 260, 261
Mook, Dr van, 63-6
Moore, Sir John, 210
Moorehead, Lt-Col, 121
Morgenthau, Henry, 69
Morrison, Ian, *Times* correspondent, 19, 212-13, 223, 252
Moyne, Lord, Secretary of State for Colonies, 166, 167, 213-14
Muar and Muar River, 151, 152, 154; fighting round, 156-7
Mukaide Force, ambushed, 155-6
Murphy, Robert, 79-80
Murray-Lyon, Maj-Gen D. M., 106, 123, 128-30, 207-8
Mussolini, Benito, 30-1
Mutaguchi, Lt-Gen Renya, 101, 172, 264-5; hopes of conquest of India, 264-5

Nagasaki, atomic bomb on, 269

Nagumo, Adm, 25, 32-4
Napoleon, 210
Narong, Col Sura, 87-8
Naval patrol-boats at Singapore, 170-1
Negri Sembilan, 55; abandonment of, 151
Nehru, Jawaharlal, 262
Nelson, David, 267
Netherlands East Indies, 18, 32, 47, 49, 56, 61, 62, 69, 72, 95, 99, 100, 144, 152, 167, 231, 245; resistance to Japan and negotiations, 63-6
Nettinate, Luang Vudiasora, 88, 89
New Zealand, 43; and Operation Matador, 96
Newall, Marshal of the RAF Sir Cyril (Lord), 51
Newbigging, Brig, 178, 179, 183
Nickel, Japanese need for, 66
Nishimura, Lt-Gen 103, 169, 171, 172, 184, 266
Nomura, Adm, Japanese Ambassador in Washington, 66, 95

O'Connor, Gen Sir Richard, 244
Ogata, 2-Lt, 107
Ogura, Japanese Finance Minister, 69
Oil: supply, 28, 69, 73, 230; Japanese need, 62-6, 68-9, 186
Ooka, Shohei, 269
Operation Barbarossa, 24
Operation Matador, 89, 113, 121, 123, 192, 207, 208; discussion of plan, 92-3; military advantages, 93; proposals to operate it, 93-4; plans, 94; and attitude of Thais and Americans, 94-9; consultations with Dominions, 96; Roosevelt's hypotheses, 97-9; conditional American support, 99; Brooke-Popham authorized to proceed if necessary, 99-100; not immediately put into force, 106, 110; not to be operated, 110, 112

Oshima, Lt-Gen Hiroshi, 25-8, 30

Osone, Maj, 119 and n.

Ostfriesland, sinking of, 39

Ostrorog, M., 80

Otani, Col Keijiro, 35-6

Oto, 2-Lt, 127, 128

Ott, Gen Eugen, 25

Ozawa, Vice-Adm, 101, 104-6; decides to land at Kota Bharu, 108-9

Pacific War Council, 17

Page, Sir Earle, 138

Painter, Brig G. W. A., 159, 209

Palliser, Rear-Adm, 106, 137, 141, 144-6

Panomyong, Nai Pridi, 74, 91

Paris, Brig, 130-3, 155, 163

Parit Sulong, 207; massacre at, 266

Patani, 93, 101, 107-9, 114, 118, 121; Japanese landings, 119, 122, 123; advance from, 128

Peacock, Maj Basil, 267

Pearl Harbour, 137; Japanese attack on, 25, 27, 32, 33, 103, 116, 139, 241

Penang 17, 55, 94, 129-31, 134; evacuation, 257-9

Perak, 55, 94, 217, 237

Perak, River, 101, 129, 132-4 146

Percival, Lt-Gen, A. E., 23, 52, 90, 106, 109, 121-3, 194 and n., 195, 213, 220, 221, 224, 230, 242, 243, 258, 262; on strategical problems of Singapore (1937), 43-5, 48, 236, 272-87; further appreciation, 45-6; appointed GOC Malaya, 55; and Operation Matador, 92-4, 97, 110; and defence of Northern Malaya, 128-9, 132-4; defence of Johore, 151, 152, 154, 155, 157-9; and battle for the Island, 160-72; and direction of Japanese attack, 162-5; decides to meet Japanese on beaches, 166; parcelling-out of forces,

166; defence of Singapore, 168, 170-2, 174; and surrender, 175-83, 187, 260, 263 qualities, 186; Yamashita's views on his tactics, 187, 188; over-estimate of Japanese numbers, 187, 189-90; on reasons for Japanese victory, 188-91; and civil population, 198; and Wavell's comments, 200-1; and Simson, 202-7, 209-12; on water supply, 212; and recruitment of labour, 218-19; on use of Chinese, 248-51; and Malay population, 255; and 'scorched earth' policy, 294-8

Perlis, 55, 74, 123; evacuated by British, 126

Pétain, Marshal, 60

Pethick Lawrence, F. W. (Lord), 15, 19

Petroleum, *see* Oil

Philippines, the, 41, 44, 95, 105, 144, 167, 184, 267, 269

Phillips, Adm Sir Tom, 101, 106, 110, 136-9, 141-6; in command of Force Z, 137; decides to sail north from Singapore, 139; change course for Kuantan, 141-2; lost with *Prince of Wales*, 143; views on air power, 145-6

Pibun, Songgram, Thai dictator, 74, 76, 83, 87

Piggott, Maj-Gen Francis, 37, 42, 229

Playfair, Maj-Gen I. S. O., 94, 100; on civil population in Malaya, 198-9

Port Darwin, 43, 106, 139, 167, Japanese raid on, 31-3

Pound, Adm Sir Dudley, 134, 136, 137

Pownall, Gen Sir Henry, C-in-C, Far East, 130-1, 203n.; Chief of Staff to Wavell, 131, 167

Prince of Wales, battleship, 137-9, 142, 143, 146; loss of, 16, 20, 36, 143, 145, 190

Pritam Singh, 260

Province Wellesley, 55

Public Works Department, 207, 211

Pulau Ubin, 164, 169, 171, 187

Pulford, AV-M C. W. H., AOC Far East, 55, 106, 139, 141-2, 145, 146, 171, 195, 220, 221

Punjab battalions, 126, 130; prisoners massacred by Japanese, 266; 1/8, 129, 133; 1/14, 124, 260; 2/16, 124; 3/16, 121

Queen Elizabeth, battleship, 137

Quetta Staff College, exercise on defence of Singapore (1922), 40, 41, 45

Rabaul, Japanese occupation of, 32, 33

Raffles, Sir Stamford, 22, 37, 38n., 43

Ramshaw, Flt-Lt, 105-6

Repulse, cruiser, 106, 136-9; loss of, 16, 20, 36, 143-5, 190

'Retreat complex' 191, 194

Ribbentrop, Joachim von, 25-8, 30, 31

Rice, 217, 238; Japanese needs, 62, 82

Rommel, F-M Erwin, 244

Roosevelt, President Franklin D., 14, 26, 28, 58-9, 63, 67, 81, 241; hypotheses on Far East, 97-9

Roskill, Capt S. W., 144

Royal Air Force: and proposals for Singapore defence, 39-40, 44, 45, 49; and defence of Malaya, 50, 118; numbers and types of aircraft, 51-2; and Operation Matador, 93; fighting at Kota Bharu, 117-19; evacuation of Alor Star airfield, 128; withdrawal to Netherlands East Indies, 160, 171; patrols over Singapore, 171; and demolition of airfields, 190, 195-6; 27 Squadron, 223; 453 Squadron, 257

Royal Artillery, 117; 80 Anti-Tank Regiment, 124; 155 Field Regiment, 124, 133; 16 Light Anti-Aircraft Battery, 150

Royal Australian Air Force, 105

Royal Dutch Shell, 64

Royal Sovereign class battleships, 137

Rubber, 199, 215, 218, 232; Japanese and German needs, 62, 64, 66, 82-3

Russia, *see* USSR

Russo-Japanese War, 269

Ryujo, carrier/transport, 32, 109

Ryuku Maru, transport, 267

Saeki, Lt-Col Chizuo, 126-8

Saigon, 75, 84, 85, 103, 114, 115, 141

Sakura Maru, transport, 118

Sasaki, Col, 268

Sayers, Dorothy L., 22

Scharnhorst, German battleship, 15, 21

'Scorched earth' policy, 294-300; balance sheet of booty, 300

Segamat, 151, 152, 154, 156, 157

Selangor, 55, 215-16, 229; abandonment of, 151

Seletar, 161; airfield, 162

Sembawang airfield, 144, 162

Sendai, cruiser, 107

Shah Nawaz Khan, 256, 265-6

Shan States, 74

Shenton Thomas, Sir Miles, Governor of Straits Settlements, 46n., 49, 75, 166, 167, 175, 195, 202-3, 212-29, 233, 240n., 248, 259; and surrender, 176; and Simson, 203 and n.; his qualities, 212-13; possibility of his removal, 213-14, 225; presentation of his case, 214-25; on works and labour, 215-16, 218-20; food control, 217; air raid precautions, 220-2; on Malayan economy, 232-3; and Vlieland, 234, 235, 237-40; and the Chinese, 252-3; and Malays,

254, 255; on evacuation of Penang, 258; and 'scorched earth' policy, 295, 298

Shiga, Naoya, 14-15

Shimada, Maj, 149, 150

Shimoda, Maj-Gen, 268

'Shonan', Japanese name for Singapore, 14, 15

Shumshu, coastal vessel, 108

Siam (Thailand), 74, 217, 229-31, 235, 245. *See also* Thailand

Simmons, Maj-Gen Keith, Fortress Commander, Singapore, 167, 168, 213, 298

Simson, Brig Ivan, Chief Engineer, Malaya Command, 166-8, 176, 177, 215, 223-5, 248; version of events, 202-7, 208-12; charges against civilian authorities, 202-3; responsibility for civil defence, 166-7, 202-3; proposals for strengthening fortifications, 204-5; and defences against tanks, 206-11; pamphlet on anti-tank measures, 208-9; and water supply, 211-12; and 'scorched earth' policy, 295, 296, 298

Singapore: decision to build Naval Base, 37-9; Johore Strait site, 39; cases for air or naval-gun defence, 39-40, 43; appreciation of defence, 43-8; civil government, 55

regarded by USA as indefensible, 63; and position of Thailand, 78, 80, 82, 86-7, 89, 96; Japanese espionage in, 88, 115.

and Japanese drive south, 106, 107; report by Japanese agents, 115; long-range defence, 121; reinforcements, 132, 138, 155, 158; role and defence of base, 135-6

battle for the Island, 160-74, 185; withdrawal of RAF, 160; reinforcements, 160-1; light tanks, 161; swollen population, 161; strength of British force, 161; defence zones, 161-2; airfields, 162; direction of Japanese attack, 162-3; Japanese take Pulau Ubin, 164, 169; Japanese artillery opens up, 164; Percival's plan, 166; rift between civil and military authorities, 166-7; civil defence, 166, 202-3, 220-3; lack of northern defences, 167-8, 192, 194, 195, 201, 210-11, 223-4; Japanese deception plan, 169; Japanese crossing, 169-71; Japanese strength, 169; defence on Jurong Line, 170, 171, 187; loss of Tengah airfield, 170; airfields untenable, 171; Japanese attack in western sector, 171; drive on Bukit Timah, 171, 172; surrender call to Percival, 172; Causeway repaired, 174; Japanese ammunition shortage, 174; British artillery barrage, 174; news of British peace envoy, 174

surrender, 13-15, 22, 31, 175-86; inevitability, 175; conferences of British commanders, 175-8, 212; administrative situation, 175-8; water situation, 176-8, 211-12; counter-attack turned down, 178; timing of ceasefire, 178-80; exchange between Percival and Yamashita, 180-3; time of capitulation decided, 183; intended Japanese attack, 183; Japanese punitive expedition after surrender, 34-6

Singapore Harbour Board, 216, 221

Singapore: The Chain of Disaster (Kirby), 165, 226, 294

Singapore, Too Little, Too Late (Simson), 202

Singora, 77, 82, 85, 93, 97, 98, 101, 106, 107, 109n., 110, 112-14; Japanese landings, 119,

120, 122, 123, 127, 134; advance from, 128
Slessor, Marshal of the RAF Sir John, 145-6
Slim, F-M Viscount, 34, 200
Slim River battle, 146-52; Japanese use of tanks, 147, 149-51; Slim River Bridge, 147, 150; Japanese attacks, 147; defective anti-tank defence, 209-10
Sloan, A., 18-19, 21
Smuts, F-M J. C., 96; on division of Allied naval strength, 138
Smyth, Brig Sir John, 158, 163
Some Personal Observations of the Malaya Campaign, 1940-42 (Ashmore), 90
Somerville, Adm Sir James, 32, 33
South Africa, and Operation Matador, 96
Southby, Sir Archibald, 17-18
Soviet Russia, *see* USSR
Standard Vacuum, US oil company, 64
Stark, Adm, 94
Stay-behind parties, 194, 250-1
Stewart, Brig I., 53, 135, 206
Story of Changi, The (Nelson), 267
Straits Settlements, 55; Volunteer Force, 161
Strategic Air Offensive Against Germany, The (Webster and Frankland), 39n.
Street, Sir Arthur, 52, 249
Sugita, Lt-Col, 180, 182
Sugiyama, Lt-Gen, 13, 81, 84-5
Sumatra, 129, 171, 184, 199, 267
Sungei Patani, 108, 113, 115, 223, 236, 299
Suzuki, Teiichi, 69-70
Swordfish bombers, 52

Taiping, 115, 130; captured by Japanese, 131
Taiwan Army Unit No. 82 (Research Department), 113
Takazaki, Maj-Gen, 268

Takumi, Maj-Gen, and Takumi Force, 101, 107, 113, 118, 119
Tamil labour, 218, 255
Tampin, 152, 155
Tamura, Col, 260
Tanks: requested for Singapore, 45-6; Chiefs of Staff cannot send, 51; Japanese use of, 147, 188, 189; light tanks in Singapore, 161; defence against, 206-11
Tedder, Marshal of the RAF Lord, 233
Tekong Island, 162, 163
Telok Anson, 47, 132-5, 237
Tengah, 172; airfield, 162, 170
Tennant, Capt, 138, 143
Terauchi, F-M, 116
Thailand, 46-9, 58, 63, 67, 74-91, 110, 112, 236; possibility of British moves into, 46, 47; irredentism, 74; war with Indo-China, 75-8; Japanese mediation and influence, 75, 77, 88; British fears of Japanese aggression, 78-80, 82; possibility of Japanese invasion, 81-2; Japanese discussions on Thailand, 82-5; Britain and Japan and Thai neutrality, 85-7; British military contacts with Thais, 87-8; Thai intentions to resist Japanese, 88-90; possibility of British assistance, 89-91
and Operation Matador, 92-100; Japanese advance and landings, 103, 108-9, 119-20; resistance ends, 120; Thais fire on Krohcol, 123. *See also* Siam
Times, The, 19, 212
Tin, 199, 215, 218, 232; Japanese need for, 64, 66, 82
Tirpitz, sinking of, 39n.
Togo, Shigenori, 26, 27
Tojo, Lt-Gen Hideki, 13, 30, 65, 83, 84
Torrance, Brig, 179, 183
Toyoda, Adm Teijiro, 68-9, 82-3

Index

Transmitter sets, 193, 194
Trans-Siberian Railway, 61
Trenchard, Marshal of the RAF Lord, 39-40
Trengganu, 55, 74
Trincomalee, 32; attacked by Japanese, 33
Tripartite Pact, 23-5, 27, 29, 56, 61, 65
Trolak, 147, 149, 150
Tsuji, Col Masanobu, 114-15, 119-20, 126, 127, 169
Tsukada, Gen, 116
Tsuruda, Goro, 263
Tsurumi, Ken, 88

Ugaki, Vice-Adm, 29, 105, 116
Uranami, destroyer, 104, 109
USA, 24-5, 245; and Germany, 25-6; economic warfare against Japan, 58, 66, 68-9, 71, 72; suspicion of involvement by Britain in war, 63; trade with Malaya, 215; entry into war, 16, 36, 230, 241; at war with Germany, 27-8
US Air Force, in Philippines, 105
US Asiatic Fleet, 110
US Pacific Fleet, 25, 32, 103, 137, 144
USSR, 64; and Japan, 23, 24, 27; invasion by Germany, 23-5, 50, 61, 82; British aircraft diverted to, 50

Valiant, battleship, 136, 137
Van der Post, Laurens, 267
Van Waerwyck, transport, 267
Varnavaidya, Prince, 77
Vichy Government, and Indo-China, 80-1
Victoria Point, 103, 245-6; airfield captured by Japanese, 119
Vietnamese insurgents, 76
Vladivostok, 27, 61
Vlieland, C. A., Secretary for Defence, Malaya, 225-46; appreciation of Singapore's defence, 46-9, 227-31, 236-7,

288-93; on danger from the north, 46-8; anticipation of events, 227, 237; and fallacy of 'fortress Singapore', 228, 231; and 'jungle' fiction, 231; on importance of Malaya, 231-2; his position, 233-5; Bond's opposition, 234-5, 238; plan to store rice at Alor Star thwarted, 238; resignation, 240; presentation of his case, 241-6

War Committee (Malaya), 236, 238
War in Malaya, The (Percival), 23, 109n., 162-3, 189
Warlimont, Col Walter, 27
Washington Conference (1921), 38
Watanabe 2-Lt, 150
Wavell, General Sir Archibald (F-M Earl Wavell), ABDA commander, 131, 154, 159, 166-9, 171, 172, 175-8, 213-14, 218, 223, 231; visits to Singapore, 163-5, 171; on Singapore's defence prospects, 167; views and statements on Malaya, 199-201; and 'scorched earth' policy, 294, 297
Wavell, Supreme Commander (Connell), 231, 297, 298
Wedgwood, Lord, 22
Weizsaecker, Baron von, 25
Welles, Sumner, 67, 80
'Westforce', in Johore, 154-8
What Malaya Did (Shenton-Thomas), 214
Why Singapore Fell (Gordon Bennett), 191
Wild, Maj Cyril, 178-80, 182-4
Wildebeeste bombers, 52, 118
Wingate's first expedition, 264
Winkfield, Maj, 149
Winterton, Earl, 15

Yamagata, F-M Aritomo, 262
Yamamoto, Adm, 116
Yamashita, Gen, 34, 35, 101,

103, 109, 120, 155, 260, 263; and battle for Singapore Island, 169-72, 174; and British surrender, 180-4; notes on Malayan operations, 187-8; underestimate of British numbers, 187; and his deception manoeuvre, 187; and distribution of British forces, 187; on reasons for British surrender, 187-8; and Percival's failure to switch troops, 188

Yeh, George, 224-5
Yoshizawa, Kenkichi, 66

Zeros, Japanese fighters, 52
Zyunyo Maru, transport, 267

Index